GET HIRED!

LAND YOUR DREAM JOB

Praise for *GET HIRED!*
by Michael Altshuler

"I was transitioning to a new career and needed expert advice to get clarity and direction, as well as how to successfully transfer my skills and qualifications…got the best answers in this book!"

— Jordan Acker

"Lots of great tips that apply to landing a dream job and also everyday life. The content is useful and will definitely help job seekers become more confident and prepared."

— Michael DiGirolamo

"During the interview I would get very nervous, and I wasn't properly articulating my responses to questions. I knew I needed help, and that's what this book gave me. End result, I got a great job!"

— Megan Hamilton

"I was hardly getting any calls from my resume and no interviews. The expert tips and strategies in this book gave me the perfect roadmap that landed me more interviews, and I got hired."

— Esteban Vaca

"I wasn't getting called back after the first or second interview. In GET HIRED I learned specific steps on how to ace the interview, get called back and get lots of offers!"

— Rebecca Johnson

GET HIRED!

LAND YOUR DREAM JOB

Insider Secrets from America's Top Recruiters &
Hiring Managers on what it really takes to *GET HIRED!*

MICHAEL ALTSHULER

THE JOB GLADIATOR

ISBN 978-1-7378307-0-2 (paperback)
ISBN 978-1-7378307-1-9 (ebook)

Library of Congress Control Number: 2021917881

Visit the author's website at JobGladiator.com

Published in the United States by Gladiator Press
Boca Raton, FL

Dedicated to you, the job seeker, who no longer wants to settle and is ready to fast track landing the job of their dreams.

Table of Contents

Engagement: Acing the Interview

Expanding: Going Digital with LinkedIn, ATS's and Social Media

Resilience: The Emotional Aspects of Job Hunting

Foreword

As an original 'shark' on the hit TV show *Shark Tank* and having had 20 companies that topped $100 million in sales, I've learned a thing or two along the way about success. In fact, helping others achieve massive success is my life's passion. So when my good friend Michael Altshuler told me about his new book that helps job seekers achieve massive success in landing their dream job and asked if I would write the foreword, of course I said, "Yes". Now, I have to tell you that I didn't say "Yes" to Michael because of our friendship (that got the conversation started), I said "Yes" because I truly believe this book is not just a game changer, it's a life changer, and there is nothing out there like it. I love getting behind things that change lives. I know this is Michael's passion as well. Let me give you a little background.

About three years ago, I met Michael at a National Speakers Association Convention. We hit it off right away, and our personal and professional relationship has continued to grow ever since. We've shared the platform together at Hard Rock Stadium, we've partnered in a business together, and have even enjoyed golfing together (me more than him—he didn't do too well). The more I got to know Michael, the more I respected him and valued his integrity, drive, and the success he's achieved. When he does something, he goes "all in" and is all about getting great results for those he serves! Add to that his passion for wanting to help people and to change lives, and you have the perfect storm for *GET HIRED!*

The reason this book stands out from other books written on the same subject is because it's not based on just *one* career consultant's advice and best practices. It's a compilation of 17 recruiters, hiring managers, and career consultants from across the country, providing their expert advice and best practices. These hiring professionals collectively have hired (or rejected) thousands of applicants and have hundreds of years of combined hiring experience. Having this book in your toolchest is like having your own personal board of directors providing the perfect roadmap for job-seeking success. Nowhere else will you find a book that pulls back the curtain and takes you behind the scenes, where insider secrets will be revealed to you by 17 top experts on exactly what you need to say and do to land the job of your dreams. So whether your challenge is getting more interviews, delivering the goods on the interview, or making a successful career change, this book provides the answers.

When I was a shark on *Shark Tank*, I always looked to invest in businesses that had a unique competitive advantage in the marketplace. Well, that's exactly what you get with this book. *GET HIRED!* gives you a competitive advantage in the job marketplace, dramatically increasing the odds of you winning the job of your dreams.

~ Kevin Harrington

A Note from the Author

Although this book was written during the COVID pandemic of 2020-21, the proven strategies, principles, and tactics contained within on landing your dream job are timeless.

Preparation:
The Essentials of a Good Job Application Plan

"By failing to prepare, you are preparing to fail."
- Benjamin Franklin

Alberta L. Johnson, MBA, MPA

Human Resources (HR) and Diversity,
Equality, and Inclusion (DEI) Consultant

CHAPTER FOCUS

- *Research, research, research!*
- *Be able to communicate how your skillset is transferable between sectors*
- *Continued education shows a growth mindset*
- *Follow your passion*

I was thrilled to chat with Alberta about making the pivot between the non-profit, government, and corporate sectors, and how those who are looking to make the leap can be successful in their job search.

Currently a Human Resources (HR) and Diversity, Equality, and Inclusion (DEI) consultant, Alberta has served as the head of human resources for a non-profit organization, where she played a key role in executive management and directed overall operations for human resources, including diversity and inclusion, talent management, employee engagement, performance management, training and development, and compliance. Alberta has a wealth of experience in diversity and inclusion, as well as in human resources and supplier diversity.

MICHAEL: Alberta, you've been in HR a long time. What have you seen as the biggest difference between people looking for

work in the past year versus people looking for work over the last 10 or 15 years? Have you seen any big changes between then and now?

> EVEN THOSE THAT ARE EMPLOYED ARE SECOND GUESSING WHETHER THEY WANT TO STAY WITH THEIR CURRENT EMPLOYER.

ALBERTA: Yes, there was actually a story on yesterday evening here in Chicago about returning to the workforce after COVID. Even those that are employed are second guessing whether they want to stay with their current employer, because they don't feel comfortable returning to the office. So, I think you're not only seeing those that were impacted by layoffs or reductions in the work force, but also those that are looking to switch employers or change careers because COVID has been so eye-opening to them. They've realized that they value other things in their life, and they've realized that their current employer doesn't value work-life balance as much. We now have a group of people job-seeking who are already in the workforce but who want a change.

So I think there is some competition out there. We are definitely starting to see the job market pickup as we see things opening back up.

MICHAEL: Yeah, that's great. That's actually the first time someone has brought up the idea that people are uncomfortable returning to the office, and I think it's really insightful. I'm actually helping my stepson. He's working for a university, and he's uncomfortable, because no one wears a mask. That's a reasonable thing to be uncomfortable about today. Now, we realize with the pandemic that people are on different sides of the fence—some are super paranoid, some don't care at all and think they're going to be fine, and everywhere in between.

Right now, we know that the folks who are working from home are starting to go back. I have a company that I consult for that is insisting that everyone must come back to work. It's a small area, and not everyone wears masks. And I can understand the concern. Depending on how seriously concerned people are about coming back to a workplace where the safety precautions aren't as great as they want, they feel they need to pivot and make a new career decision.

So let's talk about career pivoting. What advice do you have for someone moving into a new career? How can they do that successfully?

ALBERTA: Well, you have to know which direction you want to go in first, because you can't just throw darts in the air and look to see where they land. I went through this when I pivoted from a government job to the private sector. You have to understand the perspective of those that you're trying to impress, and that really takes doing some research and getting to know the industry.

> YOU MUST UNDERSTAND THE PERSPECTIVE OF THOSE YOU'RE TRYING TO IMPRESS.

For myself, in HR and in DEI in the government sector, that looked very different when I pivoted to the private sector. I found that some interviewers had a very narrow perspective of who government employees were and what they did. They were not able to see how my skills could transfer from government to the private sector. So that's where I had to be very resilient. I had to be my own champion, to show them and to explain to them that my skills were transferable and that I was marketable. You really have to advocate for yourself. IT'S UP TO THE INDIVIDUAL TO SELL THEMSELVES, AND YOU ALSO HAVE TO KNOW THE INDUSTRY IN ORDER TO DO THAT.

I did a lot of research. I wanted to understand what the differences were between government and the private sector, as well as the similarities, so that I could be well informed. I wanted to show that I understood both sectors, both industries, and that I would be able to pivot in any direction I needed to. You can make yourself marketable.

MICHAEL: **Yeah, I think that's spot on. I mean, this seems to be the common theme with all the experts I've spoken to:** JUST DO YOUR RESEARCH. **I can't say that enough, and our experts can't say that enough: prepare, prepare, prepare, and practice. And by doing that, Alberta, by understanding the difference between the government and private sector through the research that you did, you were able to effectively communicate how your experience in government translated over to the private sector. You went from government to private right?**

ALBERTA: I started out in non-profit and then went to government and then transitioned to the private.

MICHAEL: **Talk about that and how you transferred. Take us on that journey. What it was like and what you experienced and how you effectively moved to the next type of organization.**

ALBERTA: I started out working for a non-profit in a grant-funded position in Chicago. I was always on edge, wondering if I was going to have a job or not the next year, because if the grant didn't come through, then I probably would not have a job. Most non-profits have government contracts, or they work with city and state funding, that's what started to open the door for me to get to know folks in the city and state government.

As I got to know colleagues in city government, I learned about a job opening, and from there, I was able to transition into government. I was already learning about city government the while in the non-profit sector. I was learning their processes and procedures, while also learning the non-profit world. I knew that I wanted something that was more stable, and that was one of the pluses of going into government. I knew that I would always have growth opportunities because there were so many different departments. I went through four of them, because I was always looking for more opportunities.

I actually worked for the first diversity and inclusion corporate-style office for a municipality in the nation. It was started by former mayor Daley here in Chicago. I had the opportunity to work with corporate leaders who were brought in to run the office. Through those corporate leaders, I learned more about the private sector, the corporate sector, and, on a volunteer basis, got involved with the National Society of Hispanic MBAs, an organization that focused on hiring Hispanic professionals. NSHMBA primarily worked with corporate companies, and that's where I learned even more about the private sector, corporations, and their hiring processes. That's also where I first learned about ERG groups, which did not exist in city government. However, we did have an entity that was similar to an ERG group, but it was called an advisory council. Because of my experience, I have been able to identify and communicate effectively to each one of these sectors the similarities of these groups, which helped them understand the transferability of my skills.

In Chicago, city government had a hiring process that is under a Shackman decree, which stipulated hiring processes. The difference in government is that, yes, it obviously takes a bit more time to make changes when it comes to hiring processes and policies, but a lot of those same processes, policies, and initiatives exist in the corporate sector. I had to learn the terminology for the corporate sector and what each term equated to in government or non-profit. I took those steps, not only professionally, but by personally getting involved in a volunteer board and dedicating my time to not only learning and growing professionally, but also to learning and growing personally. In the end, it helped me take that next step into the private sector.

MICHAEL: That's wonderful. I mean, there are so many things I want to dive into there, but the overarching thing I got from what you just said was that ALL THREE SECTORS ARE SIMILAR, AND IT'S IN THOSE SIMILARITIES THAT YOU CAN CONNECT THE DOTS AND EXPLAIN HOW TRANSFERABLE YOUR SKILLSET IS. I love that.

I want to get in the weeds a little bit about what it's like to apply for a job with a non-profit. What's that experience like? How should you prepare for it? And what are the nuances and subtle, or not so subtle, differences in applying for a non-profit job versus a government or corporate job? Can you share a little bit about what that looks like to really get started and how to be successful in that search?

ALBERTA: I think it depends on the size of the non-profit, because I've worked for non-profits that function as corporate entities. One of them was the YMCA. Here in Chicago, I worked for what would be considered the corporate office, which oversaw 22 sites across the Chicago and Chicagoland area. The office I was in functioned very much like a corporate office. What I've seen over the years is that non-profits have adopted a lot of the same practices as corporate companies. Their structures are similar to corporate companies: they have a CEO, a COO, a CFO, CHROs, and staff to support them. Again, this is a larger nonprofit. In a smaller nonprofit, you may only be dealing with an executive director.

Smaller, non-profit organizations want mission-driven people. They want people who want to support the organization. Non-

> **SMALLER ORGANIZATIONS WANT MISSION-DRIVEN PEOPLE.**

profits do a lot of community work, so no matter what your position is in the organization, there are volunteer days where you can volunteer within the community. There is that mission-driven focus that needs to be valued by those who are brought into the organization.

You also have to be able to understand a different type of employee. You may have a lot of part-time employees, where that was not the case when you worked in the corporate sector or the government sector. When you're dealing with the community, you have community programs that only occur during the summer, like summer camps or lifeguarding, where you're hiring part-time people, or, if it's fitness related, like the YMCAs, you have a lot of turnover with instructors.

Again, this is part of doing your research. It's also about understanding the structure and the expectation of the sector. If you go into government, there can be a lot of red tape, and the hiring process can take a lot longer than it would in a non-profit. When I was going through the hiring process in city government, it took almost six months for me to get hired. Entire entities have to approve new hires, rather than in a small non-profit where the executive director or the CEO can just say, yes, we're moving forward with this candidate.

As far as the expectations for government employees, despite what some people think, I think that you're being held to a higher standard, because you are a public servant. You cannot accept gifts, like free lunches or gift cards, for instance.

Also, when you're in a public servant role, you never know what the public's reaction is going to be. If you're a government employee who's not doing the right thing, you can be reported. There's a much higher standard there, because you feel like you're always being watched. You can be accused of wasting government dollars, depending on the position you hold.

In thinking about performance management, things take a lot longer in the government sector. You could have a change in administration, and suddenly, all the work that you've been doing could be stopped.

In non-profit, you often have very tenured employees. There's not much change in leadership, so you can easily keep programs going. It's easier to get hired in the non-profit sector, but you *have* to be a mission-driven individual in order to really fit in.

The corporate sector, in contrast, wants you to be on the cutting edge, to know the trends and the best practices. If you want to climb the corporate ladder, you have to be a trendsetter. I found that in the corporate sector, that the perception of government employees was that they were slow, not as qualified, and not as in tune with best practices as someone in the corporate sector. Non-profits are, to some degree, seen as even further behind government. The corporate world sees themselves as more fast paced, where you, again, have to be trendy and have to know best practices.

I think switching sectors is about understanding what that perception of your desired sector is and getting to know people in that industry so that they can see that you are qualified and that you understand the industry, that you understand the network, the trends, the best practices, and that you can be successful not only in the private sector or the non-profit sector, but also the corporate sector. **PIVOTING SECTORS TAKES A LOT OF EFFECTIVE COMMUNICATION.** I can't stress that enough.

MICHAEL: Let's give some clarity on why you would choose one over the other if you're making a career move. When you're looking for a new career, you're asking, "Am I going to be happy? Am I going to be fulfilled? Am I going to be productive? Can I deliver well in this new sector?"

I know some people are thinking, "Why would I ever want to work for the government?" I was speaking to someone two days ago about why they work for the government. Once you have a great government position, you get great retirement. You get great, great benefits. But the job and the sector have

to be right for you. You don't want to feel like you're in something for 20 years that you hate.

Tell us why you decided to get into government? Why did you make the move from non-profit to government and then to private? What was inside your head or your heart? What were you happy with? What were you unhappy with, and what did you learn through that experience?

ALBERTA: For me, it was initially about job stability. When I first got into government, I thought, "Oh, I'm just going to stay here a couple of years and then I'm going to move on." And then a couple of years turned into 10 years, and that was because I loved the work that I was doing. I could see the *impact* of the work. It was on such a large scale. Despite the red tape that you have to deal with in government, I was seeing that impact a lot quicker than when I had been in the non-profit world.

I was part of large campaigns that were on the sides of buses. They were on billboards and in the news. I could say that I actually contributed to that program or that service. For me, it was more rewarding. Throughout the years that I worked in city government, what made me make the switch from government to the private sector was that I said, "I'm doing diversity equity and inclusion work, and the corporate and private sector companies are doing so much more than government."

It was something that I knew I would not be able to do in city government, because they just weren't there yet. They were still focusing more on the compliance side of diversity—equity and inclusion, and not more of the culture aspect of it in employee engagement. That was the area that I wanted to explore in my career at that time.

I could see that corporate companies were creating employee resource groups and business resource groups. They were creating these corporate social responsibility programs where they were giving back to the community. The city just wasn't there yet, so in order for me to do the work that I wanted to do, I had to look elsewhere. From there, I became a national diversity manager for a national law firm, which was in the private sector, but I also started working as a consultant with corporate companies, because I had learned their processes. I understood corporate hiring, corporate diversity, corporate recruiting, and corporate employee engagement. It was about me wanting to learn more, because I wanted more personal and professional growth.

Once I had learned skills from the corporate and private sector, that's when I started to see non-profits adopting corporate practices. They've started ERG groups, they have leadership and development programs, they have mentorship programs, and these were things that were not in place when I initially started in non-profit. So I came back to a larger non-profit, which was considered a corporate non-profit. I was able to lead their diversity and their employee engagement.

But I had to ask, do I really have a voice here? Because again, when I talk about how non-profits are structured differently, some of the DEI positions that I served in either reported to a head of HR, or it was a standalone position. Then my thought became, how can I have a bigger voice in this? How can I have my seat at the table? And that's when I transitioned into being a head of HR, which I've done for the past five, six years, not only in the non-profit sector, but also for consulting firms that are doing consulting for not only non-profits, but for private and corporate companies.

I took all the experience I've had over the years, and I combined them into being a head of HR and head of DEI for a consulting firm. I'm consulting for non-profits, government agencies, and private sector organizations, but, had I not taken the steps, nor learned the other industries and sectors, I would not have been successful in any of my positions.

> TAKE AN ASSESSMENT TO KNOW WHAT YOUR TENDENCIES ARE.

MICHAEL: Yeah, that's great. You mentioned that when you went to the corporate sector, that it's fast-paced and trendy compared to the more slower moving government sector. When you're looking for a career move, I would recommend, and strongly, strongly urge, you to take an assessment to know what your natural tendencies are, whether it's Enneagram or Myers-Briggs. This helps you to be able to see and have a clearer picture to what you've accomplished. Maybe you think, "I want to work for a government agency," but there are certain things about you that don't match personality-wise.

SMART PEOPLE LEARN FROM THE MISTAKES OF OTHERS. I'm not saying we don't all have a journey and have missteps. We do. But I'm saying that the purpose of this book is to show you that you can learn from Alberta's lessons. To be able to say, "you know what, maybe government, based on what I just heard, is not going to be a fit for me after I do this assessment because I'm clearly a fast-paced person. I like to be in an aggressively-growing, vibrant environment." Well, if you really want that, then government probably isn't the job for you, but <u>YOU NEED TO REALLY TAKE A DEEPER DIVE INTO WHO YOU ARE, WHAT YOU WANT, AND WHERE YOU MATCH WITH THE COMPANY AND INDUSTRY.</u>

ALBERTA: I think it depends on what position you're in in government, because if you're in a position where you can create real change, then it's worth it.

The other thing that I found to be incredibly important in pivoting to other sectors was my education. I have a master's in public administration, a master's in business administration, and I also got my DEI certification. If you're an accountant in finance, you want to get your CPA. You want to be involved with whatever organization is considered the certifiable organization for your industry. Because that supports your credibility. I was always looking for opportunities to learn and grow, to make myself more marketable.

MICHAEL: **Absolutely. Those certifications from established and respected organizations not only serve to benefit you when you're seeking a job, but they also show that you have a growth mindset, that you're willing to learn and grow and develop and transform and get better, which every company wants. As Carol Dweck points out in her book *Mindset*, it's shows a growth mindset that you're willing to put time and effort into improving yourself, improving your skills, improving your habits. And as a result of that, you're going to be a greater contributor to the company you're working for.**

I bring it up all the time that there's great organizations and educational institutions online. Many are free. You can get

education courses from Harvard, from MIT. A diploma from one of those institutions is going to be an attention getter for someone who's hiring you. It shows that you have a growth mindset, and that you're skilled in whatever course you took. I love this Mark Twain quote that I heard the other day: "The person who doesn't read is no better off than the person who can't read." If you're not reading, learning, growing, developing, and transforming (I'm talking about taking courses, I'm talking about audible.com, I'm talking about books, articles, podcasts), then you're going to be left behind. You need to commit to do that, to improve yourself. As I like to say, we're not human doings, we're human beings. WE HAVE TO BE MORE BEFORE WE DO MORE BEFORE WE HAVE MORE. So what are you doing to be more?

When you're more, you're more marketable. We all need to raise the bar and elevate our game. It can be a battle out there. You're not the only one looking for a job. There's eight to 10 million people that are looking also. So you have to say to yourself, what am I doing differently and better to improve myself, to make myself more marketable? What are companies looking for, and how does what I have and what I'm doing right now transfer and communicate to them that I'm the right and best candidate? Not just a good candidate, but the right and best candidate.

So do I want to get involved in non-profit? Do I want to get involved in government or with corporate? When we peel back the onion of that, the way we make those decisions is by understanding who we are, what we want, what we need, and what will complement our natural tendencies.

So any closing words or advice from someone who's been there and done that? What final words would you have that will give job seekers encouragement or direction?

ALBERTA: This may sound cliche, but it's definitely about following your passion. What's going to drive you? Where are you going to be most successful? It's about finding the right organization for your needs. Ask a lot of questions during the interview processes, because it's not just them interviewing you; you're interviewing them as well. You have to make sure that the job is the right fit for you, that the culture is the right fit, and that it's going to be an environment where you will be able to express your passions, where you will be comfortable and have the ability to grow, but also where you can see yourself thriving.

> YOU HAVE TO MAKE SURE THAT THE JOB IS THE RIGHT FIT FOR YOU.

One thing that has impressed me as an interviewer is candidates that know the company. They can tell me things about the company that are not just on the website, but they know that we have a partnership with a community organization or that we've had growth over the past couple of years. It's knowing the little tidbits of information that impresses the interviewer. The more you know about the company, the better. Then, the next thing that impresses me is how well you can relate your skills and your background to the position. Having these skill sets have always been impressive to me. In thinking about my career, my future, I just can't say it enough: follow your passion and make sure that you're with the right company. Do your research.

MICHAEL: As that's a common theme and that's beautiful. It's great advice from someone who's been there, done

that, but hasn't written a book yet. I love that you finished with "do your research". It's a common theme with all HR professionals that when you do that research, you're going to get what I call "competence points." You're going to build points in your favor. They're going to say, "Wow, if they did their research during the interview process, they will do that when they're employed at my company."

And that's the connection that you want them to make.

I'll say it again: do your research. That's going to be the big differentiator. You know, this information means nothing, zero, zilch, unless you actually take action and put it into practice.

Alberta, this has been a pleasure and a privilege.

ALBERTA: It was a pleasure to be here, and I wish everyone who's out there searching that you find the right place for you.

ACTION STEPS

DO YOUR RESEARCH: Know the company you're interviewing for—don't just look at the website, but also read news articles or speak to someone who currently works for the company. Showing that you're willing to work during the interview process will set you apart from those who have not done the same. If you're pivoting sectors or industries, familiarize yourself with new language and terms so you can effectively communicate how your skills are transferrable and that you are marketable.

KNOW YOURSELF: Take a personality assessment like Myers-Briggs. This can help you understand which sector, industry, or company you fit into best.

ASK QUESTIONS: Remember, the company is not just trying to figure out if you're a good fit for them, you're trying to figure out if they're a good fit for you. It's a two-way street.

STRIVE FOR A GROWTH MINDSET: Take a free, online certification to boost your knowledge of your industry. Get involved in a premier organization that represents your industry. Learn about the sectors you interact with at work that are outside of your own.

Josh Love

Executive-level Recruiter at
Prince, Perelson & Associates

CHAPTER FOCUS

- *Executive job-seeking success*
- *Resume writing*
- *How to reach somebody at the top*

I'm excited to bring you a top recruiter to share with you what to do and not to do to hear those words, "You're hired!" As a Principal of Prince, Perelson & Associates, Josh Love leads the firm and specializes in the recruitment of executives across the globe. Drawing on a decade of experience, Josh is a strategic and consultative recruiter. An expert in identifying the top tier talent with a cultural fit for the role, he is driven by a passion to exceed clients' expectations and thrives on building elite executive teams.

MICHAEL: Welcome, Josh Love!

JOSH: Thank you, Michael! It's good to be here.

MICHAEL: I'm so glad we're talking during these times with the pandemic and 10 million people unemployed, which is just unfathomable. For many people, it's not just losing a job. It's people losing their identity. They may be losing their home. They're not able to take care of their family, and

some have even contemplated suicide. I mean, it's a really serious issue. Have you witnessed that at all? Have executives or others shared with you what's going on inside their heads and, perhaps more importantly, what's going on inside their hearts?

JOSH: It's been a really interesting time for jobs with COVID and what a change of life, right? So many people were trending along, doing great in their careers, and then COVID comes along and literally wipes out their company, their job, their lifestyle. You know that feeling of not being able to find another job? In good markets, typically you lose a job, and you can go down the street and get another one. But that has been difficult with COVID, and the recession... Being through three recessions myself, I know it has a dramatic impact on your life. You're providing for your family, and you have your toys, and you have all this stuff. I don't think we're cautious enough or prepared enough for when these bad times happen. That puts people at risk in their lives.

What's unique about Utah, where I live, is that Utah's been a stronger state than all the other states, as has the West in itself. And we're seeing a lot of people move here. And so the folks that I have talked to have certainly taken a beating, and they're making significant changes in their lives, which is, if you can't find a job around your neck of the woods, they're moving here. I've seen more people coming into Utah from out of state more than ever before. It's not easy to move, you know, and that's on top of losing your job. So that's a lot of pressure for people.

MICHAEL: Yeah, no doubt. You mentioned that you do executive recruitment. Have you always done executive recruitment? Do you see a vast difference between someone who's looking for a position as an executive and someone who's mid-career?

JOSH: I've been with our firm 22 years now, and actually started in the hospitality division. You know, if you go to a conference, the servers that walk around and treat you so well? We would place those folks. Through the years, I did technology, and then I did construction, and I found a lot of opportunities in our firm to take on a variety of different recruiting roles, but I gravitated toward the executive level, because it's a little bit more of a slower pace for recruiters. Mid-level is really active. There's a lot of competition and different things happening there.

The difference is that there are more jobs in the mid-level area. Most people are trying to climb the ladder of success, right? Well, sometimes people climb too fast, and they can get stuck in a position where if you're at a C level, even VP level, there aren't as many jobs in the market for those types of roles, such as the managers, the directors, even the associates, underneath. And so, when you can get to executive level, which is fantastic, the pool of opportunity for you to find other roles is a lot more limited, because you're at the highest level.

MICHAEL: That makes sense. You're always going to have more, I don't want to say "worker bees," but more workers in management. And then, underneath the management, it's even a larger workforce of those that work for the management. So, in the sphere of executives, when they're looking for a job, what are three things you've seen that will kill their opportunity to land a job or interview?

JOSH: The number one thing is not doing your due diligence before an interview. It's such an information highway these days on the internet, and you

> THE NUMBER ONE THING YOU SHOULD DO, IS RESEARCH THE COMPANY YOU'RE APPLYING TO.

need to read up on the company. If you're not evaluating a company before you have an interview and don't know anything about them, they'll smoke you out right away. That's number one. Secondly, in this age of information, brand yourself in the market by having an appropriate resume that really represents you. A lot of executives use certified resume writers to build out a resume that says who they are. **IT'S VERY IMPORTANT THAT A RESUME REPRESENTS WHO YOU ARE AND THAT IT MATCHES THE JOB.** You have to tweak your skills to fit, and that takes effort and time. Most executives have three or four resumes that they actually build. I have a generalist resume, and a separate specialist resume that really fits those areas. You can apply to a job and never know who's on the other end of it. It could be somebody just checking boxes, just to say, "Oh, do they have a degree? Do they live here? Do they have this title?" And so what we try to coach on is that **YOU NEED TO TWEAK YOUR RESUME TOWARD THE JOB DESCRIPTION.**

Now, don't lie. We're not looking for you to come up with anything that you're not, because it'll come out in an interview. So that's the second piece. And the third piece is really showing up and being authentic. Be professional in your attire, wearing a suit and tie to an interview. It's simply said, but it's fascinating how it's gotten a little bit loose in these markets, and some people will show up in the appropriate attire. If it's a casual company... maybe ask human resources. If you're using a recruiter, we will coach you on that, because we have the relationships, and we know what's appropriate, so that when you show up, you're fitting the culture. I think those are the three significant pieces that you have to have in place.

MICHAEL: Yeah. That makes sense. Where would you recommend they go for information about the company and the people that they are going to be interviewed by?

JOSH: Great question. Number one, you start with the website. Look through that. LinkedIn has become probably the largest engine that companies use now. When I started out, it was more of a Rolodex type of relationship.

MICHAEL: You're going to have to explain that for the younger people in the audience. I said, Rolodex, they said, is that a candy? That's not a Rolodex. You explain it...

JOSH: You had this paper wheel on your desk. Right? And it had alphabetized cards. You'd pull them out and write down someone's name or a lead. You know, we didn't even really have business cards then. So we'd write on these cards, and just pack them in there. And it was interesting during that time, because it was much more relationship-driven. Things have really evolved, in my world, as far as hiring and recruiting. Now LinkedIn has opened up the back door to every company in the world. You can literally go on there and hunt, and recruiters live in there. We live in there every day, and we don't have to go back to the old Rolodex style.

We can literally look at a company, look for titles, and cold call people that way. And so, to answer your question, if you're not on LinkedIn, you're missing out, because it's an opportunity highway for not only recruiters like myself that are in recruiting firms, but also inside corporate recruiters, who are on there daily, looking for potential talent. So if you don't have a profile on LinkedIn, that's number one. Get in there.

The second thing—if you're going to interview for a company, look inside the company a little bit and see what people are working there. You can use LinkedIn for that too. There's nothing better, Michael, than walking into an interview for a VP of sales or something and saying, "I see you have 10 sales guys." If you can name their names, that would be even better. That's the stuff that will really resonate in an interview. Also, doing all this due diligence is putting all these questions in your mind so that when you sit down, it's not a one-way street where the client's just asking you all the questions; you're also trying to see if you're a good fit, right? Rather than just trying to get a job, any job, because a bad fit only lasts so long. And then that really good opportunity passed you by because you just jumped to take a job. So it's a balancing act.

There's some other software out there, if you have the ability to invest, that help you to really dig into companies, and it'll ping you and give you highlights if there's investments happening and things like that. But probably the easiest way to jump in is visiting the potential company's website and LinkedIn.

MICHAEL: **Great stuff. And you could also look at the latest news. If you read the latest thing, they just acquired a company, or they just launched a new product, you can bring that up during the meeting and say, "How did that new launch go with the ABC product?" Those are things that reflect that you did your research. It shows that you're** interested. It shows that you would do that if you worked for them. That's really what I use.

And I probably say this in all my podcast episodes, that if you're dating someone, and if you're the gentlemen and you're dating a woman and you don't open the door for her and you don't have good manners while you're dating, she should not expect that to get better. When you're married, it's going to go downhill. The same thing holds true when you're applying for a job. If you're not on your best behavior, if you're not giving it your best shot, research, communication, professionalism, they know that once you get the job and you're already hired, it's not going to get better. It's only going to go down because you already won the prize, you got the ring.

JOSH: The beauty of that too, Michael, is that it's a very, very low percentage of candidates who do research, and all it takes is literally for you to just spend a little bit of time. You put a little more effort into it, and you're way ahead of most people in the economy.

MICHAEL: That's the gem right there. If you want the advantage, which is what you want, and you need that advantage in today's ultra-competitive job market, you need to do these little things that others aren't doing.

You talked about LinkedIn. I want to go back to that. Josh, what are the things that make a LinkedIn profile good enough? What would catch the attention of a recruiter or a hiring manager and make them say, "Wow, this is great!" And conversely, what would you look at and say not to put on your Facebook or anything else if you're looking for a job? What percentage of your time do you and other recruiters look on LinkedIn profiles or other social media for the person that you're considering?

JOSH: That's where we start. If a client calls me and says, "Hey, I'm looking for this type of person," we certainly have our past relationships that we look at, but we go directly out to the market, and we just start looking for those types of titles. So that's why you need your LinkedIn up-to-date. It's as simple as making your LinkedIn profile look like your resume. This is where so many people are missing the mark. They may be on LinkedIn, but they don't put in the content. They'll just put their title. Well, there's so much more different information that recruiters are looking for when they are scoping out people on LinkedIn.

If all I see is a title, I tend to move on, because it's a lot of time and effort to go after candidates, because we're

> IF ALL I SEE IS A TITLE ON LinkedIn, I MOVE ON. YOU NEED TO FILL IT OUT.

looking for talent. So the first thing you want to do is have a professional picture on there. It's not you and the family. It's not you and your cute hubby or wife or your dog. It's you, representing *you* in the best way possible. That's number one, how you would show up to work. The second piece is really putting the info into LinkedIn, and they make it very easy. You know, the technology is great, and it simply can go to your resume to pull the content that you need. Right? You don't have to be a writer or wordsmith to do this. Just take that information and put it in, highlight that underneath each of your positions, and add your degree.

LinkedIn has put these really neat little tools in there that you can say that you're actively looking, considering opportunities, maybe where you would relocate. Not everybody utilizes that, but it's really important because as a recruiter, that's how I refine some of my searches. I go in, and I'll look, and I'll say, "Hey, I only want to see this kind of person with this kind of skill that is open to relocation." And that's going to be my pool of talent. Well, you may be that candidate, but you didn't put that on your LinkedIn. You have to really utilize it as a tool and spend the time to fill it in. It's a great accelerator for people's careers to always spend time and make sure that their LinkedIn profile is up to date.

MICHAEL: You want to put your best self forward. Do the folks that are looking for work ever call you and say, "Hey, you're a recruiter, find me a match?" And what percentage are they calling you versus you calling clients?

JOSH: Yes, they do. On an executive level, I get more email resumes than I will via LinkedIn. But phone calls don't happen anymore. No one ever calls. It's a lost art and in the world we live in, I would say it's probably about 5% of the time that candidates will reach out to me on the phone. The one thing that gets frustrating for candidates is when they don't hear anything back.

MICHAEL: When they're ghosted. I hear that a lot. I want to ask you about that. When recruiters are talking to a candidate, do you and your business, or recruiters in general, ask a lot of questions similar to what a hiring manager would ask? Do you vet them first and then the hiring manager speaks to them, and is that how that actually works?

JOSH: Yeah. When you utilize a recruiter or you get approached by one, a good recruiter should be able to paint the picture for the candidate and answer all the questions. Yes. When a good recruiter calls, they vet that candidate. That's what the client's paying you for, is to do that first initial screening. And it's not only just technical knowledge. It's also looking at a fit in the organization and talking about relocation comp, etc. We're aligning all of these things so that when we do move them forward, that there are hopefully no deal-breakers. So yeah, when we take a job order, we're asking our clients, what are you looking for? What should we be identifying in backgrounds? You know, what are the must-haves that they need to be successful? We pull that out in the interview process.

MICHAEL: How many typically get passed on from a recruiter? Why would someone call a recruiter versus a hiring manager?

JOSH: We've seen a big trend in companies actually building recruiting teams in their companies instead of utilizing outside resources, because, you know, we're not cheap. But it's kind of a mixed bag. We do a lot of confidential searches, searches that are not on the street. You also have companies that have run ads, and they're trying, and they just can't find the right person. So then they'll reach out to us and engage our services to find that type of person. So we get it all. There are very different reasons to use a recruiter for companies.

MICHAEL: Cool. I love the idea that you said, no one calls me, I'm lonely, call me, and you automatically separate yourself from the pack. The other day, I shared with you that I was on the show American Gladiators, a TV show back in the day. And I called the executive producer of Samuel Goldwyn

productions. Of the 10,000 men who tried out for the show, 22 made it. I was, as you suggested, doing my research. How many do you think actually looked up and found out who the executive director was? I actually spoke to him and said that I was donating the money to a homeless shelter if I won. I had a great story that I knew he wanted to hear. I called them up front. I didn't send him an email. Didn't send them a letter. I called him up, and I was expecting a secretary, a gatekeeper to answer the phone. Like he must have a thousand calls. He picks up the phone. "Hello? This is Anton." His name is Anton Keller. No one calls the guy.

He says, "You're really trying out for the show, and you're calling me, wow, this is cool." And to your point, Josh, we actually had a great relationship, which I believe a recruiter can be this too. You know, we're all human beings. We have emotions, and it's about relationships and trust. And he became not just someone who listened to the story. He became a fan and an ambassador. He was in my corner, and he was pushing for me with the other 10 judges, if you will, those that are making the decision of who's going to make it on the show. He was pushing for me the whole time. You got to get this guy, Michael, because he has a story.

But I loved the idea of picking up the phone. I mean, it works, and it worked there. You know, I was one of 22 out of 10,000. If you're looking for a job, your odds are better than that. You got to take the action and call or do something that will separate you. Be prepared before you make the call with what you want to say. That's meaningful.

JOSH: Spot on, man. I love that story. You know, you're the only one who calls, I'm sure, but it only takes one to make the effort. And also, if you truly believe that that's who you are when you see a job description—and I tell candidates this all the time—call that company, because not every company uses a recruiter either, right? It's as simple as making an introduction and leaving a voicemail or figuring out whose email you should send a note to. Because, like I said earlier, you can get lost in the shuffle. Some people think they apply and if they don't hear back, they're out, but if you totally believe that that job is who you are and where you want to go, you take it to that next level. Call the HR person there on LinkedIn, go to the company and look at the employees, reach out to them. You can send them a note, right on LinkedIn, or better yet, find their email address by picking up the phone and calling the company. We've gotten a little laissez-faire on that aggressiveness in the market. It used to be there. And I think technology has really kind of dumbed that down for us. But back to our point, those are the little differences that get you a job.

MICHAEL: **Yeah. You make a great point, Josh, that a lot of people who are applying for jobs get deflated and defeated when they don't hear back. They don't necessarily know about applicant tracking systems that are actually discarding your resume because it doesn't have the right keywords that are matched electronically. The loudest squeak gets the oil, and it's a concentrated effort over time and being creative. If you believe it's right for you, try multiple things. If someone doesn't get back to you, do not think for a moment that it's because they're not interested. There's just so many, because it's so easy to apply online. That's the problem. Tons of people are applying that don't even qualify.**

You're electronically vetted out with this applicant tracking system, and by you taking other actions, manual actions such as calling or emailing or sending letters, it will show how committed you are to that job. That you're the right person at the hub. They want someone with passion and belief that this is right for them. You shouldn't quit. It's going to take several attempts.

JOSH: Yeah. The market will just give you what it'll give you, you know? Now going back to resume building, if you use a resume writer, you're spot on. I typically get more marketing types of resumes, and they bring out a lot of creativity in people. Those don't make our system—every time, they bounce out. So we've had to create a little roundabout to make sure that that doesn't happen. So if you're saying, "Hey, I'm not getting any calls, and I'm sending out this beautiful resume," that's probably the problem. It might not even be hitting their inbox because their ATS system doesn't accept it. Try having more of a text-oriented resume, and again, use a resume writer to make sure it's getting through those systems.

MICHAEL: I love when you said before, that you want to have a couple of baseline resumes, and then you want to tweak them to this specific job that you're applying for, so your skills and your qualifications and your experiences all connect with and speak to what the job is looking for. Is that accurate?

JOSH: Yes. Some people have all of that in the resume, but it's buried. Bring it up to the top. We want to see that it's there. We're all human, and sometimes, as HR people spot-check it, they miss it. Tell them what you did at your last job. Peel back the onion. How much revenue did you grow? It's the resume that gets you in the door.

MICHAEL: That makes total sense. So continuing the conversation about the resume, what have you seen? We know now to tweak it to that company in that job description. Okay. We get that. How much time does a recruiter and or a hiring manager typically spend looking at a resume?

JOSH: Oh, it's five, 10 seconds.

MICHAEL: Five, 10 seconds. So I want everyone to hear what I'm about to say. It's called AIDCC: attention, interest, desire, conviction, close. If you don't get their attention, and you don't gain their interest within the first few seconds, they're not going to read any further. And then you get their desire. I think conviction is proof of sources. What you've done in terms of the numbers that you hit, the amount of money you saved while you were in this job, or how many employees you were able to lead, that's what you need to do. So, Josh, how do you see this in a resume? Do you like when they're compartmentalizing, and they have headings? How do you make it so it's clearer?

JOSH: Yeah. It should be visible on the resume right off the bat. Forget the fluffy paragraph that says I'm a smart, energetic, driven professional. You don't have to say that. Who is Michael? Put that right at the top and bold it. It can be as much as a sentence or it can be titles. But let them know, this is what I do. And then put your position title. So immediately if I look at a resume, I see the value in your market, and I see what you've done lately.

MICHAEL: That matters. So if you were a sales manager 15 years ago, and now you've gotten into engineering, and you want to get back into sales, and it's been two decades, it's kind of challenging, right, get those type of jobs? Not to say never, but it's typically that the value in your market is the last five years of what you've been doing. So you want to make sure that the header on your resume says your role in the company worked for. And what I love is when it actually says what industry you're in, because recruiters are trying to hit targets for our clients. Let's just say our client is in an apparel manufacturing company, and they want me to find a VP of digital marketing, those are the two things that I'm looking for straight off the bat.

JOSH: And if I don't see some digital marketing inside a company, you're out just that quick. Right? So if you put your title and a little bit of a blurb about the type of company you work for below that, then I go to that next level, which is typically a paragraph about numbers, growth, revenue, and other really good evidence of the role what you've been doing there. How many subscribers you've attracted to the company, and all those pieces. Add bullet points underneath. And then I look at tenure. Tenure is a big piece too. If you're a person who jumps from job to job a lot, you're probably not going to get as many calls.

Tenure used to mean a lot back in the day, and it still kind of does, so they'll judge you on that. How have you had five different jobs in six years? So that's important. When you find a job, find something that's meaningful and that you're passionate about. Something that you *want* to do, not just *a* job, because you'll burn out, and then you're looking for another job and it's this snowball effect. You might be making all this money, but you're unhappy. It hurts your value long term, because you've had all these jumps in in your career. I don't mean to go off on that, but I just see so much of it. So those are the key pieces that I'm looking for right away.

Then I look back in the resume more for other types of companies that may be industry related. If you've been in apparel for 15 years, that's awesome. If it's just been the last five, okay, but 15 is much deeper experience-wise than five. So, to recap, your resume is really just your titles, the type of companies that you've been in, and then bullet points of what you've done. That's a great resume. One to two pages is the standard these days. If you have significant experience, you should have two pages. I have people email me that have 20 years' experience on one page, and no, you really want to see the depth of a person, especially at an executive level, because it's a long story!

> YOUR RESUME SHOULD INCLUDE:
> - YOUR NAME IN BOLD
> - TITLES IN BOLD
> - A SHORT BLURB ABOUT YOUR EXPERIENCE
> - BULLET POINTS OF WHAT YOU'VE DONE

MICHAEL: What kind of advice can you give on cover letters? Should they include one? How long or how short should a cover letter be, and what do you think it should contain?

JOSH: For me, personally, cover letters are dead. Usually, cover letters are just a bunch of fluff, and I think it's just a waste of time and a formality. My clients never ask for a cover letter. They just want to see the resume. So if you do one, I would say that you build it out. Make it interesting. If you're willing to relocate, talk about that and why. If somebody took the time to take the requirements out of a job description and list their experience in the cover letter, I've seen it done well that way, and it really matters. That's a pretty meaningful cover letter. But I can send you 10 right now from my inbox. They're from back east and their cover letter doesn't say anything about relocation, so I don't know if they're even interested in moving out here. Then I have to pick up the phone.

MICHAEL: Here's what Josh is saying. If you make it quick, if you tie it in and say, "Hey, I'm willing to (whatever)," if you start out with something that speaks to him and what he's looking for, you might get a call. Josh just told you, they only have seconds to read this, and the resume is going to be the meat, or let's call it the sundae. And the cover letter is the cherry on top of the sundae.

So if you send the cover letter, say something like, "I read about your company. I love the fact that you just launched the new medical device, and I'm willing to relocate. It's a passion of mine, what you're doing, because I'm a cancer survivor." If you say that in the first sentence, you're going to hook that person, and they're going to read through, and you didn't lose them. I'm convinced the cover letters should be short, maybe one or two sentences, a couple of sentences in the middle, and then a closing line such as, "I look forward to setting up a time to talk."

JOSH: Yup. Amen! You know, Michael, that's it exactly. It's the genuine words that mean something, the words that tie into the job description.

MICHAEL: So in your role as a recruiter, do you have a favorite question that you ask a potential candidate? Is there one that just reveals so much to you about the person, maybe their qualifications, soft skills, hard skills, etc.?

JOSH: Yes. I ask them what they're passionate about. I start with the heart. I can *technically* find good people that can do a job, but it's the fit that matters. So that's what I try to get at. What are you passionate about? And where are you at? When you were a kid, you maybe wanted to be a rock star or a football player, but as your career has grown, we all kind of get off on these different paths that sometimes we don't choose. You start working when you're young, and you have to make the money and build your family, but there's always passion along the way. So I try to get to the root of what they love to do.

MICHAEL: If there's no passion for the job or for the new opportunity, then what good is it? So Josh, I would expect a guy with the last name of love to have that passion, by the way. You know, my mind works in crazy waves. I'm thinking, wouldn't it be funny if his first name was "Lotta"?

So we agree it's tough times, and there are a lot more people looking for jobs and a lot less jobs available. If there was one piece of advice in this crazy job market that we're living in right now, what piece of advice would you give the desperate or frustrated job-seeker?

JOSH: I would tell them to not rely on the system to get a job. Be aggressive. Identify those types of companies in your background, in your industry, and start there. So if you worked in plant manufacturing, and you created medical devices, it would be wise to identify those types of companies in your area, and reach out to the decision makers in that company. The CEOs typically don't get those kinds of notes, so they're not bombarded. HR *is* bombarded. So call the CEO and say, "Hey, I'm a VP of, you know, I'm in the market... I just got laid off. I've heard a lot about your company." You've done your research, so you have this little spiel. A lot of times, it's you creating your own happiness. **YOU CREATE YOUR OWN JOB BY YOUR OWN EFFORTS.** You're still using the system to see what can happen, but you're not *relying* on it. You're spending the time to really dig in in the market. I always tell people, it's like having a job when you're out of work, you need to carve out time during your day to job search. Look at it positively. Hey, you know what? I got some time off. I got some money in the bank. I'm going to go scan what interests me. It's a good time to take a break.

We all need a good break sometimes to recharge, but check out some resources and throw out some resumes. And meanwhile, I'm going to play and take some time off. That's fine. But you're only going to get the results of what the market bears, right? So spend the time, carve out at least a couple hours a day to do what I just said. Identify those markets that you could work in. Networking is massive. If you know people, and they can vouch for you when their workplace is hiring, that's fantastic. That's the stuff that matters. It takes energy to do these things. You can get kind of worn down waiting for a job or for interviews to happen. If they're not happening, you get frustrated and down, but if you're creating it on your own and bringing your own energy, then good things will happen.

MICHAEL: Yeah. I love that. So be creative; be progressive. Don't follow the normal road. It doesn't mean you don't do

the normal things. Everyone does. That's okay. BUT THOSE THAT HAVE THE GREATEST SUCCESS GET MORE CREATIVE WITH THEIR NETWORKING. THEY REACH OUT TO THE PRESIDENT OR THE CEO OF THE COMPANY, NOT JUST THE HR PERSON. And they have something prepared that will resonate with them as to why they should hire them, or at least consider them. And you better believe that if you're calling the president of the company, the CEO, you're one of the few doing that. You're going to automatically separate yourself from the masses. So, yeah, that's great. And I love what you said also, Josh, that finding a job is a job.

Effort, more than anything else, determines the outcome of whatever it is you're endeavoring to do. If you put one hour in a day, you'll have one hour's

> EFFORT, MORE THAN ANYTHING ELSE, DETERMINES THE OUTCOME OF WHATEVER IT IS YOU'RE ENDEAVORING TO DO.

worth of potential success. Two hours of the day, you'll have two hours of potential success, or four hours in a day, you'll have four hours. Whenever you put into this, is what you get out of it.

Josh... well, he's bored to death. He wants to talk to somebody, and no one ever calls him. He jumped through the phone when he realized he was going to be in a podcast show where he got to finally talk to someone and not just read an email and send an email! Josh, you've been a pleasure, a great resource with tons of golden nuggets. Any one of these will help a job seeker, a candidate, move forward to the next level. And you said also, it is all these little things that you do that add it together that make the big thing, which is ultimately getting in and hearing those words, "You're hired!" Thank you so much for your time, Josh, and your insights. I appreciate it.

JOSH: I'm so happy to share. I love to give and serve. And 20 years of being in this, this is the stuff that I love to do, you know. If I can ever be a resource to anybody out there, feel free reach out to me. I'm happy to share tools and tips.

ACTION STEPS

RESEARCH the company you are applying to, and custom-tailor your resume and cover letter for them. Ask specific questions during the interview about their latest product or numbers.

DON'T RELY ON "THE SYSTEM," or on human resources. Be aggressive and go after jobs on your own. Call the CEO yourself and tell him or her that you're interested in the job and why.

REMEMBER AIDCC when writing your resume and/or cover letter: attention, interest, desire, conviction, close.

John Maihos

Human Resources Professional

> ## CHAPTER FOCUS
>
> - *How to build your network*
> - *How to connect in an interview*
> - *Persistence is a double-edged sword*

It was a pleasure to speak to John Maihos about job hunting and all that goes with it. John is a certified human resources professional with over 35 years of experience. Starting in the newspaper industry, he worked for local newspapers as well as with publishers all over the country. After leaving the newspaper industry, John joined a direct response marketing team that grew from a 30-person call center to over 300 sales professionals in less than three years. He now works in municipal government, addressing employee concerns for a small team of 70 while handling community relations for over 30,000 commercial and residential customers. He's active in community service, his church, and as a governor-appointed Justice of the Peace in Massachusetts.

MICHAEL: John Maihos is a smart man. His company grew from a 30-person call center to over 300 sales professionals in less than three years. Wow! He's also a justice, so if you ever need to get married in Massachusetts, he's your man. He's a guy who can really change your world, your life, and

your career, right now. So John, in those 35 years, you've seen a lot. Maybe seen it all.

My sole purpose of putting this book together is to help those who are frustrated. They can't get interviews. They're submitting resumes, and they're just not getting call backs. For those folks that are getting interviews, some just can't articulate effectively during the interview. And as a result of that, they're not getting offers. And the third thing is there's some people who are ready to pivot and change careers. They see this as an opportunity to do that, but they aren't clear on what that new career path should be and how their skills and qualifications can transfer.

So why don't we start with this: what are the top three things a job seeker can do right now that would help them either land more interviews or ace an interview, or maybe get clear on a career path? Pick any one of those three and talk about that.

JOHN: The most important thing is getting yourself in the door. Your network is always important. That's a critical one. In addition to that, have a good story to tell, and then have a good way of conveying that story; your resume is your selling tool. If you watch a commercial on television, and it looks like it's just thrown together. But you know, a commercial is created with care. The producers pick the right words and use all those nice action verbs. They use metrics or statistics too. Basically, you want to quantify your experience. You need to do the same with your resume. Then you have to be able to do the interview properly, but the most important thing is getting yourself in the door.

MICHAEL: That's easier said than done. Competition is stronger than it ever has been. So... networking. Let's dive into that a little bit. What does networking look like? How do you get in touch with your network? What do you say to your network?

JOHN: That's a good question, Michael. You can build your network a lot by using LinkedIn. You've got to be on LinkedIn. Have a good profile that tells a good story or some of the things that you've done. Include some of your skills—people look at this stuff. And then, if you have somebody that you've made a connection with, ask them for advice. Don't necessarily ask for a job, but you can say, "Hey, you've known me for a little bit, give me some things I need to improve on because I really want to get this job," whatever it happens to be. And if they can give you some of those little pieces of gold. Then you can take them, work on them, and make yourself just that little bit better. Sharpen the edges. Asking people for a job isn't right, but building your network helps you make a connection with other people who might be able to offer you a job. So think about your network as a tool to get to that next position.

MICHAEL: So what about the networks that people have already, like LinkedIn? LinkedIn is a great resource for meeting people and asking people for help. If you do it the right way, people will certainly give you that help. But how about church? We both go to church, and there's plenty of people there. I think it's always wise to ask, "Do you know of anyone you could introduce me to?" You can use that as a resource. And then you have soccer games and places you've worked in the past. Everyone in your contact list. What is the best way to approach those folks?

JOHN: You hit on an important thing. Your network can't be just LinkedIn. Personal connections are probably your strongest. LinkedIn would be a secondary source. Sometimes your personal connections and your LinkedIn connections are the same, and when they mesh, that's great. But a person who knows you, who has seen what you can do, they're going to be able to give you a proper reference. So then you're utilizing that network for real.

If you haven't told people you know what you do, you should. If people know you just as the guy who brings Billy to the soccer field and doesn't interact... you've got to start these conversations, so they know who you are. You might find yourself falling into something. Networking isn't just knowing a face, having fun, and making small talk; it's telling them what you do and showing them what you do.

MICHAEL: **The answer is always "no", unless you ask. You're not only a building yourself a network, but you're adding to their network as well. And it grows exponentially. That's the easiest, and sometimes the fastest, path to get a job.**

JOHN: Right. Sometimes using your network helps the person that you're talking to, even though you intend to help yourself. And if you can do something for them, then chances are, they're going to do something for you when the time comes up.

I was in a position where I was being interviewed by a recruiter. And I said, "I can tell from talking with you that I'm not going to be your best candidate, but I know somebody who might be." When you can make that connection, you've given them something, showing them that you're willing to help them. It doesn't have to be suggesting a candidate. It could be something else that helps that person. GOOD THINGS THAT YOU DO FOR OTHERS COME BACK TO YOU.

MICHAEL: You've been in the business for 35 years. Over the years, how many people have you said "no" or "yes" to in hiring?

JOHN: Oh, golly. It's thousands of people. There's nothing more rewarding than telling somebody, "I've got a job for you." But sometimes we have to tell someone, "This isn't the place for you," or, "I see strength in you, and just because we can only say yes to one person doesn't mean you're not a top candidate." Giving a candidate just a little bit of a psychological edge is important. I'm not out to trash anybody. As a recruiter, I might only have one position, but I need to bring in 20 people. Sometimes, if I only have that one position and you're not the one, it doesn't mean you're not going to be the one somewhere else.

MICHAEL: It's very demoralizing when you get turned down, or you're not getting interviews. All of a sudden, it starts wearing on you. If it's something I'm doing now, this does not mean that you don't need to continue to improve. We all do. But that being said, because someone doesn't say yes to you doesn't mean you're bad. It just means you're not the best candidate, or it's not the right time and not the right placement.

JOHN: A hundred percent. And the other thing too is timing. You could be the best candidate, but if you come in after we've hired someone else, it's too late. So when you see a job that you think you're the person for, you have to jump on it. Don't delay. Try to be one of the first respondents. Don't drag your feet.

MICHAEL: Do you have a favorite question you ask candidates that helps weed out the bad ones?

JOHN: I think you hit on a broad topic there. I mean, obviously, you always want to get a candidate who is highly skilled or is matched for the job responsibilities. That's really important. Then another thing is a culture fit. Does the person fit into the culture? Questions that you ask are going to be based upon me learning your skills and figuring out if you are trying to pull the wool over my eyes. That might be a test. Some are going to be behavioral questions. Tell me something you did in the past. One of the ones that we always like to hear is "What's your weakness?" and "What's your strong point?"

I ask that in a different way, because no one wants to tell me their weakness. And when they do, you always know they're going to say something like, "I'm really not a good public speaker, but I try, and I've been practicing." Because that's what you need to do, right? You have to take your negatives and turn them into positives.

But to actually get a real weakness out of a candidate, you have to put them in someone else's shoes. So what I like to do is say, "This reference that you put down—Mary—I'm going to call her, and I'm going to ask her what she thinks you need to improve on. What do you think Mary is going to tell me?" Now the candidate has to frame that answer from her point of view. It's not meant to trip anybody up. It's just to try to get them to answer the question in a different way.

MICHAEL: I used to ask a very similar thing: "We're going to send you away to a seminar to improve on one, two, or

three things personally or professionally. What would you want me to send you to a seminar to improve on?" It softens the blow a little bit, but certainly gets us to understand what their weaknesses are. It also shows a person's honesty and awareness that we all have weaknesses and that being honest and transparent is a good thing. It will show a growth mindset and will help more than it will hurt.

I did have a salesman say to me once that his biggest weakness was that he was very lazy. I'm thinking, "Whoa, I give him 10 points for honesty, 10 points for stupidity." It can come back to bite you if you don't frame it correctly.

What are a few things that are an immediate turn off in a candidate?

JOHN: There's a lot of those. You can always shoot yourself in the foot. That's really easy. The interviewer knows that people are nervous. So you can't always hold on to the one stupid thing they say. My job is to try to understand why they said what they said. IF I THOUGHT A CANDIDATE HAD TO BE PERFECT FOR THEIR ENTIRE WORKING CAREER, I COULDN'T HIRE ANYBODY.

But a person who comes in and really doesn't want the job that I'm advertising for has a secondary thought in mind. They want to take this job because they really want a different job, but that job's not open, but they see it as a foot in the door. I don't need that. I need a person who can do *this* job.

The other turn off is if somebody comes in and hasn't done one bit of research about the company. I mean, nothing. They didn't even know you had a website. An interview is for the candidate as much as it is about me wanting to get the right person. So if you don't get that kind of marriage going, then that can be a failed relationship too. So it's important to actually do your research.

A third one is, I don't care how bad your past experience was, don't tell me about it. Maybe that type of an answer will come out in the question, "Why did you leave that company?" Candidates might see that as an invitation to say, "Oh man, that boss, he was no good. I wouldn't recommend the job to my worst enemy." I don't want to hear that. Especially because, if something doesn't go right at my place, I know they're going to be talking about me. Don't burn that bridge.

MICHAEL: **Interviewers, hiring managers, and recruiters are people first, hiring managers, recruiters, and business owners second. Look at things that they deeply care about as a company, things in the news, what charities they get involved with. Now, I'm going to go even a step further: look up the person who is interviewing you on LinkedIn. Look at what they're connected to, so you can get inside their head, but more importantly, get inside their heart. See what charities they're subscribed to. It shows it right on LinkedIn.**

You connect with people on passion. That's when things light up. It will change the way they see you. And as a result of changing the way they see you, it will change the way they hear you and interpret what you're saying to them. It changes the meaning of the words that you're saying.

JOHN: It really can piece things together. Sometimes doing that little dive into something that a person has done in their past might ring a bell and you then realize, "Oh, you know what? I know something about that group. I know somebody who used to work there. I'm going to talk to that other person." Now you've formed a connection in a different way, but on a much deeper level. And that can really open the door. It can really turn on the bulb.

MICHAEL: At the end of the day, it's about percentage points that a candidate's going to win. The person doing the interview is hearing everything you're saying and doing. There's a scoreboard in the interviewer's head, and they're thinking, "That's another point in your favor or a point against you, or you didn't make yourself lose any points." Well, all these little things add points, and the more points you can add, the greater the likelihood that you're going to win the game. All these little things are going to add up to bigger things and better results.

So without a doubt, go to the website. Look at the personal things that are meaningful to the company, and then connect on those things, relate to those things, whether it's your personal experience or through someone else. And that connection point will drive the relationship. And that will give you a better chance of winning the job.

What comes to mind when you think of individuals who stood out? What did they do that was exceptional?

JOHN: That's a great question. WHAT MAKES A PERSON STAND OUT IN AN INTERVIEW? WHEN A PERSON CAN TELL ME A STORY OF SOMETHING THAT THEY'VE DONE IN THE PAST AND THEN RELATE IT TO SOMETHING I NEED, THAT'S CRITICAL. That's very important. Not only are they giving me a skill that they have, but now they're relating it to me and making me realize, "You know what? Mike is going to really be able to help me out on this. He's even given thought to it." And that's pretty valuable. Not everybody does that, but if more people did that, it would give them an edge. It shows they know the company, and they have investigated something that they can maybe improve on.

MICHAEL: Can you speak to anything someone has done out of the ordinary outside an interview? Something that made you say, "Oh, I want to talk to this person"?

JOHN: Persistence can be a double-edged sword, you know? I've had people that have been very persistent about getting an interview, even to the point of going to somebody else and getting them to make me want to meet them. In a way, it can be a real pain in the neck. But I might have incorrectly factored that person out, and somebody else can help me to say, you ought to think about it from this perspective instead.

A person who is persistent can be a good thing. Maybe they were a number two candidate, and they come back to me and they show that they really want this job. They really want to work for the company. They really see something in us that they like. Then that's a good thing. But persistence can be a bad thing too, because if I know in the back of my mind I can never hire that person for that job, and they just keep showing up, then I'm eventually going to get annoyed. You still have to be nice about it, because they're still customers.

MICHAEL: As you said, you never burn any bridges. I heard this from a Ken Blanchard talk maybe 20 years ago,

and I never forgot it. He said, "Patience and persistence, patience and persistence." I said, "Wow, what a beautiful combination." It almost sounds like a paradox, but it is a beautiful combination to have patience and persistence. What does that really mean? How does that really translate into what I do and how I do it and how often I do it? So let's finish up with this, John. In terms of follow up, what is the best way to go about it?

JOHN: Well, everybody's a little different. I have a recruiter friend who always reminds me that it's their job to help somebody to get a job. So if one job isn't going to work, maybe they've got an opportunity for them somewhere else. Keeping in touch is important. For me, personally, it doesn't matter how they reach out. I suppose email is better than phone calls all the time, because I'm going to have time to look at email on my own schedule. I don't want the candidate to feel like they've been ignored either. Giving me time to answer appropriately is nice.

We've always been the type that has the ability to get back to the person and say, "Hey, thanks very much for your time. We did select somebody else for this position. Best of luck in your job search." Not everybody does that. At a certain point, if they don't have the courtesy to at least return your calls, do I really want to work there?

I'm a Justice of the Peace, right? Some couples, they get so busy, they might make an initial call to me. And of course, I want to close that "sale;" I want to do their wedding. They're very busy with 15 other things, and the last thing they're thinking about is me. I relate that to me in the workplace, with all the candidates coming to me sometimes saying, "Hey, I just wanted to check in and let you know, I'm still interested. If you haven't found anybody, please consider me. Is there a good time to talk?" And if people do that to me and do that with politeness, I'm very open and receptive to that.

MICHAEL: I love that approach. It was concise, and it was considerate.

The last question I have for you, John, is this. We are in a very challenging time for job seekers, with 10 million people unemployed. Some people don't know how they're going to take care of their families. They have no sense of identity or self-esteem anymore. It's so much deeper and more important than just a job. What piece of advice do you have for these people who are discouraged that can help them get a job?

JOHN: Don't give up. You have value. You're going to take and make that connection. At some point, you're going to get the job you want. But also, don't turn away from something you think is below you. It's okay to go back to a job you may have done before. They're going to see value in you and maybe something else opens up that you work into. It's okay to take a step back. Keep working. Work is important to people. It shouldn't define you, but it certainly is important. And when you're not working, like you said, so many other things start falling apart. Do something, keep yourself active, and be successful. You will be successful.

MICHAEL: Beautiful words to end with, John. Thank you so much for your wisdom, and for your compassion for those that are looking for work.

JOHN: What you're doing for people is a great thing. Keep doing it.

ACTION STEPS

CREATE A GOOD NETWORK by not only connecting with people on LinkedIn, but by talking to the people in your life about what you're doing and the opportunities you're looking for. You never know where a conversation might lead and who you might get connected to. Don't be afraid to ask for advice.

BEFORE GOING IN FOR AN INTERVIEW, DO YOUR RESEARCH. Figure out what the company is passionate about. Look up your interviewer on LinkedIn and note what things they're involved in. Passion connects people.

FOLLOW UP WITH YOUR RECRUITER OR INTERVIEWER VIA EMAIL. Show that you're passionate about the job. However, learn to read when the door is truly closed. Too much persistence can be annoying.

Dan Sell

An HR professional, consultant,
and principal of Dansumer Consulting

CHAPTER FOCUS

- *Looking at your job search as a marketing plan*
- *The importance of networking and how to do it*
- *Differentiate yourself!*
- *Prepare, prepare, prepare!*
- *Build a core of support people*

Dan Sell was another person I discovered when combing the nation for experts who know how to land and get the job done! He is an award-winning human resources specialist who has turned his experience into a successful consulting business. And with a last name like "Sell," you have to believe he has a lot of nuggets to help you sell your skills in a competitive job market. Here's a glance at his credentials:

- Extensive leadership & senior-level management experience, 40 years
- Honed his skills in public and privately held service and manufacturing companies
- Lending his HR executive skills in areas of pharmaceuticals, engineering, transportation, industrial distribution, and various product manufacturing industries
- Principal of Dansumer Consulting, LLC

Let's see what nuggets Dan has for us!

MICHAEL: Dan, you have helped many people with their job search. Can you share what strategies are helpful in the current economic conditions and your words of advice to help someone to be successful in job hunting?

DAN: I think there's a couple of things it boils down to. One, we often think of the term "job search," and I would suggest we consider looking at it as a marketing plan. One of the key things with a marketing plan is to know your product. When I talk to people about their careers, I always tell them to first do a self-assessment (a product assessment). Sit down, ask yourself a variety of questions in different ways, and journal your responses. If you have a profile gleaned from personality or skills test or job reviews from the past, all of this can factor into a profile. It's all about gathering as much product data as you can. When we look at ourselves, we'd like to say we're great and wonderful, but we all have blemishes. And if we're not aware of them, some interviewer will uncover them at the wrong place and time. So you need to discover those areas first so you can adjust. So do a self-assessment and be very honest and critical.

Secondly, you can't overstate the importance of networking. Successful networking is not having 800 connections on LinkedIn. It's discovering who are the top producers in your field, who will advocate for you and be your eyes and ears in the marketplace to help you with information regarding career opportunities. That network may be only eight people.

The technology used by HR departments benefits the company, not the applicant. You must be able to differentiate yourself, whether it's through the actual interview or networking. The networking comes full circle when Michael is willing to advocate for me, and the people in his organization like and trust his opinion. When Michael says, "Here's my friend Dan, I think you should talk to him," I just went to the head of the list instead of being trapped in an applicant tracking system.

> THE KEY ELEMENTS IN A JOB SEARCH:
> - UNDERSTANDING THE PRODUCT YOU ARE MARKETING (YOU AND YOUR SKILLS)
> - NETWORKING
> - DIFFERENTIATING YOURSELF

Recapping, the key elements to job searching are understanding the marketing plan and the product you're marketing, networking, and differentiating yourself. And if you think about it, getting back to the marketing plan analogy; it's the same way that you would sell somebody a cell phone, a cup of coffee, or a car. Those same methods apply to finding the next career opportunity.

MICHAEL: **Dan, that was so good; you dropped so many great nuggets. Anyone can take this information and run with it. It's enough for anyone to move further ahead in finding a job. You gave us great information, and I'd like to go deeper on a few things. You said, "Don't think of this as a job search, but rather as marketing yourself, and you are the product." Every product has pros and cons, things that aren't so good, and things you do well.**

Find the things you need to improve, identify those areas and neutralize them, and get better. So with that in mind, there

are multiple assessments; there's DISC, Myers-Briggs, and many online assessments. If you don't know your weaknesses and strengths, you can't really communicate them effectively. The self-assessment idea is brilliant, along with the concept that you are the product that you are marketing. You are the product you want the employer to buy, not some other product, not someone else. I want to dive further into the topic of networking.

Dan, job search candidates often think the process involves; create the resume, refine the resume, and then apply to all the companies that are on your target list. The thought is if you have a great resume and you apply to lots of companies, then you have a good chance of getting lots of interviews and getting hired. I'm not saying that's not important, it is important, but it's not as important as what Dan said about fast-tracking the process. If you want to put the odds in your favor, over 60% of decisions are made today based on networking and introductions, not job applications being posted on a job board. Let's take a deeper dive into networking. Let's talk about LinkedIn and what a good LinkedIn profile looks like. Let's discuss other social media, whether it's Facebook or Instagram, what are the do's and don'ts and how do you contact someone in their network? Take us through that journey of what to say, how to say it, and what to ask for.

DAN: Well, I think one of the things that's important to realize with a resume or an application, or to some extent your profiles on LinkedIn, is that you're at the mercy of the HR person's perspective. I'm not looking at the application and saying, "Wow, here's a great candidate." I'm asking, "Does this person fit? No, they don't." At a glance, I can evaluate whether or not I want to talk to that person. Understand that someone is looking at a large quantity of resumes, whether they're doing it on paper or online. They are looking at you for, if you're lucky, 10 seconds. It's going to be that first impression.

For the regular resumes it's like writing a newspaper column. When you read a newspaper column, for those who still read newspapers, you have the headline, which attracts you to the story. Next, are the important facts contained in the first couple of paragraphs, followed by secondary details. Make sure whatever communication platform you're using, that your aim is to lead with dynamic material so people will take a look at your resume and not dismiss it saying, "This person's not going to fit with my organization." Michael talked about the importance of networking. Michael, until this conversation, did you and I ever meet each other? Never. We were introduced because I happened to be on a Zoom call with somebody who's going to be the speaker at an HR conference that I am involved with. She happened to know Michael and said, "You know, you really ought to talk to this guy, I think he's someone you'd enjoy talking with." Lo and behold, I received an email from Michael, and we agreed to a phone conversation and then came the invitation to be on his program. That's networking.

MICHAEL: I'm glad you brought up that example, Dan. As a peak performance coach, I want to go one level deeper. The woman that introduced us is someone I found on LinkedIn, and I took action. I called her. I asked her who are the HR rock stars that I can invite on my podcast that can help others get a job quickly. She recommended you and one other person. Now I want to make a point. The first thing I did was take

action. After an online connection, an email, and a phone call, Dan was a guest on my podcast within a few hours. The immediacy of the whole process; I believe it's proof positive that networking works.

DAN: Right. What you ideally want to do is find someone who's in the industry or in the particular organization you're trying to get into, and reach out to that person. As I mentioned earlier, when the candidate can walk into a hiring manager's office and be presented by someone who works there, you have been vetted. Part of that process is, again, understanding the marketing plan that answers the questions: Where do I want to go? What do I want to do? Who are my targeted accounts? And the next phase of your plan is to get introduced to the right people.

If you're selling a particular product you need to answer the question, who's going to buy it and why? From a selling standpoint, that's developing a needs analysis. What are the needs of the industry and what can the product do to meet and satisfy those needs and make life better for them? And that's what you have to be able to identify when you do your job search. For example, LinkedIn is a database; interrogate it, use it, run lists that may take you to several different levels. The research is going to get you to those names and contacts, and you enter a different phase of engagement.

In our case Michael and I had someone who introduced us, a go-between. Someone looking to engage with the right person needs to identity the go-between that might be a decision maker, an influencer, or someone you may know who is a connector. <u>**A WORD OF CAUTION, WHEN YOU'RE NETWORKING, SIZE UP THE PERSON WHO YOU'RE INVITING INTO YOUR CIRCLE.**</u> If you align yourself with someone who turns out to be a real jerk, that's not someone you want representing you to others in that organization. Have a sense of your A-players, the ones who can give you a big bang for the buck. As I said, LinkedIn is nothing more than a database to assist you with your marketing plan.

MICHAEL: **Great information on using LinkedIn. Here's a tip, right on the LinkedIn page are the mutual connections. If you have targeted a particular company for your marketing plan and you learn that Mary Jones is the VP of HR, and she is your target contact, you can look at your mutual connections, and engage with someone you know who is acquainted with Mary Jones. As Dan said, make sure it's someone with a good reputation, and then ask if the person can arrange an email introduction to Mary. This strategy will unequivocally get you to the front of the line faster. The beauty of a more personal introduction is an open door versus having your resume discarded through the applicant tracking system.**

> IT'S GOLD WHEN YOU OBTAIN AN INTRODUCTION TO THE PERSON WHO IS HIRING WITHIN AN ORGANIZATION.

It's gold when you obtain an introduction to the person who is hiring within an organization. You go in with a recommendation from a mutual contact, and you secure an interview. I also wanted to take a deeper dive on the LinkedIn page. Think of it as one of the ways to advertise your abilities. I want to further explore the LinkedIn profile as a form of self-advertisement. Dan, from your perspective as an HR professional what would be a qualifier or disqualifier on a LinkedIn page?

DAN: Well, regardless if it's LinkedIn or the actual job interview you should have a list of what you have accomplished in your organization. I spent 40 years in corporate HR, and I'm convinced that HR people write the world's worst resumes, because we tend to write resumes that are very process-oriented. We always talk about the process, such as administered the benefit program or coordinated college recruiting, but we don't mention the outcomes. What was the benefit to the business as a result of the process? It's what I call the "So What Factor". So what happened as a result of your efforts? Were people hired more quickly, were the right people hired, or did you save the company money by using the process? The positive results you have achieved is what grabs someone's attention and that should be at the top of your LinkedIn page, your resume, or whatever source you're using to tout your successes. So, when you do your self-analysis, you have to take a look at what you have accomplished, and then determine the impact and the magnitude of that in dollars, efficiencies, or other benefits. Someone will take a look at those positive attributes and say, "You know, if Michael did that for his organization, that's the kind of guy I want in my organization." Another area you want to highlight on your social media or resume is how you've progressed in an organization. Have you been promoted in your position or given different responsibilities? **IT'S IMPORTANT TO SHOW JOB GROWTH, MOVEMENT, OR RECOGNITION YOU'VE RECEIVED WITHIN THE ORGANIZATION.**

I also want to advise people about what they post online. Once you put information on the Internet, good or bad, somebody's going to find it. So, be really careful. You may think posting a photo of you at a party is harmless, but it may call into question your judgment. Remember, people think in pictures and once you create an image, that image is going to stick with you. It's the brand or product image that you have created. I recommend you periodically Google yourself and look at all the different things that are out there because that's what the HR person's going to do.

Another point I want to make is related to the interview. You want to differentiate yourself so that when you walk into a room and you meet with someone, and present your material, you want to make your marketing plan come to life. When you finish the interview and leave the room, you want them to remember you. You want to make an impact.

MICHAEL: **You've mentioned some gold nuggets, and I want to take a closer look at some of the points and give you my observations. It's only natural, with your last name being Sell, that you like to sell the analogy. I don't care if you've never sold merchandise or a service, understand we're all selling. Maybe you're not defining yourself as a salesperson, but from childhood to adulthood, we're always selling, whether it's an idea, ourselves, or negotiating a better deal on a car. In sales—and this is going to help you when you're looking for a job—there's something called substantiated documentation. Dan, you addressed this: provide numbers or percentages that quantify the results of what you accomplished, what the outcome meant to the company because that's all the prospective employer wants to know. I want to give it a sales term, and I don't care if you are or are not in sales, learn and understand fabulous FAB-Feature Advantage Benefit. This is my role (Feature), these are the tasks that I performed daily (Advantage) and here's how the company grew, saved money or reduced costs (Benefit). Next, as an interviewee, you need** to tie this information to your prospective employer. Your skills and qualifications gave you the expertise to save 30% in net revenue and costs because you reduced turnover. And as a result, the company made an extra 30% in profit. That's a feature, an advantage, and a benefit. Then you tell them how you'll do the same for their company.

DAN: Michael, your example is the tipping point the HR person is looking for and will move you forward in the process as a valid candidate. And secondly, that you're going to add significant value to the organization, the features and benefits aspect is key.

MICHAEL: The company wants to hire someone who has gotten great results for the previous employer. What you did is not nearly as important as what result you got from what you did; that's what they're after.

DAN: You want to give the interviewers a little taste: here's the actions I took, here's what happened as a result of it, and here's the value that was created. You want to explain your successes quickly, and if they want more details, they'll ask for them. Don't go on, and on, beating the topic to death. Simply get that impact image in their mind, the wow factor. One of the points I wanted to make, this is really important, regardless of what career search stage you are in, whatever you say, make it true and realistic. Don't invent stuff. Don't embellish details because sooner or later, even if you make it through the interview process, you're probably going to go flat on your face when you start to perform the job. THERE IS NOTHING WORSE FOR AN INTERVIEW CANDIDATE THAN TO GET CAUGHT IN A LIE, OR IN A SITUATION WHERE IT CASTS A DEGREE OF DOUBT ABOUT THEIR HONESTY. If you never ran a project, don't say that you are a project manager. The one thing that will totally implode an interview is when the interviewer catches something that wasn't quite the way it was represented by you. Focus on the tasks that you have performed.

MICHAEL: That's great information. I want to touch on something that you said that I think is really critical. You mentioned giving the highlights of your successful results and not to go on, and on. When you just put a morsel of information out there that is appealing, you create enough interest and curiosity that they're going to be compelled to talk to you and ask you more. Remember, less is more. When it comes to your resume, those screening the applications have a limited time to look over your credentials so keep it clear, concise, and compelling. That's the whole goal to set up an interview and get them talking to you.

DAN: You're exactly right. If I can make a comparison: I have seen more commercials in the New Jersey/Philadelphia area recently for online gambling sites promoting, "Place your first no-risk bet with us." They're trying to draw you in, and once they do, then they've got their hooks in you. And that applies to an interview. You want the interviewer to be interested enough to pull you in and then make sure you back up your statements with details. If you get to the types of questions where they are asking you to walk them through the steps and methodology that gave you positive results, you're at second base. The interviewers are not just checking the box because they have to ask you the question, they want to ask you more questions and drill down. That's a good, green light when they're interested in learning more about your achievements.

MICHAEL: I love that concept of marketing yourself. You're the product. You know, when you look at ads, they promote the benefits of the product; this is what you'll get, this is what you'll be. When you look at a weight loss commercial all they show are the before and after pictures, and you want to find out how the heck did they do that? There's only 30 seconds to show the result and this is what will happen if you use our product. In an interview, you are the product, and if the company hires you, this is what they receive. It's the curiosity factor, moving us perfectly into the next phase. What you want to do on LinkedIn or Facebook is obtain that phone call to have that first conversation, to lead to an interview; that's the goal. Be focused on that goal, which is to get that call, and then show your best stuff when you're at the interview. Dan, how many interviews have you conducted in your illustrious career?

DAN: I wouldn't even want to think about all the different interviews. Let's just say I've done a lot.

MICHAEL: You've interviewed at all levels, from entry to executive positions. What would you say is your number one recommendation?

DAN: Be yourself, be honest, true, and real. Good interviewers will pick up and get a sense in the back of their mind if you're being insincere. We will probably soon be transitioning back, to some degree, to in-office interviews. But I think the workplace itself is going to transition to be more of a hybrid. So, get used to the environment of being in front of a monitor and doing interviews. I will give a shout out to Fast Company, a good source that gives a lot of great tidbits about networking, interviewing, and the current state of the job market. If you subscribe to Fast Company, or can get on the mailing list, it offers weekly news briefs, a lot of snippets, and good techniques that are helpful.

It's also important to prepare for the interview, do your homework, do your research, and know the company. The first company I worked for when I got out of college was Owens-Corning Fiberglas. We made a lot of different building material products and industrial textiles. I had one candidate who came in for an interview, and I asked him basic interviewer questions as to why would he want to work for us? He said, "My mother loves your Corning Ware and swears by it." And I looked at him and said, "That's not us, that's Corning Glass, a different company. Sounds the same, but it's a different company." He took a step back and looked at me and asked me, "What do you make?" At that stage, I knew the interview was over. Obviously, he hadn't done his homework, and he was not really interested in a career with us. In this day and age, there is so much information available online, so do your homework.

We've gone from the marketing plan of knowing the product, knowing the interviewer plan, which is a subset of the marketing plan, and knowing the organization. Next, I want to make sure we talk about preparing for that inevitable question about your weaknesses. You may be sitting there thinking the interviewer is never going to ask you about your weaknesses, but it's going to pop up. You want to be able to understand how to answer that question. I once had a candidate, who when I asked what are your weaknesses, basically self-destructed and told me all of their weaknesses. They took me inside of their psyche, a place I didn't really want to go, and they did this data dump. When you're faced with that type of question, remember—no negatives!

When a question comes that you're not sure how to answer, you can take a step back and pause before you blurt out a response.

You don't have to answer the question immediately; buy yourself some time to get back in balance. You want to have some pat phrases ready to buy you quick nanoseconds or seconds to recalibrate yourself. You might say something like, "That's an interesting question. I haven't had that one posed to me that way," or "Give me a second to think about that because that's an interesting question." Another way to handle the question of weaknesses is to give an example of a weakness and then explain how you are managing it. For example: "One of my weaknesses is I tend to over-commit, but I've learned years ago that that's my nature. So, what I've done is keep a daily planning calendar, set my priorities, and force myself into situations where I don't over-commit." Don't take the question any further; you took the question, answered the question and hopefully killed the question. Don't sit there feeling that you have to go on, and on. That's why it's vital to prepare answers ahead of time instead of doing it on the fly. IMPROV IS NOT A GOOD SITUATION.

MICHAEL: That's brilliant, Dan. One of my mentors, Zig Ziglar, used to say that some words fill time and space, but don't have any meaning. Notice what Dan said about overcoming a weakness. He addressed finding a way to solve his weakness, and it's no longer a weakness. Most interviewers aren't trying to catch you with that type of question. I think they want to see how quickly you answer, and how transparent you are with your answer. The way you answer this question tells so much about your character; that you can identify your weakness, you find a way to fix it, and you took action to solve the weakness. The weakness turned into a positive.

I can't tell you how important it is to prepare, prepare, and prepare for when someone is asked questions like, tell me the greatest challenge you've had at work and how you overcame it? What other questions would you ask, a question that you love, Dan, that would reveal so much about a job candidate?

DAN: What I want to do, from an interviewer's standpoint, is to format the interview like a funnel. You start with the open probes with a goal to obtain a lot of data. The good interviewers know that they have to shut up, sit back and log in all the information. Once you get that data, then the final part of the interview is to creep in, and narrow it down, asking more direct questions. "Tell me specifically about this, tell me a little bit more about that, give me some examples, etc.". One of the questions I like to include toward the end is, "It's been a great conversation. If I haven't been smart enough to ask you the right questions, is there anything else we should know about you?" Another question is, "If I asked people that you've worked with over the years to describe you, what words would they use?" If the candidate has felt the interview has gone well and they're feeling a little cocky, this might be the time they shoot themselves in the foot.

MICHAEL: Go back to the first question. With all the interviews you've done, tell me an answer to that question that killed the deal. The person was okay up to that point then they gave a horrendous answer. Also, give me an answer that was stellar, and you wanted to hire the person.

DAN: Let me give you the one on the negative side. Years ago, when the company I worked for was doing college interviews, we brought a group of people in for second interviews. This one guy came into to my office, and we were having a relatively decent conversation. I asked, "What is one of your strengths?" He answered, "One of my strengths is my attention to detail. And I really take good care of how I personally present myself. My appearance is very important to me. Before I came over here, I checked myself in the mirror. I made sure that everything looked right with the suit." At that point I happened to look down, and I noticed that he had missed buttoned his vest. At that stage of the game everything else went out the window, as he was still going on, telling me how meticulous he is about details.

MICHAEL: And you couldn't take your eyes off the vest.

DAN: The juxtaposition of the two scenarios; he's talking about this as a positive trait, but he obviously didn't pay attention to the details.

MICHAEL: Your brain is registering, I'm seeing one thing, but I'm hearing another. This doesn't make any sense.

DAN: From a communication standpoint, what you're telling me and what you're showing me is a disconnect; the words and the behavior don't match. That's going to register.

MICHAEL: Right? It's like if you say you're thoughtful, and you believe in follow-up, and then you don't send a thank you card following the interview, it's going to be an issue.

DAN: That's important too. There are little things, like the thank you card that can differentiate you in a positive way. Emails are the norm, but don't stand out. If you want to send a quick email right after the interview to thank the interviewers, that's fine but follow it up with a handwritten note. I̲T̲'S̲ T̲H̲E̲ L̲I̲T̲T̲L̲E̲ T̲H̲I̲N̲G̲S̲ T̲H̲A̲T̲ C̲A̲N̲ H̲A̲V̲E̲ A̲N̲ I̲M̲P̲A̲C̲T̲.

One of the other things that I would recommend right after the interview is to make a point to sit in your car, bring out a notebook, and write down the post-mortem of what just happened. What did I do well, and what didn't I do well, and later go back and review this information and learn from each experience. Even after doing a lot of interviews for a lot of years, I made mistakes in interviews. I realized what the issues were and the next time I went out for an interview, I nailed it and got the job. It's important to continually assess the product and the process.

MICHAEL: **Assessing the product allows you, even the pros, to continue to improve the product, which results in getting more job offers. Dan, the pro athletes constantly look at film and what they can do better, where they blew it, and they are making $14 million a year, when they're at the highest level, the top 1%. And if athletes are assessing performance at this level, you better believe you need to do it when seeking a job.**

> EVERYONE HAS ROOM FOR IMPROVEMENT.

Everyone has room for improvement. One of my favorite quotes, from an improvement standpoint, is from Ray Kroc, the founder of McDonald's. He said, "When you're green, you're growing, and when you're ripe, you start to rot." So I have a question for you. Are you green and growing after every interview with all the things you're doing? Are you asking others, who are objective, for feedback? Are you asking yourself, "Am I doing this better than I was previously?"

Because the more you improve, the more you're going to improve the likelihood of hearing those words, "You're hired." That won't happen if you stay at the same level, and keep doing the same thing you've always done. Inspiration and improvement, all these things are part of the process. It can be a challenge out there and you need to stay inspired and always say, how can I get better and do more.

Dan, getting back to how you would respond to the question, "Tell me something I haven't asked you about yourself." Can you think of any candidates that gave you a great response to that question and it was the cherry on top of the sundae?

DAN: That's a really great question. I don't remember a specific response that blew me away, but there is one thing that I've seen happen at the end of an interview that probably shouldn't. I've interviewed veteran salespeople over the years and many of them leave the interview, simply saying, "Thank you very much," as opposed to saying, "Hey, this has been a great time. You are a great organization. I think your marketing plan and products are spot on and the changes you made, the rebranding and repackaging, is exciting. I'd love to be part of that. What is the next step? Because you've really raised some excitement in me." You close on a high note, and you ask for the order. I think that is important. You want to leave the room with a lasting image of, "I'm really good at what I do, and I'm excited about doing it for you."

MICHAEL: I'm going to tell you something, nothing Dan has said, nothing I have said means anything, it's 100% worthless, unless you take action on these steps. I read a great Mark Twain quote, "The person who doesn't read is no better off than the person who can't read." Wow. I think the person who has action steps, has information that will help them succeed, and who doesn't take the action steps, is no better off, in fact, is worse off than the person who's ignorant. As you continue to add little things, as Dan said, those little things will add up to the big thing. Now, what you said at the end of your last comment is perfect. It's certainly not a hard close, but it wraps it up and is masterful in restating to the interviewer that you have an understanding about their company, and you are passionate about what's most important to their company. That approach says, "I did my research on connecting my passions to what your company's all about, your vision, your values, new products and services, and I'm connecting those dots in a summary. After the summary, which is very emotional because I'm connecting everything, "I believe in what you believe in Mr. and Mrs. Interviewer, and I would love to learn about what the next steps are. Is it okay if I contact you next week or the week after? And would you prefer a call or an email?" That shows your interest when it closes on a really positive note summarizes everything, and shows passion, which is what they want to see. Not just passion in general but passion that directly correlates, connects with, speaks to what they're passionate about related to the job.

Dan, is there one piece of advice that you would give someone today, to focus on and that they must do to be successful?

Dan: Please go find the biggest amusement park that you can drive to and then ride the biggest, baddest roller coaster, 10 straight times in a row. That's your job search. You're going to have days where you're looking up the track to the top, and it's going really well. Then all of a sudden it just drops down. You go from the high to the low and then you move along, and you start to go back up again. You're going to have those highs and lows throughout the process.

That's when it's important to look at who's in your network and have people in your circle that can help you go through those highs and lows. They're not necessarily the job connectors, but they're the emotional connectors, people you have a level of trust with that you can tell them how you feel. It's reassuring to have that human voice on the other side of the phone, or the other side of the table that is so important. YOU'RE GOING TO HAVE GOOD DAYS, AND YOU'RE GOING TO HAVE BAD DAYS. AND THE MORE EFFORT, THE MORE WORK THAT YOU PUT INTO YOUR JOB SEARCH, THE MORE THINGS WILL START TO COME BACK AND HAPPEN. If you take the approach, well, I'll get up and do an hour's worth of work, you might get lucky. It's the old adage, the harder I work the luckier I get. It's working eight hours, 10 hours-a-day to get this done. If you take that approach, you're setting yourself up to have a much higher probability of success.

MICHAEL: Bam, bam, bam, bam. Spot on. Right on. Rock on. I love the rollercoaster analogy. It is a roller coaster. We are not independent people. We are dependent people. You need people in your life. I just read a quote from Toby Bryant, "Everyone has self-doubt, especially when things are going bad, and you need people that will charge your battery." I call them battery chargers, and we also have battery drainers in our life. We have to cut them loose, we can't be around them, they'll drain our battery. LISTEN, LIFE AND BUSINESS ARE HARD ENOUGH. WE NEED TO SURROUND OURSELVES WITH PEOPLE THAT BELIEVE IN US, SUPPORT US, POUR NEW ENERGY INTO US THAT

HOLDS US ACCOUNTABLE. Put those people in your path, in your life, look to your network or those people you can call on and who will support you. Listen, I'm a peak performance coach, and I have those people in my life. I don't always have great days. No one has great days, every day. But when I speak to those folks, and they breathe new life into me, then they charge my battery. I don't stay as low for as long. So using the rollercoaster analogy as I'm going down, I don't go down quite as low as I did the day before. It's tough riding the ups and downs but when you're riding it with someone that believes in you, has confidence in you, it makes the ride less daunting.

> IT'S TOUGH RIDING THE UPS AND DOWNS BUT WHEN YOU'RE RIDING IT WITH SOMEONE THAT BELIEVES IN YOU, HAS CONFIDENCE IN YOU, IT MAKES THE RIDE LESS DAUNTING.

And when you have self-esteem, the ride is more enjoyable and the ride is smoother, and we'll have better results. Probably one of the best metaphors I've ever heard about looking for a job.

Dan, you have offered a wealth of knowledge and insight. From the bottom of my heart, I want to thank you, because it's not just a job people are dealing with today. It's their livelihood, their financial support for their family. A job is so significant for people today. They may have saved their whole life for a home, and they may be losing their home because they've lost their job. It's being able to take care of your kids, which is the fundamental purpose of parents. Some people are suicidal and feel hopeless, and getting a job may prevent a tragedy. Some people feel they've lost their identity with no job. Dan, you are a bright light in the job universe, helping people, sharing your time, wisdom, and insights to help people on this journey.

DAN: Thank you very much for the opportunity. My pleasure.

ACTION STEPS

LOOK AT YOUR JOB SEARCH AS A MARKETING PLAN. Understand the product you're marketing (you and your services) and move forward that way.

THE KEY ELEMENTS TO JOB SEARCHING are understanding the marketing plan and the product you're marketing, networking, and differentiating yourself.

NETWORK! Successful networking is not having 800 connections on LinkedIn. It's discovering who are the top producers in your field. Scour LinkedIn, look at the people in the HR department of the companies you're interested in. Find some connections who will put in a good word for you and have your back. Be careful of people who might have a negative association.

HIGHLIGHT YOUR OUTCOMES: It's not only important to state what you have done, but how have those actions benefited the company? Be specific with numbers and percentages, but be honest.

PREPARE! Questions like "What is your greatest weakness" can catch you off guard. This is not the time for improv.

RALLY YOUR SUPPORT: There will be ups and downs in the job search, and it can be long and exhausting. It's important to have people in your inner circle that you can call, who will lift you up and remind you of your self-worth and importance in this world.

Mastery:
Writing Resumes and Cover Letters

*"The future belongs to those who learn more skills
and combine them in creative ways."*
- Robert Greene, International bestselling author

Becky Krueger

Human Resources Director,
Champaign County Regional Planning Commission

CHAPTER FOCUS

- *The changing workforce*
- *Online courses and degrees*
- *Your resume and cover letter*
- *Articulating your earlier successes*
- *Know your vision*

Becky earned a bachelor's degree in human resources management from Ashford University. She is certified by the HR Certification Institute as a Senior Professional in Human Resources (SPHR) and holds the Society for Human Resources Management – Certified Professional (SHRM-CP) certification. Her professional experience includes over twenty years in the human resources profession. She spent 13 years at a global automotive tier one supplier as corporate human resources manager, recruiter, and benefits manager for over 14,000 employees. She spent the last nine years in the public sector where she is currently the human resources director for the Champaign County Regional Planning Commission. Volunteering in the human resource community is also one of her passions. She has volunteered with SHRM for over a decade and has served as Illinois SHRM state director and on the board of the National Conference Leadership Team. Becky is passionate about helping others achieve their career goals and is a big believer in the power of positivity. Let's see what she has to say.

MICHAEL: You're all about positivity, and I'm all about positivity. Becky, you've spoken to countless folks. What do you think is the greatest challenge that job seekers are having today?

BECKY: Today, I think they're struggling to identify where they're going with so many uncertainties that are going on in the world and the economy, particularly in the teaching field. Teachers haven't been going to school every day because of the pandemic. Women are leaving the workforce in droves. <u>OUT OF 1 MILLION PEOPLE WHO HAVE LEFT THE WORKFORCE SINCE THE BEGINNING OF THE PANDEMIC, **80%** OF THOSE ARE WOMEN.</u> What I'm hearing is that they're just not sure what they want to do. That's challenging, because when you're trying to sell your skills in the interview process, you've got to have a target and a clear focus.

MICHAEL: So there's a lot of women out there that are being displaced and not working. Why is that? Is it that they're not clear on their career path, or they are, but they're having trouble getting positions in that group? Where do you see that at right now?

BECKY: Well, I think there are challenges right now. Fifty-seven percent of the workforce are women—that's the lowest since 1988. In my own experience, I see that many women are caretakers. During the pandemic, they are often the first to say, "I will stay home and make sure the kids get their curriculums done. I will stay home with elderly parents and take care of them." And, you know, that's causing a gap. That's causing a lot of thinking about where they want to go with their careers or what their futures really look like. They don't have a clear picture of where their future's going. There are just so many elements that are impacting that.

When is this pandemic going to be over? Are my parents going to survive? When are my children going to go back to school? Full-time work schedules are really one of the biggest elements for many women. There are men who are impacted as well. However, the numbers are pointing to more women who are staying home with kids who can't go to school or daycare, and they don't know when they can go back to work.

MICHAEL: Hmm. Do you think there are opportunities for women to work then at home? Maybe that should be a pivot point; they're at home, they're taking care of the kids. It's not full-time, but it's a decent amount of time, so maybe there's something they could do that is remote where maybe it wasn't remote before. A lot of companies are allowing more work to be done remotely. Now, do you think that that's something that they should be looking into, and what advice would you offer there?

BECKY: According to the Society for Human Resource Management, it shouldn't be a surprise that many employees have pivoted to at-home work. They've got to have those technical skills, communication skills, and the ability to work in this new environment. People who are making the transition to a new position are going to be adding to those technical skills that you can get online. You can complete a master's degree online nowadays. I finished my degree online while working full-time. It was great, because my schedule allowed me to work on research and papers from 10:00 p.m. to 2:00 a.m., which fit my schedule well.

People with families might be able to use the downtime from the pandemic to start working on technical skills that they need for all of the jobs that are now going online or working from home. We don't really know what the future is with this new normal. We're getting reports that large, medium, even small companies are going to consider hybrid work; some employees will return to the office, while some employees will continue to work at home. For the people returning to the office, there will be culture decisions that will be individualized for each organization. I think that, for sure, anywhere you work nowadays, you're going to have to have a high-level of technical skills.

MICHAEL: **Yeah. Let's talk about that for a second. We have a partnership with one of the top online education services, and they work with Harvard and MIT and offer 3,500 free courses. You can learn practically anything. If you want your diploma, you pay a little bit for that—$50 to $250 on average, but** <u>YOU GET FREE COURSES ONLINE, AND YOU CAN GET A DIPLOMA, A DEGREE FROM HARVARD, FROM MIT, FROM STANFORD.</u> **I mean, this is crazy. You don't have to pay tens of thousands of dollars like you did for this years ago. So there are opportunities. I don't think people are tapping into that, but it's EDX.org. That's one place that you can go, and there are others.**

But my point is this—I couldn't agree more that people need to get educated with this new normal, and no one knows, no one has been able to point at what new normal looks like, but we know it's not going to be the same as it was. How different? No one knows, but we know it's going to be

different. We know that there is going to be more video than there was before, like we're doing right now on Zoom.

So let's say you decided to take these courses. How valuable is that from an HR perspective, when someone you are interviewing tells you they are doing that? What does that say to you as someone who could potentially hire someone? What can you discern from that?

BECKY: I put a lot of stock into people who choose to be self-motivated and invest in themselves. That's a big positive when I am interviewing and searching for qualified applicants for our organization and run across people who take the initiative to improve their skills. That is typically a behavior that is reoccurring in our organization. We are a learning organization, constantly investing in training and state-of-the-art technology, to make sure that we're sustainable and agile so that the organization will go on for another 50 years. So we want people who can learn and who enjoy learning. That's a huge plus for me and our management team.

MICHAEL: Yeah. I liked what you said there, because really, what that translates to is when you take an outside course, you're improving on that skill that might be a necessary skill for the job or jobs you're applying for, which is a huge plus, because everyone wants someone that's qualified and knowledgeable about what they're being hired for. But the second thing is that it shows a growth mindset, that you're willing to grow, learn, get better, transform. That means you're going to have that same disposition, that same attitude, that same energy, that same goal, that goal-minded effort in the new job. I mean, that's the reality. Success leaves clues.

If you're doing it before you get a job, it's likely you're going to do it again. And if you're not doing it now, chances are, you're not going to do it when you get the job.

Let's talk about interviews. When you interview someone, what would you say are the top one, two, or three things that are total turnoffs? And then we'll go to the flip side of that. What are one, two, or three things that you really like when you see them?

BECKY: Number one is communication. You have to be a good communicator. You've got to be clear. I have to understand that your communication with me is genuine. I want the applicant to explain to me the experience that supports their motivation. Just saying, "Hey, I'm here. I want the job. Here's my resume. I can do that." All those, warm, fuzzy words don't really work anymore. I am also looking for the employee to be able to sell themselves, to demonstrate confidence and belief in themselves. I'm looking for words, not only on the resume, that are tangible and productive in nature, but I'm looking to see if the applicant can tell me about their accomplishments. I'm looking to hear about things they've improved.

During a job interview, I'm looking for examples of where they have demonstrated leadership skills, something over and above their normal job duties. I want to hear that they are interested in becoming an expert in their field and are looking for increased responsibility. I want to know if they can influence people. Do they have the ability to take that initiative to influence?

For entry-level positions—we all know that change happens at the employee level, because these are the people doing the work, and they find ways to improve upon things. So as you can tell, I'm a bottom-up type of leader, not about top-down. I'm looking for people to tell me, "Something is wrong with the process, and I have an idea," rather than the process

TOP 3 THINGS INTERVIEWERS LOOK FOR IN AN INTERVIEWEE:
1. GOOD COMMUNICATION SKILLS.
2. LEADERSHIP QUALITIES.
3. WILLINGNESS TO LEARN.

goes on for five years and it's wrong and we've lost productivity, we've lost employees, and we've lost clients.

Communication is tremendously important in any organization. Several HR professionals interview for communication skills. Interviewers are screening for knowledge, skills, and abilities. We are looking for people who can move the employer's vision forward and ensure the organization is sustainable. We can no longer hire people, put them in a job, and expect them to just kind of learn as they go along. Our job as managers and leaders is to ensure that they are properly trained and successful. I'm looking for people who are willing to learn and who are motivated by learning.

MICHAEL: **Yeah. I love that. I just want to tap into that a little bit more about qualifications. Those fluffy words don't work anymore, and you really need to have something quantifiable and substantive. Like, I did this for the company, and the result was that they achieved 30% reduction in turnover, 50% higher production, 150% of quota. You know, when they see those tangible results that you've achieved, an employer is able to discern from that, that you have certain talents and abilities, otherwise, you would not have gotten those results. So if you're 120% of quota, you don't have to tell me** that you're a hard worker. Believe me, you don't become a 120%-of-quota achiever if you're not a hard worker. Likewise, if you've reduced turnover by 30%, then you don't have to say you're a team player or a good leader. Those are the kinds of things that really resonate most with a hiring manager and a recruiter, these quantifiable results that you've achieved for a previous company and how that translates to the job you're applying for in the new company. Is that something you would agree with, Becky?

BECKY: Absolutely. Keep in mind, interviewers are learning from the applicants. It is a huge plus to learn from the applicants during the interview process. Applicants can present things that maybe we haven't thought about. Applicants have ideas that we can bring forward and implement to improve productivity or to reduce turnover. So I think interviewers should keep that in mind; they should be open to learning. You never know what an applicant's experience is going to bring to you during the interview conversation.

MICHAEL: Prepare and bring some suggestions that you found that might be a neat improvement in the company. That's going to raise some eyebrows, and they're going to say, wow, this person has done work before they came in, and it is already bringing value. We haven't even hired them, and they're already saving us money, coming up with ideas, and whether it works or doesn't work, it doesn't matter. The fact that you cared enough to do that, and that you developed the habit or showed that you had the habit, that's a real plus.

So let's shift gears. Becky, what are one, two, or three taboo things in an interview that you've seen that just cause you to you shake your head in disbelief?

BECKY: The number one concern in an interview is when you've posted the pay grades, you have conducted a pre-screening probably by phone or nowadays Zoom, and you've confirmed that the applicant can work between a certain pay range, and we get all the way through the interview process, we are ready to make a job offer, and they say, "Oh, no, can't do that."

When the applicant agrees to the pay range at the beginning of the interview process and declines to move forward at the end of the process, that is a lot of money spent and wasted resources for the organization. Typically, the hiring manager is not happy, and they're calling me and saying, "How many times have we discussed the pay rate?" So don't lead a recruiter all the way through the interview process and then pull out and blame it on pay rate. You know, maybe that's the easiest way to get out of the applicant process. Maybe an applicant has another job going on, however, they should be honest about their intentions with the recruiter the entire way through the interview process, because if the recruiter does not believe in you, it's hard to get that door open any further.

MICHAEL: **Right. Speaking about that and open doors, how important do you think resumes are today compared to years ago?**

BECKY: I believe applicants must communicate their knowledge, skills, abilities, experience, and education, whether we call it a resume or a LinkedIn profile or social media presence. Somehow, you've got to get ahold of that information. We recruiters will often look at them all. But I think resumes are still a big part of getting a job. I received one of the best resumes ever this morning.

MICHAEL: **What are some of the things that made it outstanding that just kind of blew your mind?**

BECKY: It was so positive. It was in multiple colors. There was a photo of the employee being her normal self in her natural environment. The photo was amazing and eye-catching. It wasn't your typical drab, black and white resume, with the name at the top, experience, education, hobbies. It stood out. I loved it. It told me a little bit about the person's personality, their motivation, and their tone in life. She got the job! I appreciated the applicant's approach to their resume. Particularly early professionals entering the workforce are using innovative strategies to stand out to a potential new employer and find their edge to get into the employer's door.

MICHAEL: **Yeah. I love that. You have to be different and in a good way, in a way that someone would look at it, and see that you are marketing yourself. Let's face it. It's called AIDCC. I've said it before: it's attention, interest, desire, conviction, and close. So the first thing you have to do is get their attention. If everyone has the same resume, what's going to make you stand out? If you're an orange and then someone comes by and they're a watermelon, who's going to stand out? So you want to be that different resume that stands out, that a grabs the attention and then their interest, and will hook them.**

BECKY: You asked me about other things that are not good about resumes. I have seen typos on resumes that make a huge difference. We recently were recruiting for a high-level public-sector leader, and they were describing their experience in the public sector, and they spelled public wrong. I'm going to leave it there. Needless to say, the interview team could not get over that particular typo.

MICHAEL: Wow. Unbelievable. But also sad. That's a major, major thing. You have to make sure that you're using a grammar check or something to double check your spelling. Your grammar should have another set of eyes look at it. What do you think about having different resumes for different job applications? Why do you think that's important?

BECKY: In my experience, it's obvious when applicants may have not been appropriately advised on their job search, and they're just sending the same resume for all positions for which they apply. The applicant is only doing a disservice to themselves when they do not revise their resume to be relevant to the specific position for which they are applying. You can't send out a resume for a manufacturing position if the company is really looking for someone to fill an administrative position. It just doesn't make sense. The recruiter must be able to connect the dots and sell the applicant's knowledge, skills, and abilities to the hiring manager. The applicant must take the time to adjust their cover letter and resume to the job that they're attempting to land. The applicant should be sure they are speaking the employer's language. Applicants should use the jargon from the job postings and the job descriptions.

MICHAEL: That's critical in sales. We call that mirroring, that you want to speak back in the manner of which they're speaking to you. Those are great suggestions. You take what they want, and you're saying, this is what I deliver. Obviously, you shouldn't lie, but just use the language they're most comfortable with, the lingo. I love that. And every organization and industry has different lingo. So that's why I think it's important to, like you said, have different resumes for different companies, different jobs that speaks their language, taken from the job description.

> TAKE THE LINGO FROM THE JOB POSTINGS AND THE JOB DESCRIPTIONS AND MAKE SURE YOUR LINGO MATCHES WHAT THE EMPLOYER'S LOOKING FOR.

BECKY: That ties in, Michael, to other practices and strategies. Our recruiter frequently uses keywords while utilizing LinkedIn and college websites, looking for qualified applicants. Our recruiter uses keywords and jargon that come directly from the job description.

MICHAEL: Yeah. That's critical. You talked a little bit about cover letters. Some like them, some don't. Some say they use them, some say don't use them. I'd say have one. And if they don't use it, then they don't use it. But at least you'll have one for the ones that do use it. What do you like to see in a cover letter that would make it successful in today's age?

BECKY: Well, you're absolutely right. Michael, some cover letters are specific to the individual and sometimes to the organization, but the key thing in this entire process of getting a job is that you have to be prepared for everything. So have your cover letter ready. <u>YOUR COVER LETTER IS YOUR SALES PITCH, YOUR AMPLIFIED ELEVATOR SPEECH.</u> In my experience, I have found that particularly hiring managers spend more time on the cover letter. They're looking to see the tone of cover letter. They're looking for quantifiable results. They're looking at what the applicant's specific objectives are, if they've done their homework, and whether or not they're applying for the right job and the right company. So cover letters, in my opinion, are still valuable and should be done concisely and should be aimed at marketing yourself at the very highest level. It's your first and maybe only sales pitch.

MICHAEL: Here's a few things that I'm going to pull out: one is to be concise. Remember the HR manager/recruiter spends an average of seven to 10 seconds on a resume and cover letter. That's not a lot, so you need to hook them right away. That means there needs to be lots of white space, not a full page of text, one line in the middle for the space and maybe two or three lines and close it with one line, that's it. But it has to be compelling. I like to use alliteration: clear, concise, and compelling. So if it's clear, concise, and compelling, that's what's going to resonate. So what makes it compelling is another thing you said, Becky, which I love, is show something that's customized for that company, specifically something you read about that company.

And also give something quantifiable that you've done, such as a certain accomplishment. Customize it to something specific—a new acquisition or company that you're excited to learn more about or contribute to. And then talk about a great accomplishment. Add numbers, statistics, something that you did in terms of a quantifiable result. I think those are going to be the things. This is what you need to ask yourself when you do a cover letter: if I read this cover letter, will it compel me to read the resume? And when they read the resume, the question you need to ask yourself as well is, will this compel me to call this person in for an interview? Those are the questions; reverse engineer it. What is going to be most compelling? What's going to make me stand out?

And those are the things that Becky's taught me about: be clear, be customized, make sure you tie into your qualifications and how they match, give quantifiable results and how they'll match what the company is looking for as well. If you're 120% of quota for your current company, then you want to use that with the new company, and they will hope that you're going to get the same results for them. You're going to be over quota. What are your thoughts on that, Becky?

> THERE IS A WAY TO SELL AND MARKET YOURSELF, BUT YOU STILL HAVE TO BE HONEST ABOUT IT.

BECKY: Michael, I can't agree with you more. But I think you referenced this earlier in our chat today when the word honest came up. You cannot lie on your resume. Everybody should write this down. There is a way to sell and market yourself, but you must be honest about your knowledge, skills, and abilities. So when you're talking about those quantifiable experiences, you must be genuine. When human resource professionals check references, they are going to verify your prior achievements with the organization, make sure that every element on your resume and cover letter is something that can be verified and will be a value to the organization. Let's use an HR example here. If you put on your resume that you reduced turnover by 95%, you better have the data to back yourself up.

Several people have left a position and have a gap month while they were looking for a job. The coronavirus has created gap years for many people this year. Applicants should be honest about gaps on their resumes. When reference checks are done and there's a month off, many recruiters will call and ask for clarification, so again, be genuine about gaps on your resume.

MICHAEL: **If you were going to ask one question that reveals a ton about a person you're interviewing, which question would that be? Do you have one or two?**

BECKY: I have to give you two questions. I always like to hear about their most successful moment in their career and what that entailed. I love hearing their success story and what they did to make them successful. I also like to hear about if an applicant worked with a team, if they had a mentor, if they had a coach, and how that felt. That tells me a lot about their motivation, their thought processes, their positivity. On the flip side, I also like to know how they handle situations when things do not go so well. Tell me about your biggest nightmare and how you handled the situation. These two questions also tell me a lot about their character. We know we're all human. We're not going to have a perfect day. We're not going to have a perfect career. I like to work with people and hire people that are realists. It's not going to be a perfect day every day, but it tells me a lot about how they handle it when things do not go well. Some people say, "it's not my fault" or "I didn't do this." They're all doom and gloom. I want to hire people who can manage those emotions, be strategic, identify necessary resources, and work as a team.

Employees must be able to move challenges forward and work as efficiently as possible.

MICHAEL: Okay. So tell me some real-life experiences where you've asked those questions, some responses that you got that were just phenomenal, and then others that you think the person needed to practice a little bit more on how to answer this question.

BECKY: I love a good success story. I love seeing employees grow. Our intern received a full-time job offer because he was able to write code and develop an intake program that would take all of our services and plug it into one place and automate a tremendous amount of paper processes. On the flip side, when an applicant tells me something horrible has happened, it usually ends up being something like, they chose communication styles with members of management that didn't go so well, that it wasn't their fault, it wasn't their responsibility, but communication had failed. Those types of unfortunate stories just don't cut it. If you're telling me that something did not go so well, and it was your responsibility, and you are not accountable, that causes a bit of pause. There's definitely a maturity and a growth opportunity in this situation.

MICHAEL: Right? And there's always going to be hiccups. There's always going to be roadblocks. Nothing, no company, no position, is going to be perfect, but it's how you deal with those, how you progress through those challenges and obstacles, that reveals the most to someone like yourself and any HR director in terms of, if you didn't handle it, if you pointed the finger at your old company, that it was someone else's fault, it's the company's fault, it's the culture's fault, it's

my bosses fault. Then you're not going to get the nod with this company, because you need to accept some responsibility and say, "I could have done something a little differently." I guess, in the HR person's mind, you're going to be that same way when we give you the job.

BECKY: DURING THE INTERVIEW PROCESS, YOU HAVE TO BE AT YOUR BEST. In some cases, you're only going to get that one opportunity to sell yourself to the potential employer. My message to applicants is you've got to be prepared to be your best, and be honest about your knowledge, skills, and abilities. But to be honest with you, there are people out there that just are not at that level of professional development to clearly speak about their accountabilities and make it a learning experience and move on. You've got to make a decision whether or not you can work with someone who needs that professional development, or is that going to be a core characteristic that we're not going to be able to get over?

MICHAEL: **Everyone needs to work on that. There's no doubt. You said: preparation, be yourself, communicate clearly.**

In finishing up, are there one, two, or three things that you could say to those folks, maybe the majority of them women or the total pool of those looking for a job during this pandemic, as things are freeing up a little bit—what words of advice would you have for them to really keep them uplifted, to give them the best shot at getting that job of their dreams?

BECKY: You've got to find your edge. What makes you different and competitive in the workforce? Find that edge that also brings you joy in your life. I believe that a job is not a job if you love

> I DO BELIEVE THAT A JOB IS NOT A JOB IF YOU LOVE WHAT YOU DO.

what you do. I know that's an old saying that I really believe in; find something that you love. You've got to have a clear vision of where you're going, because if you can't articulate that vision in an interview, it's very hard for a recruiter to say, this is what they want to do, and this is how their career paths fit in our organization. YOU'VE GOT TO BE ABLE TO ARTICULATE YOUR VISION TO A RECRUITER. Write down those career paths, and write them down with some detours. If one route doesn't work, this could work. This is the road I want to go down, but it could go this way. Most importantly, you must have a clear vision.

MICHAEL: Yeah. That's, great. Well, Becky, you gave really valuable insights, inspiration, and positivity, as you like to refer to it, for those looking for work. I want to really thank you for caring. You know, it's one thing to offer advice and another thing to really care about the welfare of those that are looking for work. And you know that it means much more than just a job. Some people are losing their home or on the verge of losing their home. Some can't take care of their family. Some have lost their identity. So whatever it is, we know this information will help people get back on their feet, have hope, and have a better roadmap to getting that job and hearing those magical words, "You're hired." So I want to thank you so much for your time and all your valuable, compassionate input.

BECKY: Thank you, Michael. It was an honor to work with you today! To all of those job seekers out there, just keep your focus, get that vision together. You've got this. You can get it done!

ACTION STEPS

THE WORKFORCE IS CHANGING. You may need to take educational courses and learn new things so you can work remotely or online, especially if you're applying to a company that offers a hybrid or at-home work option. There are some great, free online courses.

YOUR RESUME should not just show your education and experience. Add quantifiable data to it, such as if you helped a company increase sales, retain employees, or more. That speaks volumes. It should also be grammar checked by another set of eyes before it goes out, to avoid embarrassing mistakes. Be concise. A hiring manager or recruiter usually only looks at it for seven to 10 seconds before they decide to continue reading or not.

YOUR COVER LETTER is your first sales pitch about yourself. Make it clear, concise, and compelling.

BE HONEST AND BE YOURSELF during an interview. The hiring manager will probably fact check the examples of your successes that you mention. And if you've been out of work for a month or two, tell them why.

KNOW YOUR VISION: Be able to articulate where you want to head in your career. This will not only help you land the job of your dreams but will help hiring managers and recruiters know if you are a fit for their companies.

Linzee and Steve Ciprani

Co-Founders of Ciprani Consulting

> ## CHAPTER FOCUS
>
> - *Effective answers to the dreaded "strengths and weaknesses" question*
> - *Resume aesthetic—how to make your resume stand out*
> - *LinkedIn—how to keep your social resume clean*

I had the pleasure of speaking with Linzee and Steve Ciprani about how to make yourself stand out in a sea of candidates. They offered priceless tips on how to make the most of your resume, LinkedIn, and other social media profiles to get recruiters interested.

Linzee and Steve are the Founders of Ciprani Consulting, a recruiting and training company that specializes in the field of small business building and recruiting. The company has placed and trained over 3000 talented individuals within the small business community. In addition, Linzee is the Founder of the Linzee Ciprani Team—a real estate team within Keller Williams Realty Inc., that uses the processes and systems of Ciprani Consulting.

MICHAEL: **Because of the pandemic, we have around 10 million people still unemployed. As someone in the business of recruiting and training, Linzee, what are the top three**

pieces of advice you can give to someone currently seeking a job?

LINZEE: Obviously, first, having a really great resume is key. We believe that you should bullet point and bold the things that should stand out to a recruiter or hiring manager right away. We have a great resume course on our website, if anybody would like something like that.

Secondly, once you apply, it's very important to follow up. We always say that the squeaky wheel gets the grease. It's very important to continue to say, "Hey, I just want to make sure you received my resume, and I wanted to see if you have any questions. Let me know if I can answer anything. I'm really interested in the position." Most people just send something, and then they just leave it, and they expect a phone call. YOU HAVE TO BE PROACTIVE IN THIS MARKET. And that was the third thing I was going to say—be proactive. Make sure the recruiter knows that you're very interested in the job. Following up on those things is really important.

MICHAEL: **Perfect. You've talked a little bit about bullet points and bolding themes. A recruiter or hiring manager only has about four to six seconds to spend on each resume because of how many they're receiving. Steve, what are your thoughts on the top three things applicants today can be doing?**

STEVE: I think the weird thing about the pandemic is that there's been this convergence of all the different areas of our lives. We're all working from home, and if you have kids, they're running around in the background, and there's lots of stuff going on.

We're really present in a virtual world right now, and I think you can use that to your advantage.

First and foremost, <u>PAY ATTENTION TO THE LITTLE THINGS.</u> If you're doing an online interview, as a recruiter, I'm looking at you, but I'm also looking at what's behind you. So be very careful with the little things. The more things change, the more they say the same. Be prepared. If you just took a shower, and you've left your towel behind you, and I see that, and you say you're really organized, I'm going to question you a little bit there, right?

Secondly, you do need to sell yourself. Even if you don't like thinking of yourself as a salesperson, you have to be able to sell yourself in this job market. If you don't think that way, the people who do are going to get the jobs.

> GO AFTER POSITIONS THAT ALIGN WITH YOUR VALUES.

Thirdly, be authentic. Go after jobs that you really want. Go after positions that align with your values. If you're brand new to sales, and you're applying for a director of sales role, you're probably not going to get it. All the time, we see people who are forklift operators or something like that applying for a hundred-thousand-dollar jobs. Grow into that. There's nothing wrong with starting somewhere and growing from there. <u>**BE REALISTIC ABOUT WHERE YOU ARE AND WHERE YOU WANT TO GO.**</u>

MICHAEL: It is all in the little things. And, as we know, all the little things add up to the big things. Success leaves clues, as they say. But today, the market is a lot more competitive than it used to be. Before, you had to make yourself stand out from 50 people, but now, that number is up to 250. How

do you get through that? How do you become that beacon of light amongst all these other lights? How do you get noticed in this sea of candidates?

Is there one particular question that you like to ask candidates that reveals a lot to you? Different people have different questions that they use to flush out transparency and authenticity. We'll go to you, again, Linzee. What are your favorite questions to ask a candidate that you find reveals a lot about them?

LINZEE: I have a lot of favorite questions. And they really stem from what position I'm hiring. I have a favorite question for an operations person and a favorite question for a salesperson.

For an operations person, I want to know exactly what systems they have created. And then it's all in the follow-up that comes along with that. Somebody can tell me, "Hey, I've created an onboarding system for new real estate agents." Then I'll ask them to walk me through what system they used and how they did it. What was the first step? How did you plan it out? And you really dive in, because a lot of people can say that they created things, and they didn't really create them.

For salespeople, I love to ask them, "What's one question I should have asked you today that I didn't ask you? What's one thing I should know that I didn't get to know about you?" The answers we get from that are just awesome. They'll say, "You know what? You don't know anything about my personal life. I want you to know about my kids," and then boom, now I've got their values. So that's become one of my very favorite questions to ask people. In fact, I ask it for almost everything that I do, because if we can get one more piece of information that's going to help us understand them better, it's gold.

MICHAEL: That's great. I like this because, like you said, it shows you a lot about the person. What you're doing behind the scenes will be reflective of who you are. When you're looking to get hired, if you're not putting your best foot forward during the courtship period, then recruiters are going to see you as sloppy. They'll think you're going to be sloppy at work.

So, Steve, how about you? What would you say is your favorite revealing question to ask candidates?

STEVE: I would say one question you're going to get (and this is maybe not one of my favorites but is something you should be prepared for going into an interview) is about what your strengths and weaknesses are. That question is as old as time, so sometimes, we'll rephrase it and say, "What's something you can do that someone else can't do?"

I want to point out how many people miss that real opportunity to sell themselves, because they don't think through what makes them unique as a candidate. EVERYBODY HAS THEIR OWN UNIQUE EXPERIENCES. It doesn't matter if you're just starting your career or if you've been doing it for 30 years. You have to package that information in a meaningful way.

Another thing I would say is to make sure you not only know what your strengths are, but that you can back them up with an example. Recruiters are always looking for specificity. So if I say I'm really passionate, and I don't give you an example, how can the recruiter know I'm telling the truth? If you're a passionate person, give me an example of a way that you've changed someone else's business, or if you're really detail-oriented, tell me about something that you did to go above and beyond for your boss. So I think that's what we're looking for on the other end. And I think that's what, if you're a candidate, you should be really thinking about.

MICHAEL: **I would add one thing to that: when you tell a story about a time when your passion created a great result for your company, use numbers to back it up. For example, say "I saved the company 40%, and we increased production by 60%." So when you give that information, you're adding emotion to what already is a great accomplishment. Also, if you can tie your answer back to what the job description is, then that's even better.**

I think something that's really important that a lot of people don't think about is, don't just say the exact same numbers or the exact same things that are on your resume. Have something different up your sleeve. You can't list everything on your resume, so during the interview, it's a great time to say, "In addition to what you saw on the resume, I've also done this," which is a great way to continue to brag about yourself.

STEVE: Absolutely. So many people will say, "I don't really know what makes me different," so they've already given up. It's like when you're going to perform something and you say, "Hey, I'm sorry, I didn't really warm up that much for this song that I'm about to play for you, but just give me one second." People don't realize that they're on camera, so make your interview a little bit

> PEOPLE DON'T REALIZE THAT THEY'RE ON CAMERA, SO MAKE YOUR INTERVIEW A LITTLE BIT OF A PERFORMANCE.

of a performance. I want to see you at your best here. And if this is what you're bringing to your best, that is going to make me worry about where we're going to land in office.

MICHAEL: Yeah. I've said it before, and I can't say it enough: prepare, prepare, prepare. Tom Hopkins says it: practice, drill, rehearse; practice, drill, rehearse; practice drill, rehearse. All the greatest athletes in the world take a thousand shots, whether it's in golf or basketball, because they know that practice and preparation keeps them the best in the world. So there's no way to get away from that. THE MORE YOU PRACTICE, THE MORE YOU PREPARE, THE BETTER YOU'RE GOING TO PERFORM.

No one likes to do it. Everyone's excited at the beginning of a marathon, but it's the middle part that's arduous. IF YOU DON'T FEEL LIKE DOING IT, CHANCES ARE, IT'S THE RIGHT THING TO DO. So do it. You'll get the edge, and you'll move forward on getting a job.

Now for weaknesses. To soften the blow of this question, I usually ask candidates, "If I sent you to a seminar to improve on a few things right now, what kind of seminar would it need to be?" This question can be a little intimidating, but I also think this is an opportunity for you to shine, acknowledging that we all have weaknesses, but pinpointing how you overcome them and how you actually got better as a result.

So, Steve, why don't we start with you. Share with us, when you ask that question, how do you ask it, and what kind of response would be the best response?

STEVE: I'm in line with your thinking there too. I actually usually say, "an area for improvement," because I don't look at it like we're flawed and can't be fixed. We all have things we can work on. What I'm typically looking for is authenticity. Be honest in that response. There's plenty of opportunity to sell yourself on the things you're great at.

We want someone who's humble, hungry, and smart, and that's where I'm looking for that humility piece. If you can show me that you're self-aware and that you're humble and that you're growth-minded, then I don't care how unorganized you are, because I know I can work with you as your leader. What I want to know is can I build into you as a new employee?

So, again, be authentic, and be humble. We're trained to figure out if you're not telling us the truth, and we will point that out to our employer.

BE AUTHENTIC, AND BE HUMBLE.

MICHAEL: Let's role play, you and I, that I'm interviewing you.

Example: How to answer the dreaded "weaknesses" question

MICHAEL: **Steve, I want to ask you what areas you think that you could use improvement in and why? Where are some of your greatest challenges?**

STEVE: Well, Michael, thank you so much for asking. This has been something that's just part of who I am, but one thing I've been training myself on in my own personal development is being more structured. That is typically something that doesn't come naturally to me. One of the things I do to work on that is that I block out time on my calendar. I set an agenda every day.

I love connecting with people, and I think I'm really good at it. I value relationships, but time can fly right by when you're focused on spending time with the people you're with. So one thing I've started to implement is to be more disciplined and more organized with my calendar, and that's helped me a lot. That would be something in this position that I would love more coaching on.

MICHAEL: **I appreciate you being honest and open about that. We all have challenges, and that's something we can help you with. We're glad you have good relationship skills, because that's harder to teach than organizational skills. And I can relate to that. Thank you for sharing, Steve. You're hired!**

STEVE: The reason I answered the question that way, Michael, is because it's not just, "Hey, this is what I'm doing to address that." You could see that I'm authentic and self-aware, that I know this is an area for growth, but in addition to that, I told you what I'm doing to get to that next level. And that shows a mature individual that you would want to work with.

MICHAEL: **That's great. Linzee, I'd like you to share your thoughts on greatest weakness and how to deal with that question as well.**

LINZEE: Many people give you just one weakness. The truth is, if you're going to be authentic, there are probably a number of things you can say. I actually really appreciate the people who say, you know what, there are three or four things that I've been working on for a while, and here's what I've done to manage them. I love it when somebody says, "My last boss has given me these five things to do, or these five things to work on to continue to get better in those areas."

In other words, if I'm a salesperson, and I'm going for an amazing sales job, it's okay for me to say something like, "When I have somebody take that paperwork off of me, I'm unstoppable." I love it when they change the script on me and then say, what can you do for me? Or what could the company do to help me grow in that area? Because then, all of a sudden, you throw the other person back on their heels and then they start selling to you. **WHOEVER'S DOING THE TALKING IS DOING THE BONDING,** so let's bring them back into the conversation and make them engage with me. When I have somebody do that, I think, "All right, you're good."

MICHAEL: **Like Linzee said, share right in that moment that you're engaged with a coach, reading or listening to a book, listening to a podcast, watching videos online, on how to**

> SHOW THAT YOU'RE WILLING TO
> LEARN AND GROW.

improve in this area. It shows so much to an employer or a recruiter. It says that you're growth-oriented, that you're willing to learn and grow. It shows that you're clear and aware of your weaknesses.

Understand that when you're asked that question that you're being put in a position where you can shine. You can show how real and authentic you are, and show that you're vulnerable in a positive way, and that we're all human. And WE CONNECT ON A HUMAN BASIS BEFORE WE DO ON A BUSINESS BASIS.

You're looking for progress. So continue to practice over and over again. Don't bury your head in the sand: listen to yourself, Zoom yourself, see how you would look to the prospective person hiring you, and if you don't like the way you look, do it again and improve. That's what you should do if you want to shine.

STEVE: Yeah. You hit a lot of awesome things there. I agree with you about a growth mindset and reading. READERS ARE LEADERS.

MICHAEL: It's interesting that in both coaching and leading, the ones who you would think need it the least, do it the most. Why would Tony Robbins still need to read or be coached in areas like finance? We can't see our blind spots. And by getting coached, that's the way you get better. And when you read, you get better.

So let's get back to resumes now. How have things changed? We know a lot of things are being done on Zoom. A lot more people are competing for the same job. What makes a good resume? Rate its importance on a scale from one to 10. Where do you think a good resume falls, Steve?

STEVE: Probably a nine or a 10. I would still describe the resume as the currency of employment. So it's still the way that we are doing all the things that we do. People are doing some different things with resumes now—people are doing virtual resumes a little bit more, and people are spicing up their resumes. But you still want something that's going to hit the applicant tracking system the right way if you're applying to bigger corporate jobs. It's still the way that we recognize people in the eight to 10 seconds we consider you as a candidate.

MICHAEL: So, Linzee, how about you—one to 10? Where would you rank resumes on that scale?

LINZEE: I'm going to back it down a little from a 10. I'm going to say that it's probably a seven—still very important, but I do believe you can also get a position by knowing somebody. IT'S WHO YOU KNOW THAT GETS YOU IN.

There's proactive approaches, and there's reactive approaches. I believe that you can be very proactive, but only a small percentage of the world will choose to be that way, which means that resumes are still very important. So you've got to make them look great. You've got to have a great LinkedIn profile too.

MICHAEL: Absolutely. We've heard that "your network is your net worth" and all that. At your church, in synagogue, at the soccer field, talk to your colleagues, your past employers, and tell everyone what you're doing. Get it out there. There's a lot of jobs that are not publicly on a job website.

Now, Steve, talk about what it really takes to have a great resume. With the X number of seconds that a recruiter is looking at a resume, what do you think needs to stand out?

STEVE: If you're applying to a corporate position, I would go with a more business kind of resume that's going to look simpler. It's not going to include a picture of you or something like that.

If you're applying to a small business, there's all different kinds of ways that you can find to stand out, and your resume can become a tool for that. You can:
- Add a picture of yourself
- Find a great template
- Put a little design into your resume

We love a website called Canva.com. You can go on there and just type in "resume" and find 500 examples of what a great resume should look like.

I'm a big believer in that we've moved in the 21st century toward a connection model. I think that means that people want to know you. They want to know what you look like. They're going to probably look you up on Facebook and LinkedIn anyway, so just put yourself out there. A great professional photo is a little, simple thing in the small business world to say, "Hey, this is who I am." Again, that authenticity idea.

I am someone who believes that brevity is still best. So I would say keep it to one to two pages. Simplify your work history down so that I can understand it. Of course, your resume is a marketing tool. It isn't about

> YOUR RESUME IS A MARKETING TOOL.

everything you've ever done in your life. This is a tool to get you to the next step of the process. And that's another useful way to think of it. You're marketing yourself to the team.

MICHAEL: As you said, there are pros and cons to putting a picture on your resume. I think a picture can cause a problem for applicant tracking systems. So if you were applying for a job with a big company that uses an applicant tracking system, if you don't have keywords in your resume that match keywords in the job description, there are certain things like graphs and grids and pictures that will automatically send you in that black hole. One way to get a picture in is in your email signature. However, smaller or mid-sized companies are less likely to use an applicant tracking system.

Also, who says you only have to have one version of your resume? Maybe you have a more standard one that gets submitted online. Once you're in the interview process, what if you gave them a more fun, spiced up version of your resume? How cool would that be? It still depends on what you're applying to. Make your resume specific for that job. You may have a good baseline resume that speaks to the industry and to the job at large, but each company has their nuances.

The more your resume speaks to the company and their specific needs, the higher the likelihood that it's going to resonate. And that's what we want. We want it to resonate, and we want you to stand out. Customization takes time,

and most people don't put the time in. Here's your chance to differentiate yourself.

Steve, how many seconds, again, does a recruiter spend on a resume before they make a decision?

STEVE: We joke around about this and call it the once-through comb-over. What that means is that you're probably going to get about six to 10 seconds to stand out. You have to think about the person on the other side. They might be looking at a hundred to 200 resumes or more per day. So in order to get me to stop whatever I'm doing in my resume mode, there's got to be something that sticks out. If you want me to notice your hair, you've got to at least put the comb through one time.

Step one—grab the recruiter's attention.

Step two—once you've got their attention, then they're going to look at the actual content. Most recruiters are not going to go through line by line. We don't have time to do that. You want something to connect with them. Then they might spend 30 to 60 seconds on your resume, and that's going to also separate you from others.

MICHAEL: **The first thing you mentioned, Steve—you have to get their attention. What would you as a recruiter look for in a resume that would get your attention? Give the audience a practical example.**

STEVE: When I say aesthetic, I mean is your information organized? If you're using bullets at one point and then you're using stars the next, that's just going to annoy me, and you don't want to annoy your recruiter before you've even talked to them.

If you're going the small business route, you might be able to put a little bit of color in there or your picture or something that's going to make you stand out. We always look for a LinkedIn profile as well on a resume. Have a clear header. Include a summary statement. State your experience, your education. Recruiters are going to look for all of those things. But if it's not organized in a thoughtful way, I already feel like you haven't spent that much time thinking about your resume.

MICHAEL: Do you like to see a summary? What would have you saying, "Wow, this is a great summary"?

STEVE: There's different opinions on that as well. Personally, I do like a summary, but again, it has to be meaningful. If you give me a some generic, watered-down version of "I'm looking for a job," well, of course you're looking for a job. I've seen resumes that have had quotes on them from other people they admire. That's stood out.

One time, I hired a salesperson whose summary statement said, "I book leads—good ones." And that was it. I loved that, because they knew what they did well, and they communicated it. So you can be a little cheeky. SOMETIMES IT'S OKAY TO TAKE A BIT OF A RISK. That's how you get yourself to stand out.

MICHAEL: Einstein had a great quote: "Everything should be made as simple as possible, but never simpler." That is so profound and so powerful. That's how your resume should be: as simple as it can be, but not simpler than it should be.

You have to have the core content that will help someone make an educated decision in your favor.

Linzee, what would be the best customized information that you could put on a resume that would get a recruiter or hiring manager's attention in the five to 10 seconds they spend looking at it?

LINZEE: I'm going to take this from a different place. The reason we started this business is because when I was applying to positions, I got really good at this stuff.

When I was applying to social media positions, for example, my first five bullets were things I did to help the social media of my previous company grow. And I would put the stats right there, and I would bold the stats. Every single time, I would get calls, because I was really strategic about what my resume said every time. And I changed my resume every time.

If you're going to do something, it's gotta be able to capture a recruiter's attention. I really want to stress, don't let your resume just go through portals like Indeed or ZipRecruiter. They make your resume look not as good. Get your resume, the pretty one, and try to figure out how to apply directly to the company. They all have websites. They all have email. Send it in. Follow up with a phone call. That's how you get hired.

MICHAEL: That's great. One of the things you mentioned that's certainly been echoed before, is follow up. Go the extra mile. Don't just submit your resume and wonder why you never receive a call back. It's those that are doing the extra, creative things, who call the CEO, who send flowers, and so

on, that get noticed. BE CREATIVE. BE BOLD. BE ADVENTUROUS.
BE EVERYTHING THEY WANT TO HIRE.

Let's shift over to LinkedIn. As a recruiter, what percentage of the time do you look at the potential candidate's LinkedIn profile?

Steve: All the time. Honestly, it's usually the first thing they're going to look at after the resume phase.

> MAKE SURE YOUR SOCIAL RESUME IS CLEAN.

The next stage is your social resume. We've seen people that are amazing candidates fall out of the process because of one Facebook post. Be careful what you put about politics on your Facebook or your Twitter or whatever. Make sure that LinkedIn, or your social resume, is quite clean when you're applying for positions. Because if they're not, someone's going to find out.

MICHAEL: That's great advice. Think, "what would an employer think if they saw this about me?" Everyone looks at LinkedIn, but even your Facebook and your Instagram, if you have stuff that's controversial, that's stupid, that's edgy, or has profanity, you're going to lose points, and in most cases, lose an opportunity. Even if you had a great resume, they're going to say, "This is the true reflection of who this person is, and they don't match culturally with what we're looking for at our company."

So elaborate on LinkedIn. What would make a great LinkedIn profile for a recruiter and for a hiring manager?

STEVE: Well, have you actually completed all of your LinkedIn profile? That's a simple one, but again, do you actually have a banner photo? Do you have a nice professional photo? I always start with the simple things. You can really tell that some people have just done the bare minimum, and then other people have really filled it out in more detail. Have you filled in content about your career history? Is all of your information up to date?

I encourage people who have just graduated college not to include an education email. Always list your own private email or some kind of professional one. Not to knock on Hotmail too much, but Hotmail was a thing in the 2000s. So when I see that, I think, this person hasn't progressed beyond that. You may want to set up a more current email, like Gmail. That's going to show you're current with technology.

MICHAEL: Yes, don't have an email like hotbaby@gmail.com or StanleyIntheSun. If you have a name like that associated with your email address, be conscious of that. Just use another, more professional email address.

Here's another question. Do you like seeing testimonials on LinkedIn?

STEVE: Having people testify to some of your skills is another thing that will set you apart. I think great companies hire for talent more than for skill base, but if you have a public speaking skill or you've done Toastmasters or something that sets you apart, like, hey, have people recommend your skill base. That's definitely something that can make you stand out too.

MICHAEL: Linzee, what makes a great LinkedIn profile? Do you agree that recruiters always look at a candidate's LinkedIn?

LINZEE: I go less now to LinkedIn, believe it or not, and more toward Instagram and Facebook, because I think they tell a better story than LinkedIn. It's really easy for us to be professional there, but the moment you go to Instagram, it may be a disaster. So I actually go there more now.

MICHAEL: **That's really interesting. So you need to have a very professional, well thought out, online presence. It's your advertisement for you, so make sure your LinkedIn has all the things that are important to recruiters. List your education, your skills, your qualifications, and make sure your picture is professional.**

LINZEE: I once had a recruit who had a love for the medieval period, and I mean, weapons and costumes were all over her Facebook page, but she was amazing. As a recruiter, I had to actually force my client into meeting with her because his perception from going to social media was so bad. So I think you do have to think about it. Something like that might seem harmless to you, but to a business owner who's been around for 60 years, it might be a red flag.

MICHAEL: **Unfortunately, perception is reality. It's kind of a paradox. Your social media should be a reflection of you. I want it to reveal truly who I am—the doofy, the smart, the aggressive, the caring, the loving. I want everyone to see every part of me on my social media. And now I want to tamper with that if I'm looking for a new job. Now I have to think,**

"How are other people going to view my social media?" Do I need to clean it up a little bit and make it a little more professional, but still not lose my identity? How do I do that? Would that be something you guys agree with?

STEVE: I was thinking the same thing. Glad you said that. You don't need to whitewash your life. It's okay for you to have a life. But just keep in mind that social media is public knowledge, and once you put it out there, it's there. If you're aspiring toward a more professional career, you want to consider these things.

MICHAEL: **What bit of advice would you give a job seeker today?**

STEVE: As recruiters, we're not in the business of tearing people apart. I think the one thing I would encourage anybody who's looking for a job is that it'll happen. So just have faith. If you really are pursuing this with all your mind, it'll happen. But to make it happen, DON'T BE AFRAID TO PUT YOURSELF OUT THERE. TAKE SOME RISKS. DON'T BE AFRAID TO FAIL. A lot of our clients have said, "Oh, she was really nervous, and I liked that, because it means she cares about the position."

Believe that you will get the job. I know that it's been frustrating for a lot of people. Especially last March, it was really hard. So believe, number one, that it will happen. And number two, put yourself out there, take some risks. Don't be afraid to look a little silly. Your employer or future employer will notice that you care.

MICHAEL: **Well said. And what bit of advice would you give someone who is frustrated in this challenging time, Linzee? What would you say to them?**

LINZEE: I know I've been banging this drum about being proactive this whole time, but it really is important. I think it's also important to get specific and really figure out what you want as an employee. What are your values, and what kind of job do you want? I think this market has caused people to just try to find any job. It doesn't matter what the job is. But I think it really matters what job you get.

What do you want to do? What are you gifted in? What are your values? Are there companies out there that match that? Then go be proactive and get that company to talk to you. Start at the ground level, answer the phones, just get in there because they align with what you want to do. **SHOW THEM THAT YOU WANT TO LEARN HOW TO BE A PART OF THEIR WORLD.** I think a lot of people are missing the boat on trying to figure out what they really want to do and what they're passionate about.

MICHAEL: **As you guys have said, it's all about patience and persistence. Don't be deflated or defeated. Remember that the road to success is all uphill. The elevator to success is broken. You've got to take the stairs. Follow the advice that these two experts gave you, and you'll see yourself inside the job of your dreams in no time. Steve, Linzee, this has been a joy. I can't wait to see how many lives you can change together.**

STEVE: Absolutely. Thank you for having us.

ACTION STEPS

BE PROACTIVE—follow a submitted resume with a phone call to make sure it's been received.

PAY ATTENTION TO THE LITTLE THINGS—what's in the background of your Zoom call?

THE "WHAT ARE YOUR GREATEST WEAKNESSES?" QUESTION IS A GOLDEN OPPORTUNITY TO:

1. Sell yourself
2. Show humility
3. Demonstrate that you're actively working to grow by providing examples of how you're overcoming your weaknesses
4. Turn the question around and ask the interviewer how the company will be able to help you to grow in that area
5. Showcase more than one weakness—showing that you're self-aware and want to improve

MAKE YOUR RESUME STAND OUT BY:

1. Highlighting or bolding the most impressive or relevant pieces of information
2. Adding a professional photo of yourself (for businesses not using application tracking software only)
3. Put a little design into your resume by finding a great template (Canva.com is a great resource)
4. Being consistent with your design choices—if you start with bullet points, don't switch to dashes later on
5. Customizing your resume for each position you apply for
6. Adding a splash of color

MAKE YOUR LINKEDIN PROFILE STAND OUT BY:

1. Filling out the entire profile
2. Including a header
3. Including a professional photo
4. Having friends add testimonials about your skills
5. Listing a professional email (do not use an education email or a non-professional email)
6. Keeping your profile clean and professional (this goes for Facebook, Instagram, Twitter, and other social media as well)

John Baldino

President of Humereso,
Keynote Speaker

> ## CHAPTER FOCUS
>
> * *Building a professional online presence*
> * *Telling a story through your resume*
> * *Skill vs. Will*
> * *Owning your failures*

I was delighted to discuss professional online presence, resumes, and interviewing foibles with John Baldino. With almost 30 years of human resources experience, John has a passion for setting contributors and companies up for success. John is a keynote speaker for US and international conferences, where he shares content and thoughts on leadership, collaboration, and innovation, employee success, organizational design and development, as well as inclusion and diversity. He is the most recent winner of the Greater Philadelphia HR Consultant of the Year award. John is currently the President of Humareso, a global human resources consulting firm, and the proud father of three amazing young adults.

MICHAEL: **So let's start from the beginning. What three things make a candidate jump out to you, whether in a resume or in an interview?**

JOHN: Online presence is one. LinkedIn is obvious, but also, wherever you are presenting who you are to the world. I know that there are people utilizing online portfolio management systems right now, particularly on the creative and technical side of things. Managing that can be a real game changer. We do look for thoughtfulness. So if you do that well, it's a standout.

I think the resume is a necessary evil. If you feel like you're like throwing your resume into the wind, and you don't hear anything back, there are thoughtful ways to create your resume to stand out. There is something visual to it. So if you're just doing job title, 48 bullet points, job title, 48 bullet points, it's not really going to get anybody's attention. Think about the way you do your headers or the way you use the margins. You need something that helps to draw an eye to your skill set, something for us to hone-in on.

Thirdly, <u>DON'T UNDERESTIMATE THE COVER LETTER.</u> In an online world, so many people are just clicking "apply". You can't put all your hopes on that. That is not going to be the answer for you. There are a million people clicking to apply who have no skillset whatsoever for the job that they're applying to. So you'll just get lost in the mix. Have a tight cover letter. Don't just send the resume. Give a little bit of an intro. <u>TELL SOMETHING INTERESTING IN YOUR STORY TO MAKE US PAY ATTENTION.</u>

MICHAEL: I've interviewed lots of HR experts and recruiters, and there's a common denominator they all agree on, and that's preparation. No one ever argues with "be prepared" and what that looks like and sounds like. But people do have different opinions about cover letters. How can you get your resume past the applicant tracking system? How will

the resume design impact its ability to get past the applicant tracking system?

And then I want to drill into the resume and the cover letter. There's going to be certain recruiters and hiring managers that want to see a cover letter and certain ones that don't care. So the bottom line is, if you submit it and they don't care, they discard it. But if they're the ones that want to see it, you need to include it. So I would say, unless they don't have a place where you can include it, always include a cover letter.

Throw a number out there of how often you look at a perspective hire's LinkedIn page.

JOHN: I'm going to say a hundred percent. If you are hiring for an entry level position, or something more technically driven, you're probably not going to be searching for LinkedIn profiles. But I would say a hundred percent for relevant roles, however. Recruiters also use some level of sourcing technique through LinkedIn to find candidates as well.

So that's why your profile matters so much. If you are in an industry or you have a passion for a particular skillset, you're going to want to advertise that. I liken the thoughtfulness of it to what a company needs to do for job marketing. Most companies just post the job description and there's nothing sexy about it. There's nothing that draws a potential applicant in. So if you have a marketing department that partners with your talent acquisition or recruiting departments, and really puts together some job ads that are thoughtful, you get a bigger bang for your buck.

Now on the candidate side, it's the same concept. You're putting something that is marketing in nature out there. YOU'RE ADVERTISING WHAT YOU KNOW HOW TO DO AND WHY YOU KNOW HOW TO DO IT. And the story behind it. That's going to draw a potential employer in, and then you can get job descriptions and alignment around competencies.

MICHAEL: I think one other interviewer said that it's an advertisement, too. The bottom line is advertising. There's something called AIDCC—attention, interest, desire, conviction, and close. There's tens of thousands of people looking for a job. So how do you stand out? How do you then grab a recruiter's attention to get them to read your resume? What does that look like? What kind of header do you use? How do you get them to want to call you?

JOHN: On the recruiting side of things, as they look at LinkedIn profiles, there is a sensitivity today that's different than five years ago. So they're looking at your profile and thinking, "I have to be thoughtful not to allow a profile picture to affect the way in which I'm going to read this information." But that leaves room for them to be affected by something else, which is the way you market yourself.

Let your profile tell your story. Don't add anything distracting

> LET YOUR PROFILE TELL YOUR STORY.

to your profile. Pictures should not include who you voted for in the last election, etc. Why would you create a barrier like that?

Statistically, when there is a list of job duties and responsibilities that someone wants to address, for men, if they match 20 to 30% of what's on that list for the job, they will apply. Women, however, will only apply if they match around 80%. I'm going to actually add another group—veterans. They only apply for jobs they match almost a hundred percent. They want to match every bullet point that's listed there. And if they don't, they don't apply.

What I want to say to those individuals that have such a high percentage of match before they'll go forward, don't restrict yourself, because you're having a whole bunch of guys submit to a 20 to 30% match. Those folks get into the mix quicker because they put less restriction on themselves. I'm not saying apply for every single job you see. There are some guys that ought to take a minute and reread what it is that they're applying for. But that's a reality that we're dealing with on the hiring side of things. We want to draw in more vets, we want to draw in more women. So we're trying to figure out ways to advertise to that.

On the candidate side, **DON'T BE AFRAID TO TELL YOUR STORY.** Take a bullet point or two, and thread a story that you think will align with the job description. Even if at first blush you think it doesn't connect, you'd be surprised. Tell your story.

MICHAEL: **You mentioned LinkedIn. This leads to the question of what to have on Facebook, Instagram, and other social media sites. How many hiring managers and recruiters will look at other social media to get a deeper look into a candidate? They're going to look at Facebook and say, "Is there anything there that would indicate that I shouldn't hire this person?" What is your take on that? Because a lot of people have Facebook, and I know it's free speech. I know you're big on diversity, but you want to improve what** you post, because that could offend and disqualify you to a recruiter.

JOHN: Certainly, there are sites that are being looked at by recruiters. I'm all for free speech too. I get it. But be restrictive where you can be. If you choose to post something a little risqué on Facebook, make sure you set it to only be seen by your friends. If everything is public, then just understand that means public, and everybody's going to see it. And it also won't give someone who's looking at it the opportunity to understand the story. For instance, you've applied for a role as a forklift operator. The hiring manager takes a quick peak online, and they see you posted a picture from a couple of weekends ago of you smoking a blunt.

Could you have a medical reason why you're on marijuana? Yes. Is that recruiter going to take the time to understand your medical condition, which by the way, is protected by HIPAA? They're not going to do that. They're going to think, "Oh, that might be a safety issue for the forklift position that he's applied to. He may come in high. He may be impaired. I don't know if we want to walk that route."

You can tell me all day long that that should not matter. I understand that, but I'm telling you, you're asking a recruiter who could be 25 years old to make some sort of discerning decision based on what they see, so why give that information legs? Make it a restricted picture. Go through your Facebook and Instagram and take things down.

I have a friend who works with college students in career counseling. He meets with every senior. The first thing he does when they sit for their appointment is go to Facebook and LinkedIn and bring up their profile. He had one guy whose profile picture was him naked, smoking a joint, and wearing a sombrero. It's not an inviting picture for any potential employer, unless he was doing some sort of male modeling. Maybe it would work for that. But by and large, do you want to be seen as less than you really are?

MICHAEL: **So if you were an employer and you saw this picture, would it add points in your favor? Do you think it will make them more likely to call you? I've seen many people curse a lot on social media. If I saw that when I was hiring someone, and I had a value system in my organization that didn't embrace that type of language, it would be a negative mark. Would it be a deciding factor? Probably not, but it wouldn't be a positive or a neutral. It would be a negative one.**

JOHN: I'll go one step deeper. If you're applying for a role that is communications oriented, that's what I would be more thoughtful about. Do you have the right to drop the F-bomb all you want? Yes. But someone who's looking for communication as part of the job description could look at that and not be able to see the nuances of language and your mastery of it. Think about the job itself, as opposed to just someone being offended by something.

I want to make sure that I say very clearly, though, for everybody listening, that I'm not asking you to take down everything that you think someone might find questionable. So for instance, if you are a same sex couple, I'm not asking you to hide that. Frankly, if there's a company that would feel they couldn't hire you because of that, they are walking a line on discrimination that is going to come back to bite them, and you may be the one to bite them. But the other piece of it is you've found that it's not a cultural alignment. It isn't going to be worth the energy and effort for you to join an organization and be immediately frustrated by what you're coming up against. Obviously, that'll come out in other ways in the company. <u>SO DON'T APOLOGIZE FOR WHO YOU ARE.</u>

MICHAEL: **Of course. That brings up an interesting point, John, that as much as you want to be a match for this job, they need to be a match for you as well.**

I think everyone listening has a clear idea that social media is important. It can be a qualifier and a disqualifier. So spend some time going over your accounts and seeing what you need to eliminate. **Remember, LinkedIn and your resume are an advertisement. That means you have to have a header that grabs your attention. Put some things that are substantive in there.**

> LINKEDIN AND YOUR RESUME ARE AN ADVERTISEMENT.

JOHN: Yes, you even want to add graphic pieces or lines to break things out into sections. I think visual interest is really helpful there.

MICHAEL: **Talk a little bit about resumes. We've heard before that they're necessary evils. You have to have a resume. You have a lot of practical experience with applicant tracking systems and how to create a resume. Talk a little bit about that in terms of what makes a great resume and how a resume can get past the applicant tracking system.**

JOHN: There's so many ways to respond to that. The first thing I want to make sure that I say is that we live in a world where, depending upon the role that you're applying for, you could be up against more machine learning than ever before. For instance, in 2019, Amazon hired 10,000 employees, and no one ever spoke to a real person until their start day. Everything was responded to by chat bot and auto tech services.

There may be jobs where you may not ever speak to someone personally. So what can I do to help my resume? How can I get a positive hit? You want to be careful about repetitive language. Look at your resume and note how many times you start your bullet points with, the same word (ex. "managed" or "performed"). Use synonyms. There may be words that are auto programmed into the software that you're missing by being too repetitive.

Be careful about how long your resume is. If you have under eight years of professional work experience, and you have a two or three page resume, there's no reason for that. You're saying too much, and probably a third of it is not true. It may not pass the sniff test.

There's a rule of thumb that you've probably heard of don't go back past 10 years on your resume. But if you're applying for a specific job where experience that you had 15 years ago would be relevant, put it in, because that algorithm is going to look for some of those terms that have to do specifically with what you were able to do or display. So put it in there. **DON'T LEAVE IT OUT, BECAUSE YOU'LL BE LEFT OUT.** You can also have different versions of your resume for different kinds of jobs. Don't limit yourself to the same one everywhere. You may say to me, but

John, it's hard to do that on Indeed. Okay. If Indeed isn't paying your bills, then you need to figure it out.

MICHAEL: My dad used to say, "If it were easy, then everyone would be doing it." Good news for you. Everybody's not doing it. And if you want to stand out, and you want to get a job, and you want to get the interviews faster than everyone else, customize your resume. WHEN YOU CUSTOMIZE YOUR RESUME, YOU'RE SPEAKING THEIR LANGUAGE. When your resume speaks their language, it gets through the applicant tracking system, and it gets to the eyes it needs to get to.

JOHN: Your resume is a marketing tool, just like we talked about with social media. So market yourself.

MICHAEL: The end game here is to have multiple versions of your resume that speak to different job opportunities and to what those companies are looking for in terms of skills, qualifications, and experience.

So how many pages should your resume be? What I've heard most frequently is that your resume should be around two pages. What are your thoughts on that?

JOHN: I'm not a three-pager. I don't care if you've been a professional for 40 years, you do not need a three pager. Nobody's reading it. I'm a high-level HR manager. If I'm leaving that to apply for another senior HR role, why does my resume still say things like," I can do open enrollment," etc.?

But if I'm going from strategic senior HR role to strategic senior HR role, why am I wasting space with that stuff? Get rid of that. Put in the things that are going to align more to what I'm looking for.

MICHAEL: I think the key words there are, is it relevant? Is it meaningful? If it's not relevant and meaningful to the job that you're applying for, get rid of it.

What amount of time does a hiring manager or recruiter spend on a resume?

JOHN: Recruiters are going through hundreds of resumes a day. So they're spending maybe seven to 10 seconds on each one.

MICHAEL: We want people to have a clear picture. If they're only spending seven to 10 seconds on a resume, there is only so much stuff they're going to be able to read. So you have to get their attention. Your highlight reel has to speak to them and hit them between the eyes. That's the marketing piece.

> YOUR HIGHLIGHT REEL HAS TO HIT THEM BETWEEN THE EYES.

JOHN: Absolutely. There's a difference between tripping the algorithm and buzzwords. People may think that the profile section at the top is where you put buzzwords like "multi-tasker" and "detail oriented." Those kind of advertising slogans are what everybody else is using. So take that space and tell your story. If there's a specific incident that captures a lot of what the job that you're applying for would require, take a paragraph and tell me a story.

MICHAEL: I would just add that it should be a short, specific story. That's what they're looking for. Tangible, quantifiable

results, not the fluff that you talked about earlier, that everyone is saying.

JOHN: There are some roles that are easier to do that with. Let's be honest, right? Sales is super easy in terms of having a clear metric, but for those of you that feel you don't know what kind of metric you can use, I'm going to say, look at things like retention. If you were supervisor for a small group of people, what was retention? Say, "My folks tended to stay on average 3.6 years."

MICHAEL: I tend to talk more about sales since I come from that background. But also you have people applying for factory work and engineering jobs. And when you do that, you can say, "I didn't miss a day of work for three years" or "My attendance was perfect" or "I always exceeded whatever metrics they use in terms of production."

JOHN: Keep a copy of your performance reviews and appraisals, because invariably there's going to be some sort of stat that you can use to help put together what you're describing.

I remember being a senior in high school and sitting at graduation. Four people had perfect attendance from kindergarten through senior year. I remember thinking, *What losers, why the heck would they never take a day and cut school?* If there is a relevance for someone understanding what reliability looks like, my encouragement would be, if your attendance plays into that, put it on there, but also help them understand that it was more about just being present from a reliable standpoint.

I think because those terms can also work against you too. You tell me you're a go-getter, and I look at your resume, and I see in seven years that you've had five jobs. Now, there could be reasons, but seven years, five jobs, and you're a go-getter. I'm going to question that. You can't just depend on the verbiage. You have to show it.

MICHAEL: **Look at your resume, and have other people look at your resume. We don't see the world the way it is, we see the world the way we are. You're seeing your resume with your lens, your perspective. You need an outsider, preferably someone who is an HR person or a recruiter, and ask them, "What do you think of this? What's glaringly good? What's glaringly bad? How should I change it? And why should I change it?"**

JOHN: On the other side, don't apologize for what your career progression may be. I have listened to folks quite honestly and effectively share that their first two jobs that they were only at for a year were what they thought they wanted to do at the time. And then they realized that they didn't, so they made a pivot. I get that. I'm not going to give you a hard time. I can guarantee that for everyone.

I think that there's a lot more reasonable people than you may believe out there who can understand that story. The other piece is sometimes candidates do themselves a disservice by the way in which they put their resume together, where a company was acquired by another company. And so they break out by company, and it's like, "Oh, I actually never left my desk. It's just that who owned us kept changing."

MICHAEL: If you have had multiple jobs and, for legitimate reasons, you changed careers, that's understandable. What we're saying is be prepared. It's going to be a concern. It's going to be a question. Be prepared to answer that with something that makes sense. That way, it goes from a negative potential in someone's mind to a neutral. And perhaps even you could make it something that's positive: "Hey, listen, I want to do something I'm passionate about. I tried it, and I wasn't passionate. We've all done that, and now I'm on the right track. I want to find the right company to spend my career with." And that's a great story. But you have to be prepared.

JOHN: I interviewed someone not that long ago for a role where everyone else who had made it to the final cut had a bachelor's degree. Now the role was advertised as bachelor's degree preferred, not required. And so this one individual was a high school graduate and had taken some classes here and there. I asked the question, "Tell me why you didn't go to college. It is a preferred component of qualification." He was ready with an answer, and it was a phenomenal answer, and it made sense all the way through, and he got the job.

MICHAEL: Let's talk about that for a second. What does it mean that a degree is preferred but not required? Is it possible that someone can get through who doesn't have a degree, but still is qualified in all the right areas?

JOHN: Yes. Unfortunately, so many companies just recycle their job ads. And so they don't really change some of the stuff that it says. More companies are actually being pushed about these job requirements from an inclusion and equity standpoint.

I just was working with a company who required 15 years of experience for a position, but they were hoping to have a diversity-based candidate. And I said, well, let me ask you a question. Were you hiring black people 15 years ago in these kinds of roles? And they said, no. And I said, so if you weren't doing it, where do you think these people are going to come from? Tell me why 15 years? Could it be 12 years? And they chatted for a while and said, "Yeah, I think we'd be okay with 12 years of experience." I said, "Awesome. Tell me the difference between 12 years of experience and 10 years of experience."

More companies are starting to look at that because they're recognizing that it's keeping some kinds of candidates—talented, skilled people—far away from even applying because of what they see in these qualifications. So we're seeing more companies do a review of that.

I'm going to say to you, unless you know that a degree is really, really going to be relevant, like in engineering, if you're applying for a management role and it says bachelor's degree required, that's a lie. They just haven't updated the requirements.

MICHAEL: **Talk about skill and will. Everyone wants someone who has a growth mindset. Someone who's willing to put the time in and shows a track record of growth, of learning, of development, of advancement. And if you can convey that in some way, then what you lack in skills, you have in will, and you're willing to work harder to be a major part of what they're looking for. And you've done your research about the company ahead of time, and you know what the key points are, then that's going to be something that is a plus.**

What are two or three things during an interview process that you've experienced where a person came in and had the perfect answer? What are three major turnoffs during an interview?

JOHN: I interviewed someone for a sales-based position some years ago. I came up front to meet him and take him back to my office. My assistant was there and met him first. Then I came to meet him, and, as he shook my hand, he looked around and said, "This is a nice effing (he used the full term) place." I said, "Well, thank you very much. I had a hand in the design."

Now I can see my assistant, who's not in his eyesight, doubled over, dying of laughter, because she can already tell this is going to be a train wreck. I've decided I need to see this train wreck all the way through, because I'm intrigued now.

He really wants this job, and every question I'm asking him, he's like, "Ah, I can do this. You don't have to worry about that. I can do it. Don't worry. I can do it." And I was like, "Oh, okay, awesome, good. I won't worry then."

I said to him, "Are there any limitations that you've experienced and that you recognize are still areas you need to work on?"

And he's like, "Well, I don't want to deal with Asian people."

And I said, "I'm sorry?"

And he said, "Yeah, it's just, if I get this job, I want to make sure that people who call in aren't Asian, but I'll take every Puerto Rican that calls in."

And I said, "Oh, I don't know if we can filter for that, but I absolutely will look into it."

So obviously, he didn't get the job for a variety of reasons. That's a memorable one. I'll never, ever forget that.

MICHAEL: **There are basics of what you need to do in an interview. Look professional, speak professionally, don't be robotic, be real.**

What is your tell-all question to ask a candidate that reveals a great deal about them?

JOHN: There's quite a few that I have. In some way, I'll usually ask, "What do you consider to be your greatest failure? And whatever just popped into your head is the answer that I want, whether professional or personal. Walk me through what you took from it, how you got through it, if you got through it, and where you sit today, and if you need to deal with it again."

I'm always fascinated by the things that people share. Not that this is the goal, but it's not a shock for me to see someone tear up, because they're being honest about relationship failures or expectation failures.

> WE ALL MAKE MISTAKES, SO LET'S TAKE OWNERSHIP OF THOSE MISTAKES.

I appreciate that because it shows a wherewithal. **I LOOK FOR OWNERSHIP OF FAILURES,** because whichever kind of company you're applying to, they can't be an organization that doesn't have an expectation of failure. Things are not going to work right every time. So I want to have people on the team who aren't afraid of it and can deal with it. Don't take it to mean that it's an albatross around your neck. What do we do with it? And how do we move forward from it? I love that question in some shape or form. And people tend to be either honest or uncomfortably avoiding an honest answer.

MICHAEL: **Right, it reveals honesty and openness and transparency, which is important and translatable. These are the types of people we want working for our company. It shows some vulnerability, that we all make mistakes. Let's take ownership of those mistakes.**

JOHN: And it gives people an opportunity to share with relativity. For example, if I'm dealing with someone who may be a younger, entry-level type role, they may not have had enough life experience to have some earth-shattering failure. When I was 21, there were things that were failure-oriented to me at that stage in my life, where now, as I'm almost 51, I probably wouldn't list any of those things.

MICHAEL: **Right. These answers also show tenacity, resilience, and persistence. It's probably one of the best questions.**

John, I appreciate you being part of this journey with me and with all our listeners.

JOHN: Thanks for having me. It was my pleasure.

ACTION STEPS

CURATE YOUR ONLINE PRESENCE—don't be ashamed of who you are, but be mindful of what you put on Facebook, Instagram, and other social media websites. Utilize your privacy settings or remove posts that might turn a recruiter away from you as you job search.

DON'T UNDERESTIMATE THE COVER LETTER—tell a story that will draw a recruiter in. Differentiate yourself from the pack.

HOW TO CREATE A RESUME THAT STANDS OUT

- Be careful of repetitive language. Use synonyms. There may be words that are auto programmed into the applicant tracking system that you're missing by being too repetitive.
- Keep your resume under two pages, no matter how many years of experience you have.
- A rule of thumb is not to include anything on your resume from more than 10 years ago. However, if you have relevant experience from 15 years ago, include it on your resume so you aren't filtered by the applicant tracking systems.
- Keep a copy of your performance reviews. These can be used later to track specific stats that you can include on your resume.
- If you've had multiple jobs over a short period of time, be prepared to be questioned about that. Prepare a logical, well-thought-out answer.

WHEN YOU'RE ASKED ABOUT YOUR GREATEST FAILURES, DON'T BE AFRAID TO OWN UP TO THEM. Good companies realize that everyone fails. They want to understand how you deal with your failures, and how you learn from them and move forward.

Engagement:
Acing the Interview

*"Putting your best foot forward
at least keeps it out of your mouth."*
— Morris Mandel, educator and journalist

Andrea Hoffer

Founder and CEO of
AHA! Recruiting Experts

CHAPTER FOCUS

- *You can only customize if you research*
- *Navigating short tenure*
- *Get ahead of negatives on your resume by addressing them*
- *The one-way video interview: What it is and how to ace it*

I spoke with Andrea Hoffer about the pros of great interview preparation and the newest trend in interviewing: the one-way video interview.

Andrea has been in the business of hiring, leading, and motivating people for over 25 years. She is currently the Founder and CEO of AHA! Recruiting Experts. The core purpose of AHA! is to give leaders their time and freedom back by helping them attract, engage, and retain team members who believe in and support their mission. Andrea, a former spa owner where she managed 35 employees, knows first-hand the everyday challenges of motivating employees, exceeding customer expectations, and meeting business and revenue goals. She often struggled with high-turnover and lack of good candidates.

After some research and a lot of trial and error, she perfected a hiring process that gets results. Andrea is now using that experience and knowledge to help companies recruit, hire, onboard, and engage their team members. Her talks speak to business owners, CEOs, and organization leaders. She will inspire you to take action with her clear-cut action steps that have been proven to get results.

MICHAEL: Andrea, if there were three things that you could say are absolute musts for job seekers in this competitive job market, what would they be?

ANDREA: Number one would be to know what type of job you're looking for. You want to know more than just the *industry* you're looking for a job in. What kind of work environment are you looking for? What kind of culture? Are you looking to work from home or are you happy to go into the office? What are your non-negotiables, and what are the nice-to-haves?

When you start looking for jobs, show employers that you really care about *their* job. Don't just send out mass resumes that are the same thing over and over. Really personalize it. Write a cover letter that's customized to the job that you're pursuing. Explain why you're excited about the opportunity and how you can bring value. It sounds so simple, but I rarely see it, even when we're interviewing. The first question I always ask is, "Could you share why you are you passionate about this job?" I often just get candidates who go into a 10-minute story about their experience, but none of it tells me why they want to work here or why this job is right for them at this point in their life.

MICHAEL: Absolutely. Everyone says customized and personalized, customized and personalized. It seems simple,

but it will make you stand out. **Customization takes more time, yes, so if you do it, you are more likely to resonate with the person on the other end.**

ANDREA: Yes, definitely. And the only way you're going to be able to customize is if you **DO YOUR RESEARCH**. Make sure you read the job posting or whatever information they have out there, because you don't want to walk in and have all these questions that are answered on the job posting. You want to have deeper questions. Go

> GO BEYOND THE OBVIOUS AND SHOW THAT YOU HAVE AN UNDERSTANDING OF WHAT THE JOB IS.

beyond the obvious, and show that you have an understanding of what the job is. Often, people show up for an interview and ask me what job they're interviewing for because they have so many. If you have all these opportunities, I want to feel special. It's almost like dating.

MICHAEL: **I use the dating analogy quite often too. If a candidate doesn't show that they've done the research, if they don't show that they're able to communicate effectively, then you're not going to want to see them again. If you don't have good manners on the first date, and you're not doing all the things that are important, there probably won't be a second date.**

Once you get married (meaning, you're hired), they know that things are not going to get better. So they know that what you show prior to the marriage/getting hired is not going to get better afterward. It's going to get worse.

Andrea, what percentage of people come to you who don't know about the job they're interviewing for?

ANDREA: I don't know if I can put a number to it, because we have a bit of a different approach when it comes to recruiting. We put a lot of front-end effort into making sure the information is out there about what the culture is like at our client's place of business and what the job is about. So I think our numbers are a little higher in that when people apply or at least get to the interview stage, most of them do have a good deal of information. I'm guessing that about 10% come in who don't really know much about what the job really is.

I'd say another 50% just have very basic knowledge. They don't click on the links that bring them to the website, the client, or really get a feel for what the job is about. They just saw one thing in the title that they thought they could do and didn't go any further. So <u>YOU REALLY CAN STAND OUT IF YOU PUT IN A LITTLE EFFORT.</u>

MICHAEL: When you do the research, you're not only identifying and being able to communicate back what you know about the company, but you also know where the connection points are, where your skills and qualifications and experiences match up to what they're looking for. And you have quantifiable data to show that you've excelled in those areas and will do the same for them. When you're doing this research, you're also able to determine if you're a good fit, and therefore, you save yourself all that

> REMEMBER, THE INTERVIEW PROCESS IS A TWO-WAY STREET! YOU WANT TO KNOW ABOUT THEM, JUST AS THEY WANT TO KNOW ABOUT YOU. DO YOUR RESEARCH!

time and perhaps frustration of going out on something that really is not a good fit. Remember, it's a two-way street.

ANDREA: Exactly. You want to make sure this is right for you. If you do get an interview, you want to be interviewing them as well to get more information and to get a feel for what it would be like to be there every day.

MICHAEL: What are two or three things that turn you off of a candidate right away?

ANDREA: We will get resumes that say a candidate has 20 years of experience in the specified industry. Then we look at the resume, and, if you add it all up, sure, it might add up to 20 years. But it's eight months here, one year here, nine months here. We call that poor tenure—jumping around from job to job.

All of our clients come to us because they want people who are going to stay a while. For most jobs, it takes at least a year for somebody to get good at what they're doing. You don't want somebody leaving after you finally put all this training and effort into them. We want to find people who want to be there for a while. We know people don't stay places for 15 years anymore. It's very rare, but at least three to five years would be great.

MICHAEL: What do you recommend if someone has jumped around quite a bit? Do you just say, "You're screwed because you should have stuck it out for a few more years?" What do they do? I happen to be coaching someone right now who shows a ton of experience a year here, a year there. I said, "This looks horrendous," because, you're right. Companies don't want to put time, money, and energy into you just for

you to leave. So, what would you say to someone who is in that situation? What do they put on their resume?

ANDREA: I would put some sort of explanation for the jumping around, whether it's on the cover letter or in an email. Maybe your spouse or partner moved around a lot for their career. I would include that you're ready to stay for a while. If you're currently employed and you can, I would highly recommend sticking it out at least two years before you start looking for something else to at least show that you can say someplace for two years. I even recommended this to my nephew, who at the time was 16 years old. He wanted to leave. It was his first job at a grocery store. He'd been there a year. I said, just stay another year. He responded, who's going to care at 16? He's probably right, but I wanted him to start getting into that thought process of not jumping around. Don't keep chasing the buck. There are other things you can get from your job.

> IF YOU DON'T LIKE YOUR BOSS IN ONE PLACE, THERE'S NO GUARANTEE YOU WILL LIKE YOUR BOSS IN THE NEXT PLACE.

MICHAEL: The grass is not always greener. If you don't like your boss in one place, there's no guarantee you will like your boss in the next place. Bosses can change.

I also like when people address the elephant in the room. When you're rehearsing your top questions that are asked during an interview, I suggest not only rehearsing it out loud, but you can get a free version of Zoom and watch how you look. And you're not going to like how you look or sound. No one ever does the first time or the second time, and that's okay. But remember, if you don't like the way you look or sound, don't think the interviewer will either.

So that's the way you improve. Look at yourself, and say, "Oh, I can answer that a little better. I can sit up a little straighter. I can articulate what I'm saying a little better." And that's the way you improve and deliver a great interview.

I like the fact that there's a challenge on your resume. If you have five jobs you left after a year, every recruiter and hiring manager is going to pick up on that. Identify that upfront. Acknowledge it, and deal with it in an honest and forthright way that will neutralize it, not making it a negative anymore.

If someone is applying for a technology position and they're 55 years old, there's a paradigm or perspective that a recruiter or hiring manager could possibly have: what does this older person know about technology or social media? What would you recommend? What would you suggest to an older person who wants to get into that field?

ANDREA: I'd suggest the same things that I would suggest to anybody at any age. Put down what certifications you have, what education you have in those areas, what experience you have working in these areas, even if you did it as a volunteer. If you have experience in social media, website development, anything like that, keep a portfolio of examples you can share, send that on over and put it right in your resume, so somebody can just click and take a quick look at it.

The other thing is sometimes you will get screened out, and you may think that you know why. Don't be afraid to reach out to the recruiter or the hiring manager. They won't always get back to you. I know I can't guarantee that, but just say, "Is there anything that I could have improved on, because I really feel like this is the right fit for me?" Or even ask them for a second shot. Is there something that was missing that maybe I can share with you that would help you give me a second shot? And sometimes it works.

I recently hired a recruiter who I initially screened out because she had tons of experience as an HR manager, but she didn't have a lot of recruiter experience. And so I rejected her. She reached out to me and showed me that within that HR position there were quite a few jobs that she recruited for. And I actually ended up hiring her. So sometimes it could work out for you, because WHEN YOU'RE TALKING ABOUT A RESUME, YOU'RE REALLY JUST TALKING ABOUT A PIECE OF PAPER. I mean, an electronic piece of paper nowadays, but OFTEN YOUR RESUME DOESN'T COMPLETELY REPRESENT WHO YOU ARE AND WHAT YOU CAN DO. So, if you can take little chances like that, it might pay off for you.

MICHAEL: We know if you don't take that chance, it won't pay off. One of my favorite quotes is from Wayne Gretzky: You miss 100% of the shots you don't take. And the answer is always no, unless you ask. So, if you accept the no on the resume, but you really feel strongly that this is the job for you, then it doesn't hurt to ask. We know applicant tracking systems and other things will kick you out of the system.

When a person sees your human side, and they hear your passion, your voice, it can change their mind. Those things can't be demonstrated in a piece of paper, like a resume.

ANDREA: Definitely. If the hiring manager or interviewer says that you're just missing this certification, or you just need a little bit more experience in this particular skill, then go and focus on those areas. Then, six months or a year later, reach back, and there's a good chance you'll be hired. Because then you show that you're willing to put in the effort, that you listened to what they said, and they'll be impressed.

MICHAEL: **So, give me the background on AHA! Recruiting Experts, and how the name ties into what you're doing.**

ANDREA: I have a very good friend who is an amazing designer. Over ten years ago, I was brainstorming with him for our logo. And I said, "Well, maybe we could do something with my initials." He said, "Andrea Hoffer. Andrea Hoffer Associates. Aha!" So it was really his idea. And then he designed the logo, and we eventually dropped the Andrea Hoffer Associates and just called it AHA! Recruiting Experts.

MICHAEL: **So, it really has a double meaning. I didn't even pick up on that.**

What would you say out of all the questions that you ask is the question that gives you the most information about a candidate?

ANDREA: I don't believe in just one question. I believe in a pattern. And I'm going to share with your audience a secret here that I usually share with employers when I'm teaching them how to interview. I always tell the employers that their power phrase is "specific examples." So, if candidates come and have specific examples ready of things they've accomplished, things they've had failures with, but what they've learned from it, and how they do things differently, then they will stand out.

> AS A CANDIDATE, YOU SHOULD LOOK AT THE JOB DESCRIPTION AND BRAINSTORM DIFFERENT THINGS IN YOUR BACKGROUND THAT COULD APPLY TO THE JOB.

As a candidate, take a look at the job description and brainstorm different things in your background that could apply to the job. When we train employers and hiring managers to interview, just about all of the interview questions that we help them prepare ask for a specific example. If an interviewer uses those words, "specific example," don't talk in generalities, talk in details and specifics of actions you took in the past

EMPLOYERS WANT TO KNOW WHAT YOU'VE ACCOMPLISHED IN THE PAST, WHAT YOU'VE EXPERIENCED IN THE PAST, AND WHAT YOU'VE LEARNED IN THE PAST, SO THEY CAN GET A GOOD FEEL OF HOW YOU'LL SHOW UP IN THE FUTURE. But often people speak in such generalities when they are interviewing. They look things up on the internet, and they use all the buzz words. As soon as I'm hearing all buzzwords and nothing specific, then I start to know this isn't the right person for the job.

I was training a new recruiter last night. We were interviewing a candidate for a sales position. The candidate came across as very poised and confident. And you know, somebody who's not as savvy at interviewing may have thought it was a very strong interview.

After the interview, I asked the recruiter-in-training what she thought of the candidate. She said, "I thought he was very strong." I asked her, "What specifically did he say that made you think he is good for the position?" She couldn't think of anything. She started looking at her notes and realized he had spoken in generalities the entire time. He's not the right person for the position. I did not get any feel for how he would show up in this job. That doesn't mean he couldn't do it, but he didn't interview well. He just kept trying to sell himself to us without really telling us what he could bring to the table.

MICHAEL: Right! Give me a specific example, something I can sink my teeth into. Tell a story, good or bad. If you didn't get a good result, we know that situations aren't perfect at work and in our lives. But the fact that you persevere, the fact that you learned something, the fact that you can articulate that, and you grew from that, and that you serve your company at a higher level as a result of that growth, that's a win.

Your loss becomes a win. And the fact that you said you're a great leader, a great salesperson, that is one 10th as impactful as if you said, "I achieved 120% of quota for the last three or four years. I was number one in my company. I love to win. I know you hear that a lot, but my results speak for themselves. I did win. And I won because these are the things that led me to be the top salesperson. These are the actions I took on a daily basis. I committed myself to improving my skills. I made more calls. I had a routine in the morning. These are all the things I did."

ANDREA: Exactly. Because that not only explains the results, but you said the actions that you took to get there. That's the part that often people will forget. And so they might share some results, and it's not always their results. It might be the results of a whole team or a whole company. So I always try to pull out of the candidate, well, what were your actions that contributed to those results? What actions did you specifically take?

I know we're all taught to give credit to everybody. I always give the candidate the benefit of the doubt and just say, "You know what? I understand. I love the fact that you have a team mentality. This is an interview, so I'm going to give you permission to say "I" when it was your own action. I just say that once. If an interviewer says that to you, take them seriously, because they want to know what you actually accomplished.

I always recommend this to candidates. I had a notebook (this was also before computers) where anytime I had an accomplishment at work or something that happened that I felt like this is something someday on an interview that could be helpful to me, I jotted it down. I kept it in a portfolio so when I did have interviews, I brought it with me. It sounds like a lot of work, but you're documenting your accomplishments. How great is that? And then you have something you can look back on. It will make it easier when you are going for an interview.

MICHAEL: I've had some people call that a brag book. An interview is the time to brag, so take notes when you accomplish things.

In today's difficult economic climate with a lot of people unemployed, if you were to give one bit of advice, something different than what you've shared already, what bit of advice would you give?

ANDREA: This might be a bit unusual, but the hiring process has changed a lot over the last few years. It's changing very quickly now. That's because of a few things. There are a lot of balls in the air. Sometimes hiring managers and employers don't have a lot of time to do what's necessary to find the right people. So, there's all this technology that filled in the gaps.

One of the things that's becoming very popular in the hiring process is one-way video interviews. We started using this in our process at least two years ago. And I will tell you that about 20-30% of our candidates will send in a video. But then another 5-10% will just write back saying, "I don't do one-way interviews. I'm happy to meet with you through Zoom or by phone, but I don't do one-way interviews."

We don't care how great their resume looks. We tell them that's just part of our process and that we won't be considering them further. They've lost an amazing opportunity. They could have been great. I understand the reluctance. It's not easy to be looking at a camera and not at a person, but it's becoming a big part of the interview process. And we have found that it helps the candidates more than it hurts them.

> WE'VE FOUND THAT ONE-WAY VIDEO INTERVIEWS HELP CANDIDATES MORE THAN THEY HURT THEM.

THE ONE-WAY VIDEO INTERVIEW IS AN EXTENSION OF YOUR RESUME, because like I said, resumes are just an electronic piece of paper. It can't tell us everything, but we can see your personality. We can see how passionate you are about this particular job. We can ask a couple of questions about what your non-negotiables are, and decide, is it worth it for both sides to continue this conversation?

My advice would be, if there are different things in the process that you're not used to, look at it as a challenge and just do it. If it's a job you really want, then don't give the recruiter or the hiring manager the idea that you feel like you're above it, and that you're not going to follow the process that they've laid out. That might be a little controversial, but it really is valuable to the recruiter and the hiring manager to get that video upfront. It helps in getting a better feel for the candidate going forward.

MICHAEL: Right. Companies have policies and procedures. And if you don't adhere to those policies and procedures, you're actually saying, "I don't want to be part of your company." They have a vision, values, standards, and policies or procedures. By you accepting a position in the company, you have to follow them. You're part of that company culture. If you're unwilling to be part of the process upfront, then chances are, you're not going to be a good employee.

I want you to tell me what a one-way video interview looks like, because I and many of our listeners are not familiar with them. Explain a little bit about what that experience is like.

ANDREA: Not every company is going to have specific one-way video interviewing software. Some may ask you to do a Zoom and record it. If the hiring company recruits in higher volume like we do, they may use a particular video interview company that's made to do it. It was very important to us to make it as user-friendly as possible. You can do it with your phone, the words pop up, we let you practice. We even give you a second take.

We typically will not ask more than three or four questions. Our first question is, "Could you share with us why you're passionate about this position?" The second one always is, "What are the three most important things that you're looking for in your next job?" Because we want to make sure we're bringing you the right job. And then the third one typically is, "What research have you done on this company? What stands out for you?" So it's nothing too terrible. It's just to give us a feel for you.

MICHAEL: **Great. Just** <u>BE PREPARED WITH ANSWERS TO COMMON INTERVIEW QUESTIONS.</u> **Recruiters don't want a robot answering these questions. They want a human being who's real and genuine and authentic. But at the same time, know one, two, or three key talking points around those core questions or topics that you can elaborate on during the video interview.**

What do you recommend that candidates wear to a one-way video interview?

ANDREA: Be aware of how you show up on camera. Look at that camera. Make it appear like you are looking the interviewer in the eyes. Not all jobs are going to require that you wear a suit and tie for the interview. It's the same thing with a video. Wear a nice top and something that looks professional for whatever the position is you're going for. But we often do see suit and ties, which is nice, even for positions that you would never wear a suit and tie to the job.

The worst that we've seen is people who are in a raggedy T-shirt, all wrinkled, and in bed. They're just lying in bed. I had one person who seemed like she was half asleep. She was just lying there and there was no energy in her voice.

Recently, we had somebody who said, "I don't really know why I'm doing this video, because I don't really want the job." I've never seen that before. The other thing is to be aware of your location. Not everybody's going to have an office or a separate area to do an interview, but try to find a quiet place. Sometimes people do their interviews in their cars. That's okay. If you have to go out to the car because that's the only quiet place, just don't be driving your car.

You can even say, "I apologize for the background. I just wanted to make sure I wasn't disturbed." And most recruiters will understand that.

We once had a wife who was trying to do an interview, and every two minutes, her husband would be screaming out to her, and she would scream back, saying, "I told you I was doing an interview!" You have to make sure everybody in your household knows what you're doing and that you're not to be disturbed for that time period.

MICHAEL: **Sometimes it seems like these things are basic, but you'd be surprised at the number of people who don't think about them. Look at your background. You don't want to have your college partying pictures where you're passed out on the ground with a bottle of tequila in your hand behind you. Have a professional background as best you can. Make sure your surroundings are quiet. And if you do have to be in your car, announce that upfront. It shows thoughtfulness. All these things are going to add points in your favor when a recruiter or a hiring manager is looking at you.**

What about posture, eye contact, and articulation? What can you tell us about those things?

ANDREA: Show some energy with your posture. Sit up straight, and show that you're taking the

> SHOW THAT YOU'RE TAKING THE INTERVIEW SERIOUSLY.

interview seriously. We send an email with some tips when we invite people to do these one-way interviews, and we even have a short little video from a stylist who talks about what to wear and how to keep your background professional.

If a recruiter or a hiring manager sends you information to help you be more successful, then take a few minutes and follow what they say. They're giving you a roadmap to success. So you might as well take it, because a lot of people won't.

Definitely smile. That's one of the biggest things. We put that as a final sentence in our invitation email, saying, "Don't forget to smile," because people get so nervous about the video that you can see the stress and not their personality. What if we're sending this person on to a CEO or a hiring manager, and they have a very fun culture? And they see somebody in the video who looks like they're very serious. The hiring manager is going to say they are not going to fit into their culture. They're all about fun. And that person could be the most fun person in the world, but they didn't show their personality on the video.

MICHAEL: **Mother Teresa had a quote that evangelization begins with a smile. A smile conveys a thousand words. A smile will warm someone up. We're emotional human beings, not intellectual. We're more emotionally driven, and emotions come from what we see and how we internalize those things.**

<u>WHEN YOU SMILE, YOU'RE CREATING AN ENVIRONMENT THAT'S MORE CONDUCIVE TO ACCEPTANCE.</u>

Tonality is also important. You don't want to be monotone. There's a study that shows that only 7% of the way we communicate is through words. 38% is tonality and 55% is body language. When our parents used to say, "It's not what you say, it's how you say it," they were right.

Andrea, this has been a pleasure. You've created a golden roadmap to success for job seekers.

ANDREA: Great. Thank you so much.

ACTION STEPS

KNOW WHAT KIND OF JOB YOU'RE LOOKING FOR. Identify your non-negotiables and your nice-to-haves.

SHOW EMPLOYERS THAT YOU REALLY CARE ABOUT *THEIR* JOB. Don't just send out mass resumes that are the same thing over and over. Really personalize them. Write a cover letter that's customized to the job that you're applying for and that explains why you're excited about the opportunity and how you can bring value.

DO YOUR RESEARCH. Make sure you read the job posting. You don't want to walk into an interview and pose questions that are answered on the job posting. You want to have deeper questions. Go beyond the obvious and show that you have an understanding of what the job is.

FOR THOSE WHO HAVE JUMPED FROM JOB TO JOB, INCLUDE A STATEMENT IN YOUR RESUME OR COVER LETTER EXPLAINING WHY. This can help you get ahead of a negative opinion by addressing the issue openly.

IF A HIRING MANAGER SCREENS YOU OUT OF THE PROCESS, DON'T BE AFRAID TO REACH OUT AND ASK WHY. You could take the opportunity to either learn what you need to work on, or to plead your case, explaining why you think you're the perfect candidate for the job. You never know how something is going to turn out unless you take a risk.

USE SPECIFIC EXAMPLES.
- Look at the job description and brainstorm different things in your background that could apply to the job. Don't generalize. Show why you, specifically, bring value.
- Keep a log of your accomplishments at work. That way, when it comes time to interview, you have specific examples to pull from.

HOW TO ACE THE ONE-WAY VIDEO INTERVIEW
1. Prepare for common interview questions. Practice on Zoom. See how you look.
2. Pay attention to your appearance. Wear something nice and professional for the position you're interviewing for.
3. Pay attention to your background. Make sure you're in a quiet location. If you have to take an interview in your car, that's okay, just address that up front.
4. Pay attention to your tonality. Smile. Speak with expression. Show that you're enthusiastic about the position and excited to be there.

Twila Alexander

*Manager of HR and Talent
for the nonprofit EDUCAUSE*

CHAPTER FOCUS

- *How to get past the vast number of applicants to get the interview*
- *How to ace your interview*
- *The right way to create your resume*
- *The importance of the cover letter*
- *Automated Applicant Tracking Systems*

Twila Alexander is full of energy and great ideas. When I interviewed her, I was thrilled with all the advice she offered regarding what hiring managers are looking for in an interviewee. With more than 20 years' experience working in human resources, people development, and recruiting, Twila knows how to prep people for job interviews. We were blessed to have her share her insights with us.

Twila Alexander is the Manager of Human Resources (HR) and Talent for EDUCAUSE, a nonprofit association that works with higher education IT professionals and industry partners to advance technology in higher education. She holds a master's degree in Human Resources and Industrial Relations from Loyola University, Chicago, and started her career receiving resumes through the mail. Twila's professional interests are centered around improving organizational diversity through re-imagined recruiting, hiring, and training practices. She currently enjoys working from her makeshift home office (Don't we all?) near

Boulder, Colorado. Here is what she has so graciously shared with us.

MICHAEL: It's so good to meet you, Twila! I'm thrilled to hear what you have to say about finding a job in the super competitive job market that we have now. You've been at this for twenty years, so have interviewed a lot of people. Let's kick this off with what _not_ to do. What are your top three things?

TWILA: The biggest thing I see is that people apply for jobs that they are not at all qualified for, because they're hoping to get into the resume database. They're hoping to get in front of a recruiter and magically get matched to a job. Recruiters don't really have time for that. I get resumes all the time from people who do not match the requirements of the job, and I feel bad for those people, because they obviously took the time to apply, but they're just going to get rejected. And also, I work in nonprofit. People apply to these nonprofits and higher education organizations because they think it's slower-paced or they think it's nice. So they think it will be fun. It's like, no, no, this is hard work! We have leaner staffs and less budget, and you're probably working more hours than the big job that you're getting rid of because you think you want something more fun. Those kinds of things just blow my mind. We don't have time to really spend on someone who isn't a hundred percent in the game and ready to come and really work for us.

MICHAEL: Yeah. Two phenomenal points that are enlightening to me: one, it's easy today to apply online. So because it's easy,

people are doing it for jobs they aren't even sure they want, but really, it's not only a waste of their time as a job-seeker, but it's a waste of the recruiters' and the hiring managers' time as well. The reality is, <u>USE YOUR TIME WISELY. MAKE SURE THAT THE JOB, YOUR SKILLS, YOUR QUALIFICATIONS, YOUR INTERESTS, AND YOUR PASSIONS MATCH.</u> At least then you have a shot at what you're applying for, so put your time into that. The other thing is, you said if you have the inclination to work for a nonprofit, don't think that nonprofits work less, because they work *more*. Now, let me ask you a question: for someone looking for a job in nonprofit, is it a different application process? Do they say and do things that are different than when they're in a for-profit? They have to be passionate, I guess.

THE FOUR THINGS TO AVOID IF YOU ARE APPLYING FOR A JOB:

- DON'T APPLY FOR JOBS YOU DON'T MATCH THE REQUIRED EXPERIENCE FOR.
- DON'T APPLY FOR JOBS YOU AREN'T PASSIONATE ABOUT.
- DON'T APPLY FOR MANY DIFFERENT JOBS IN THE SAME ORGANIZATION. WAIT UNTIL THE JOB YOU FIT BEST COMES UP.
- DON'T MISTAKE "NONPROFIT" FOR EASY WORK. USUALLY, IT'S MORE WORK AND MAY NOT BE FOR A LOT MORE PAY.

TWILA: That's the third thing. If it's a higher ed or nonprofit job, certainly passion helps. We want to know that you're interested in our job, that you're interested in our mission, and that you are on board with what we're trying to do. But still, that's not enough, right? We get a lot of people who apply because they really want to work for our organization. They love the organization. They're familiar with the organization. That's great, but you still need the *skills*. You still have to be able to do the job that we have for you. Sometimes you have to wait for the right job to come up at your dream company so that you can get a job *in* your dream company, but don't apply for *all* the jobs. Because my fourth thing is, applying for multiple, multiple jobs within an organization just means I'm rejecting you over and over and over again. And I'm a human being. And that makes me sad. Like, oh, here's my fifth rejection for the same person, because they keep applying for jobs that they're not really matched for.

MICHAEL: Great stuff. So let's flip the table. What are the one, two, or three things that you've seen during your interview process that makes you say, "Wow, this just blows my mind!" It helps if you're talking about points; when you're hiring someone, you're either adding or deducting points in terms of what they're saying, those qualifications, soft skills, hard skills, you know, there's always this in your head. "Oh, that's a plus," or, "Oh, that's a red flag." What are the top three things you look for?

TWILA: Okay, here's my three. First, especially for nonprofit, I think most companies like you to be prepared, as far as doing the research. YOU CAN'T ALWAYS BE THE SMARTEST OR THE BEST QUALIFIED CANDIDATE, BUT, BY GOLLY, YOU CAN BE THE MOST PREPARED. You can do the research and anybody sitting in the interview room with you knows if all you've done

> **TO MAKE YOUR INTERVIEW POP**
> *PREPARE! PREPARE! PREPARE!*
> - RESEARCH THE COMPANY THOROUGHLY.
> - BE PREPARED TO SHARE YOUR OWN JOB EXPERIENCE IN DETAIL.
> - HAVE YOUR PAST WORK STORIES ABOUT SUCCESS AND FAILURE READY TO SHARE *BEFORE* YOU GO IN.

is looked at the website, or all you've done is looked at the first page of the website. We *know* what the first page of the website says; don't read that back to us. Go beyond that first page, go to YouTube, go to the internet, go to LinkedIn, and find out what we do and what we've *been* doing, what our market is, what our challenges are. Because even if you have so-so skills, the capacity to learn, the capacity to research, and the passion is going to make you float to the top of the application pool.

The second thing is to be really prepared about your own experience. I see this a lot, especially for people reentering the workforce, or if they've had a break where it's been a while since they've worked, they don't remember their best stories or their best skills or their best successes. You can tell they're coming up with a story on the spot, and sometimes it's not the best story, right? It's something that just came to them, but it's not really the one that they should have shared. It's not really the one that showcases their talent. And that's all about prep. Interviews are very often behavioral, and they're going to ask you, "Tell me about a time that you succeeded or that you failed." The applicant should spend some time coming up with those stories and practicing them. Prepare so it's really top-of-mind and fluent, so that we can tell that you actually thought this through, and you just didn't show up today hoping for the best.

MICHAEL: Yes. But also, learn what's new in the news about the organization, and like you said, what are their greatest interests and passion projects they're working on now? You know, when you read this stuff and you then share it back to the person that is interviewing you, that shows them you are prepared. What other things does that show you as an interviewer?

TWILA: I think many candidates get a little jaded or burned. They don't realize that for hiring managers, sometimes it's like dating, right? We always talk about job searches as dating. And for hiring managers, they're really nervous that they're going to fall in love with a candidate and that candidate has ten other suitors, and the candidate is going to take somebody else's job offer. So when somebody comes and says, "I've researched your company, I know a lot about it. I'm really invested," then that person floats to the top, because now we feel like we've got a really good shot with this person. If we decide we like them, we know they like us too, and they're very likely to come work for us, even if our salary is a thousand dollars different. They're going to come because they want to work here. And we get burned just like candidates, where we bring people all the way through the process, and at the end, they say, "Oh, I took another job. Sorry." So being really invested and showing that you've done the work is kind of what makes that bond. And it gives people more confidence that you're going to take the job, which means that they have more invested in you, and they'll bring you further through the process.

MICHAEL: **It becomes a mutual thing. It helps them, and it helps you at the same time, which is great. Let's go back to the dating example, which I love. If someone sucks on a date, and they don't hold the door open for you, or they don't have good manners, you should not marry that person. Let me repeat, do not expect that behavior to get better once you're married.**

TWILA: Absolutely.

MICHAEL: What I love about your example, Twila, is the fact that when someone demonstrates during an interview that they love to do the research, love to be prepared... the habit of doing those things is going to be reflective, not only in getting the job, but also once they're in the job. And I love that that skillset is proven. They've already established that. It also shows that they're thinkers. Ultimately, what we want to do in any job is to continue to accomplish our objectives and exceed our objective goals. Who do I need to bring in? What resources do I need? If they did all that to get the job, then chances are, they're going to think of that and do that once they do get into the work. I love that.

Over all these years, what would be the one question that has given you more information about the candidate than any other?

TWILA: I think for me, it's always *what they've done*. I always ask a candidate, "What have you done in your last job that left it better than you found it? What did you add?" For so many candidates, their resumes are just a list of their position descriptions. I don't care what their position was. I want to know what they *did*. So I challenge them to tell me what kind of process they put in place or what kind of improvement or what they brought to the table that was really value added for their employer. Because that's what we're looking for—someone who can add value to us.

MICHAEL: Brilliant. And to your point, unless you're preparing this ahead of time, how many applicants fail? Because I hear it all the time as a coach; they get tongue tied. Of course you get tongue tied. You're being asked questions that look back over 10 years. What's your favorite story? Or why do you want this job? And if you haven't thought of that in advance, even the best person in the world is not going to be able to come up with the best story.

TWILA: <u>YOU HAVE YOUR ONE SHOT TO MAKE A FIRST IMPRESSION, AND IT'S GOTTA BE YOUR BEST.</u> You'd have to bring your best to that first interview.

MICHAEL: That's beautiful. And I love the depth that you go into with the website; go real, go high, deep, and wide in that. Be prepared with those stories, because stories tell a lot versus just a regular answer. So with that in mind, tell me if you've ever asked this: why do you want this job? Or why do you feel you're qualified for this job? Is that a question you ever asked? And what kind of response have you gotten that makes you think, "Oh my gosh, you really should have thought about this." Or, conversely, what are some great responses?

TWILA: I always ask people, if you're changing jobs, why do you want this job? Like, what are we offering you that you don't already do? And certainly I get answers like, "Well, I'm just looking for a job," and it's probably the curse of living in a beautiful part of the country where people say, "I would like this job because I really want to move to Boulder." That does nothing for me. Thank you. You know, I don't want to pay your relocation so that you can come live in Boulder. I want to know that you're ready to grow into that next step, that there is a

> I WANT TO KNOW THAT YOU'RE READY TO GROW INTO THAT NEXT STEP, THAT THERE IS A CHALLENGE OR AN OPPORTUNITY THAT YOU DON'T HAVE IN YOUR CURRENT JOB THAT YOU'RE GOING TO COME IN FIGHTING FOR.

challenge or an opportunity that you don't have in your current job that you're going to come in fighting for. I'm not looking for somebody who's in a bad situation and needs to get out. Even if that's the case, you need to come up with something better. Just say, "I've got these skills, and I think I can put them to better use in a new opportunity."

MICHAEL: **When someone's applying for a job, they have to look at it from the hiring manager's or recruiter's position: what's in it for me? All they care about is: what can you do? And why can you do it better than any other applicant? Anything outside of that is not going to move the needle. Whatever you're sharing in the interview, make sure it's something that will move the needle in terms of what they're looking for. Not what you're looking for.**

So have you ever asked the question: What's your greatest weakness?

TWILA: I don't like hiring managers asking that because you're putting the candidate on the defensive. So when I am walking a candidate through that question, we just turn it around and say, "What is something that has not gone the way you wanted, and how did you fix it?" Or, if we're looking at emotional intelligence, "What's something that you know about yourself, and how have you improved it?" If you ask it the other way, candidates will say something like, "My greatest weakness is perfectionism." Right. It's like, stop it. I want you to actually tell me that you can learn from your mistakes. And so I think it's important for candidates to know that when they're asked that question, it is about growth. We want to know that you can learn from your mistakes, that you can make the changes, and that you can improve, that you can be honest with yourself and grow. That it is not a way of pegging you as, "That's your failure." Instead, it's a way to highlight that you can actually change and that you can actually grow in what you're doing.

MICHAEL: I used to ask people, "If I were going to send you away to a seminar and you were going to pick one, two, or three topics that you need improvement on, what would those three topics be today?" That's a nice, soft way of getting them to share. I'd be the first to raise my hand and say, "I need to improve." And if they share, "I have this weakness, but I'm reading a book right now." Or "I listen to podcasts," it shows me that they have a growth mindset. And all those things, believe it or not, they turn that weakness around.

TWILA: Absolutely, because WHAT WE'RE LOOKING FOR IS SOMEBODY WHO HAS THE ABILITY TO CHANGE AND GROW. So if they can sell it, then that's great. And again, be prepared so that it comes off as genuine, but still it's your best.

MICHAEL: Yeah. And practice, so you don't come off as robotic. I even suggest people Zoom themselves on video. And if you don't like the way you look, the recruiter or hiring manager won't like the way you look either. So do that. And no one likes the way they look the first time. So do it, and know that that's okay, and do it over and over again until you're comfortable and say, "I'm looking better. I'm improving!" That's the best way to do it.

So let's shift gears a little bit from the behavioral questions. People are talking about resumes today, and you hear across the board how important a resume is, but some say it's not so important anymore. So I'd like you to share a little bit from your perspective, about what makes a resume important and what does it either accomplish or not accomplish for the job seeker?

TWILA: I think a resume is always going to be something really important. I don't think you can get away without it. I review resumes, and I can tell when people are getting more innovative in their resume. I just want to bang my head, because we still need to know: what's your job history? How long were you there? What skills did you use there? For example, if you were a computer programmer, well, how many years was that? Was that just the last job or for five jobs? And even as we go forward, we don't exactly need to know where you went to high school or what job you worked on then, but we still need to know your depth of experience. I still need to know what you've been doing. So I think the resume is still really important.

And if I had to just give people insight or advice, it's to please be kind to your recruiter and format it in a way that people can read so that I'm not having to spend a lot of time deciphering it. People don't realize that a recruiter has only about 15 to 45 seconds to decide if we want to read this resume or not. So if it's something so stylized that I can't even tell what you do, I'm not going to get very far. I'm not going to get past the top third of your resume. If you've buried all your good stuff at the bottom, it's not going to get seen. If you're hoping that people read your cover letter and that makes it all make sense, it might be that your cover letter's not getting read either. **THE BOTTOM LINE IS, I NEED TO KNOW WHAT YOU'VE ACTUALLY DONE, AND I NEED TO MATCH IT TO THE QUALIFICATIONS WE PUBLISHED**, because we have to go with what we said we wanted in a person. I need that to match that up to your resume.

MICHAEL: That's right. Make it easy so that the recruiter or the hiring manager can go right to the section they need to get to and quickly see the information they need to see to make a determination. Correct?

TWILA: Even more so as a recruiter, I've been reading resumes for twenty-something years, hiring managers haven't always. And so if the resume is not really easy to navigate, or if, again, your information is buried where you have to translate it, a hiring manager has no idea what to do with that. Because that's not what they do every day. So it has to be something that the hiring manager can read and understand and say, "Oh, that's what this person does. That's their job. That's their skill. That's what they can bring to the table." If it's convoluted, it's not going to get very far. And I see that a lot with really good people who have really bad resumes.

MICHAEL: So let's talk about cover letters. How important are they?

TWILA: As the recruiter, I will only look at a cover letter if someone looks interesting, or if I have a huge question and am interested enough to open another attachment. But for my hiring managers, cover letters are huge. They want to see that you can write. They want to see that you can communicate. Those are great skills. And in a lot of ways, they like that cover letter even more than a resume because it reads like you can understand it. But again, as a recruiter, if you're hoping that someone's going to read your cover letter, and that's going to explain your resume, it's not, because we have to look at your resume first.

Cover letters are your way to shine. It's a way to tailor your experience to what the job is, and to show that you can write and communicate. But it *cannot* take the place of your resume. It's a little bit of a sales job that you're doing.

MICHAEL: **Right. A cover letter really is reflective of if you can communicate, because a resume is really segmented, it's key points. And are you able to communicate in a succinct manner? So let's talk about a succinct manner. We've both seen cover letters, and then we've seen cover essays or cover short stories. Now with the limited time**

> YOUR COVER LETTER SHOULD NOT BE A COVER SHORT STORY!

today, especially with hundreds of people applying for the same job, what do you think? I have my feelings on this as a career coach, but I'm very interested in what you think. What would be the proper amount of text in a cover letter that would convey the message?

TWILA: I think there's that sweet spot. Like the Goldilocks story. I think if it's too long, people don't have time for that. That shows me that you have no idea what I do and how busy we are. But if it's too short, then I wonder, why did you even write it? Back in the day, you'd see cover letters that were really like your fax cover sheet. "Hi, I'm applying for this job. Thank you." Too short. What works best is about a page long, a three paragraph essay that says: "This is who I am. This is what I can do. This is why I'm interested in your job." That's perfect. It's enough to give me a lot of information that I didn't get on your resume.

It's your opportunity to show that you did do your homework. You do understand the job. You do want to work for me for a particular reason, and you customized it.

MICHAEL: And again, I want to reemphasize, cover letters are icing on the cake, a cherry on top of the sundae, but it could squash the sundae if it's not customized.

Now let's talk about follow-up. Candidates should not respond right away. You have to respect the fact that recruiters and hiring managers are super busy. So with respect to that, but yet cognizant of the fact that you want to show that you have good follow-up and follow-through skills, and that you have an interest in the job... when do you think first follow-up should be, and how it should be?

TWILA: That is a great question. I think it's nice for hiring managers and recruiters to be mindful and to let people know where they are in the process, and when they're expecting to make a decision. That being said, though, in the real world, searches always go two or three times slower than we imagine. It just takes *so much time*. The fastest reply you're going to get is the rejection. But once you're in the process, who knows? So I appreciate when a candidate is showing that they are really interested in my job and not just applying.

But on my end, I can't do that much. The wheels of the machine are going, and I can tell you that we're supposed to be meeting on Wednesday, but that meeting might get canceled, and I should have gotten back to you on Friday, but that one hiring manager did not get back to me. So it's next week now. I think it's great for a candidate to reach out to you and say they are still interested, they are still working on learning more about the organization. "Let me know as soon as you know, because I'm super excited," versus "Can you let me know? Can you let me know? Can you let me know?" Because no, I can't, I'm sorry. And that's just one more email and one more thing I have to do. And one more guilt trip that I really didn't need to take.

But follow up is great. And I think it shows the interest, especially once you're in the interviewing stage. Sometimes, I will admit that I look at someone's resume in the pile if they reach out. That doesn't mean I can get them any further than that, but at least I can look. But once it becomes more than a couple of times, then that's not something I really want to work with. It's the dozens of people that we're interviewing or the hundreds of people that we're screening. And we can only do so much for them.

MICHAEL: **What, then, is a good follow-up? Is it a quick email? Is it a phone call? Is it one sentence, two sentences?**

TWILA: Yeah, my favorite follow-ups, where I do kind of give that person a positive check, is a brief email. Something short, such as, "I know this week you were going to have your meeting with your hiring managers. I'm hoping you have made a decision. And if you do, can you let me know as soon as you can?" Those are great because that tells me they are interested, but they also understand it's not all about me. I'm not saying you have to sweet talk your recruiter, but it is nice when people understand that it's a bigger process, and we don't always have an answer right away.

If they want to go a little bit further, what I like to see after an interview is for someone to acknowledge, "I learned more about the job in the interview, and I'm even more interested." Now we know you're kind of pushing us along, and I think that's a really nice way to be persistent but also to show that you have a little patience.

MICHAEL: **It also showed that they paid attention. Do you like people taking notes in the interview?**

TWILA: I do, because I'm a note taker. For a lot of hiring managers, it makes them nervous when somebody is writing furiously, so a lot of the training we do is to help people give candidates a little bit of room to do that so that they have a chance to think through their answer and to make a note of something that they want to follow up on. I think it's very fair for someone to take notes in an interview. Just make sure you don't lose eye contact or you're not losing the flow of the conversation because you're taking 10 minutes to write out your thoughts before you answer the questions.

MICHAEL: **Like Cliffs Notes, just put key points down. What is a good question to ask after an interview is done? Maybe, "What's the normal follow-up process?" or, "When would it be okay for me to follow up?" Is that a good question that you would recommend a candidate ask?**

TWILA: Absolutely. It shows that the candidates are forward thinking and that they are interested. I think they should ask that type of question at the end of every interview. Or, "Is there anything that I need to forward to you that I didn't give you the first time?" And be sure you know who you should follow up with.

MICHAEL: **Okay. Is there anything else at the end of the interview that might wow a recruiter or hiring manager?**

TWILA: On my recruiting scorecards, I always make a note on the questions the candidate asked. When you're in the hot seat, when you're being interviewed, I know it's hard to absorb the information that people are telling you. And in hiring managers, again, like in dating, they want to tell you all about their project. They want to tell you all about what they're doing. And I think as a candidate, sometimes they're glassy-eyed, just waiting for our next question. But if you're a candidate who can offer a question that shows you synthesized some of that information, that's huge. That's impressive. We hired somebody in our organization because at the end of the interview, he told us all the things that we could be doing better. And I'm sure he was very respectful when he did it, but it just showed that he was thinking it through, showing, "I've done my research and now you're telling me these things and I'm putting it together."

MICHAEL: **Brilliant stuff! What one piece of advice would you give a job seeker in today's environment where they're competing? Most people don't know what an ATS is. Do you want to give us an idea of what it is and how it scans and screens for resumes?**

TWILA: ATS is the applicant tracking system. It's a database of the resumes as they come in. It can be built in lots of different ways, so there are some applicant tracking systems out there where, when you apply, you answer a few questions, and if one of those questions doesn't match up, you get a rejection right away. But there are also applicant tracking systems where there's a little bit more human interaction and your resume is going to go in. It'll probably be screened into a PDF so we can actually see your formatting. Sometimes it doesn't, or your resume just has some really pretty graphics and that don't come through. I think it's really important to understand that it's going to go into this huge database, that there's a lot of candidates that are also applying.

My advice for somebody who is applying to a big company, is to make sure that your resume highlights the things that you actually want to be doing so that the keywords are there, and the experience bullet points are there, because the applicant tracking system searches for different things. For example, if the job ad said they needed somebody to do instructional design, you need to have instructional design on your resume. Or if you need to work in a certain kind of platform, you need to show that platform on your resume so that it can be picked up that way. There are still a lot of human elements in resume review, but for some big organizations where they get hundreds and hundreds of applications, it will come through a system, and it will be screened sometimes by applicant screening questions or by keyword searches. So it's really important that your resume really showcases the best of you and has those keywords without being a data dump of everything you've ever done.

MICHAEL: Right. You want to match your keywords in your resume to the job posting, but you don't want to just throw words in there that don't reflect who you really are and what your qualifications are.

Just so everyone understands, applicant tracking systems are there for medium or larger companies to help vet out the tons of resumes that they get. And it's not even seen by human

eyes. So a recruiter and a hiring manager is never going to see your resume. If you got a quick rejection, chances are, you didn't hit what's called a score, where you answered some questions wrong or didn't have the right keywords. So you need to make sure that you have a professional or someone with a scanning device look it over. But the whole point is be aware of that.

TWILA: Exactly. If you're getting rejected automatically, or if you're getting rejected eventually, you really do need to go back and look at, did I really qualify for that job? Was this like a stretch or a dream job, or am I really qualified? And if you are, then you need to have somebody look at your resume to make sure that it actually shows what you can do, because there is a little bit of that automatic matching, whether it's an applicant tracking system or a very tired recruiter. And if we can't tell it's on your resume, then you're not going to get very far.

MICHAEL: **Finally, if there was one piece of advice during the pandemic, what would the one piece of advice be?**

TWILA: The thing that I'm most excited about is that we are not place-bound anymore. Companies are not all going to go back to having people work at an office building. If you haven't thought about working remotely at this point in time, I think that this is a good time to do it. I think companies are starting to see that this is an opportunity. So if you have a good skill set and there's a company and a job that you're really interested in, apply, even if they're five states away, because they may very well be going to a fully virtual model or at least a hybrid model very soon.

MICHAEL: I'm so excited to be able to talk with you, Twila. It's like a customer telling you exactly what you need to say and do. This is the best advice you could ever get to get a job. If you follow this advice with Twila Alexander, you hit pay dirt. Follow the advice she gave you, let it be your roadmap. And my wish to you is that you land that job of your dreams faster than you ever imagined possible. Twila, this was really, really special. And I really want to thank you for your time and all the valuable information you shared with our audience.

TWILA: Thank you, Mike. This has been great. I appreciate the opportunity to help some people get some really good stuff.

ACTION STEPS

You don't just want to meet expectations, you want to *exceed* them. Here's how:

IN THE INTERVIEW: Research and prepare! Make sure you know all about the company, not just what their website says. Look them up on the internet, in the news, on LinkedIn. Then, have some good stories about yourself to share. What were your strengths at your last job? Was there a time you failed, and how did you fix the problem?

IN THE RESUME: Make sure it's easy to read and that your information is not hard to find. Don't bury your skills at the bottom. And be sure you list what you do and what you want to do, not just where you have worked or gone to school. You should highlight your skill set.

IN THE COVER LETTER: This is your chance to show that you can write, that you can communicate. It should be readable and succinct. One page in length is usually sufficient. It should be personalized and not a form letter.

BE AWARE OF THE APPLICANT TRACKING SYSTEMS: Sometimes a machine looks at your resume first, so make sure you match keywords to the job description.

Douglas Baber, SHRM-CP

Director of Human Resources
and Risk Management for St. Lucie County

CHAPTER FOCUS

- *Situation-based interview questions*
- *How to stay relevant in your cover letter, resume, and interview*
- *Show your passion*
- *The art of the tactical pause*

I had a great conversation with Douglas Baber about county government and how to stay relevant in your cover letter, resume, and interview to make you stand out. Douglas is currently the Human Resources & Risk Management Director for St. Lucie County. Doug has over 16 years of high-level human resources experience in the public sector and is a certified Lean Six Sigma green belt. He has worked in a variety of capacities, specializing in compensation, benefits management, recruitment, and employee retention.

MICHAEL: **Doug, you've been doing this a long time. What are you doing differently now in making hiring decisions than you did two, three, or five years ago?**

DOUG: As a bit of background, in St. Lucie County, in February 2020, the unemployment rate was sub 3%. Now we're around five or six percent. There are a lot of jobs and a lot of people moving into this area. It was harder to find people a year ago, but now, those folks aren't really looking for jobs right now. They're still on unemployment and getting paid pretty well for it. The $12 an hour jobs are harder to fill than the administrative and the managerial jobs these days.

MICHAEL: Yeah, I've heard that. People who are the lower-wage earners can sit at home, not working, and make as much or more.

DOUG: We're doing pretty well with hiring right now. For certain jobs, we have to target wherever we're looking for. We've actually started looking in other parts of the country. Like, if we can't find somebody to be a maintenance worker, we look at other parts of Florida or of the country that are trying to fill those jobs.

It's the same thing with the teachers. I talked to the HR Executive Director for the local school district. They try to post jobs when it's snowing outside in most of the country, to attract people to Florida. We also do a lot of hiring from within. We do a lot of programs here in the county, like mentorship and leadership programs that build our people up. We're targeting folks that are already working in the County, as well as networking between the other cities.

We have a program that we do through career source. It's called "The Summer of Success." We host this program for eight weeks, and six weeks of those they do actual work. Two weeks of it, they do training to teach them how to manage a bank account, teach them how to write a resume, and teach them interview skills. They go through the full gamut of everything to help them learn. A lot of those who take this course are teenagers who just graduated high school.

A young lady that worked in my office from the program last summer, she was great and did a wonderful job. At the end of the summer, we were doing an exit interview with her on what she thought of the program. She said, "Honestly, I never thought county government did this kind of work. I thought it was just the sheriff and the parks." So, we opened this young lady's eyes.

We're doing those kinds of things to open people's eyes to alternate job opportunities, to try to make ourselves a little bit more attractive. We're a Best Places to Work in our county and pride ourselves on receiving that award for the past five years in a row.

Local government week happens in May, so we like to go out to some of the local schools to let them know that there are jobs in county government. They may not have known that you could be an HR director for the county. We continue to open more eyes, making local government careers look a little more attractive. Government doesn't always pay the best, but the benefits are outstanding.

MICHAEL: **I've heard that it can take some time to get a position in government, because of all the approvals a new position needs. Can you give listeners a sense of how long they can expect the interview process to be for a county job?**

DOUG: There's some good stats on that. When I started working for St. Lucie County, I looked at the number of days it took to hire someone. It was around 86 days to hire an employee from start to finish. So, it was quite lengthy. Currently, we are down to 38 overall days to hire. That number even includes a prospective employee giving a two-week notice to their current employer.

I admit, it does take a while to successfully gain employment in a government organization. However, please remember we do extensive background checks, drug tests and complete physicals for every position. If you have worked for government before, we request public records on each employee and that generally takes a little while longer to process those public records requests. Basically, if we have to pull some information like that, it significantly slows down the process.

MICHAEL: **My son just went through a six-month process in a corporate environment with a recruiter. They did Myers-Briggs and other assessment testing. From what I've heard, that certainly sounds competitive with the nonprofit and the corporate or private sector.**

What are two or three things that immediately make a candidate stand out to you? What makes you really impressed or what grabs your attention? What things are immediate turnoffs?

DOUG: Well, we're in government with all types of public records. I'm going to throw a disclaimer out there that not everything is public record but we do get a lot of resumes. Our application system is NEOGOV. There are quite a few government entities as you can imagine and this software system connects them. So other job seekers can see your job posting and immediately reach out by emailing you their resume. I'm a big user of the NEOGOV software.

Talent acquisition is huge right now. When you're pulling in all these applications and you're sifting through them, it's key to ask certain questions about the job. Do you have a certain number of years of experience, or other qualifying factors related to each posting?

We generally ask those kinds of pre-qualifier questions to help us identify what we're looking for in a click of a button. In the application, the number one turn off is when you're filling out an application online and you just put "see resume." That's a no-no in my book. Yes, I'm going to see your resume anyway, but take the time to cut and paste it for me. I don't care if you cut and paste it or not, just put it in there. Don't put, "see resume." That's a huge turnoff in the HR world.

It's annoying because then you've got to dig into the application and find the resume. I'm going to get to it eventually, but take the effort, show some interest. Another big thing to watch for is people not thinking about the email address that they're using. I see people putting email addresses that you would not believe. You have to think about that kind of thing. Are you professional? Does your application present in a professional manner?

One of the things I am looking for when we read applications: I want to know what you did while you were at your previous jobs. I can actively ask you questions in the interview, more situational-based stuff. I do a lot of situational-based interview questions, and I push that for all my hiring managers around the county.

I want your application to tell a story. I don't want to know you worked for the City of Boca Raton for six years and that you did payroll. I need to know *what* you did. Take the time to spell it out for us, because we could be getting a hundred or up to a thousand resumes for that one job. You need something that makes you stick out over the rest. Take the time to put in your certifications. If you don't meet the requirements, a combination of education and experience can help you qualify a lot of times, especially in government. Government's big on that. You can use the total number of your educational years plus your years spent working in a job or officially volunteering for a number of months or years that can be certified by an employer.

If I were trying to get a job in the Parks and Recreation department, and the job wanted a bachelor's degree as a minimum plus two years of experience, but I've never actually been paid to work in the parks department, but I have a degree in parks and recreation, plus I have volunteered for two plus years and they will vouch for it, then you may be qualified. Make sure you spell it all out on your resume. Don't sell yourself short.

Your cover letter is your one and only chance to brag on yourself outside of the actual interview. A lot of recruiters don't read those, but I do. I hate the ones that say, "I'd love to come to work for Nassau County," and the job is actually for St. Lucie County. Spend some time on your cover letter. If you're looking for a job and you really want it, put some effort into it. Those are my do's and don'ts.

MICHAEL: You mentioned the applicant tracking system that you use. For those who don't know, an applicant tracking system is software that scans your resume and matches keywords and phrases to the job description. What you want is to mirror—be honest, of course—and match what they're

asking for in that job posting with your resume. So that's going to take customization. We talk about this all the time. Take your time and customize your resume.

IF YOU WANT IT TO BE IMPACTFUL, YOU BETTER DOT YOUR I'S AND CROSS YOUR T'S AND GET IT RIGHT. You better watch your email address. And if it's something that won't show you in your best light, forget it. Check everything. That includes your social media. Make sure that doesn't have anything offensive on it.

What percentage of the applications and resumes that you receive actually get through the applicant tracking system to you and your hiring managers? Can you throw a number at me for that?

DOUG: We actually have to review every application that comes through. We do use the system as a feature to weed out those that don't meet the minimum qualifications, but we review every application that comes in, and we send out a letter to them. There's some that get weeded out through the minimum qualifying questions that we ask, like the years of experience, but we go back in and double check those too. Maybe you made a mistake and answered the question wrong. Like I said earlier, it's tough to find people as it is, so it helps to double check for simple mistakes if your pool is light.

MICHAEL: That's interesting. If I can say this, I think you're held to a higher standard in government, so you have look at everything and make sure to dot your I's and cross your T's.

DOUG: Right. If I don't interview a veteran who meets the minimum qualifications, that's on me. I'm the one that's going to get the lawsuit.

MICHAEL: So, you get tons of these interviews. Let's talk about what precedes the resume, and that's the cover letter. I've done many of these interviews and some say, definitely, do a cover letter, and some say, oh, they're not as important as they used to be. If you're applying for a job and a cover letter happens to be important to that recruiter, then you need to have a cover letter. So always have the cover letter where you can. And if they don't look at it, they don't look at it. But if it's important to them, you want to make sure you have it. It can't hurt.

DOUG: <u>TAILOR YOUR COVER LETTER TOWARDS WHAT YOU'RE APPLYING FOR.</u> For example, I have a cover letter that's for the public sector and one for the private sector. If I'm sending it to a government entity, it's going to be the one that talks about mostly government and HR, risk management and city/county management, and things like that. And if it's a private sector job, the cover letter focuses more on my country club management that I had early in my career.

MICHAEL: Success leaves clues. Every HR professional will say that you have do your research. You must take the time to customize, because it will give you a better result. It will be more meaningful to the person on the other side, more impactful.

DOUG: Absolutely. Nothing turns an interviewer off more than when you say, "I haven't really looked into what your organization does." You're putting yourself out on the line to get that job. So, IF I COULD RECOMMEND ANYTHING TO ANYBODY, IT'S TO DO ONE THING, DO YOUR RESEARCH.

You definitely want to be able to dig deep and know what you're talking about. You've got to have talking points, because you don't know what questions they're going to ask. They're going to say, "Tell us what you know about our collective bargaining agreements," and I'm going to be able to say, "Well, I see you deal with the Teamsters for your general employees. I did that when I worked with such and such organization" or wherever you say that is relative, and you now have a connection with them. So, they think, "Well, he's familiar with what we do." If you make a connection with them, that's what they're looking for. Somebody that's going to be able to make a connection and has done their research.

MICHAEL: **Relate-ability is so important. People often say, don't say anything negative about the competition, but you can actually ask permission to do that. And if they grant you permission, then it's never looked at in a negative way. So, you could say to the hiring manager, "Listen, I read about the collective bargaining that you do right now, and I work with Teamsters, and they did something in a very interesting way that I thought could potentially be beneficial for your organization. If you haven't done it already, may I share that with you?" And then you're doing it in a way that can never be looked at as offensive. You're asking permission to share. You're also giving background as to why you're qualified to share. And all those things are going to earn points in your favor.**

Once, I noticed a few typos in a website. So, what I said was, "As I was researching the company to learn more about it, I noticed a couple of typos on the website that I thought you may want to know about, because I know how much you're interested in quality." I was doing it to benefit them, not to tell them something. We all make mistakes. "I know you guys are going at a hundred miles an hour. And I just thought that I'd spend a few minutes and share that with you." You'll earn more points with more people if you do it the right way.

Let's go back to the cover letter. What are some of the things in a cover letter that really resonate with you? Length, how it starts, the ending, et cetera.

DOUG: I mentioned a little bit earlier, that your resume should tell a story. You want to talk about why you're here, why I'm looking for a job and then you're going to highlight some of the things that you're really good at, like talent acquisition, recruitment, etc. You're going to say some of those things, but in a broader way that says, over my 15 years in government and throughout my education, I've grasped knowledge in these areas that I think would be beneficial to whoever you're asking to work for. I think you'll find in my attached resume these items and experiences that would be something that your organization would be looking for in a candidate like me.

So, when I get to your resume, I'm immediately going to go look for your 15 years of government experience. Then I'm going to go look for any certifications that you mentioned that you might have that could help me further my business.

You want to draw people's eyes, because they're going to glaze over after the fifth resume that they've looked at. They're already not even paying much attention by this point. They're looking for Steve that they've interviewed before. You've got to sell yourself. **YOU ONLY GET ONE CHANCE TO BRAG ABOUT YOURSELF, AND IT'S IN THAT COVER LETTER, WHICH IS LIKE YOUR FIRST INTERVIEW.**

MICHAEL: Each thing you do is to drive you to the next step. The goal of the cover letter is to get them to then look at your resume. The goal of the resume is to get them to call you and set up an interview. As Covey says in his book, *The Seven Habits of Highly Effective People,* start with the end in mind. Your objective with a cover letter is to grab their attention, gain their interest, and make them want more. Then

> YOUR OBJECTIVE WITH A COVER LETTER IS TO GRAB THEIR ATTENTION, GAIN THEIR INTEREST, AND MAKE THEM WANT MORE.

you ask that question and reverse-engineer it. What would make them want to hear or read more about me? What are the things that are most important to them that I've done that will translate over to what they're looking for?

How do you feel about offering quantifiable results in a cover letter? Like, as a result of x, I was able to improve processes and efficiencies and save the company 30% in turnover.

DOUG: Yeah, absolutely. That's huge. Don't make it irrelevant. If I'm going to be a talent acquisition director, and my job is to get people on board and in seats as quickly as possible because we're a high yield company, then that's what you would target.

MICHAEL: As you're doing everything, you have to ask, "How does this relate and how is this meaningful to the company, the position, and the position requirements?" And if it's not, get rid of it.

How much time do you spend on a cover letter and a resume with the influx of the hundreds or thousands that you've received?

DOUG: Really, only minutes. It's a scan more than anything. Does the formatting look nice? Does it look professional? I make piles: people I want to talk to, people I could talk to, and people I don't want to talk to. It's probably three to five minutes, maybe less.

MICHAEL: That's more than most have admitted to. Some have said literally seven to 10 seconds.

Let's move on to the interview process. You love situational questions. What are some questions that glean the most information from applicants?

DOUG: I ask the general questions. I want to know why you're looking at this job. And I want to ask you to tell me about yourself. And then I get into the ones that are more job specific. For engineering, I want to know about a big project that you've been on. Tell me about a time in your life when you managed a project over $5 million dollars, and what was your role in this project? If you had a chance to do it again, what would you do differently? These are performance based interview questions.

When I think about the most grandiose $5 million dollar project I ever did, I built a bridge over here on this road, and they're telling me that they did all this stuff. And if I'm an engineer on the other side of the table, I can really tell if what they're telling me makes sense or not. If the things that they're saying make sense, then maybe I'd take it a little deeper. I'll say, "We've got a bridge we're working on. And this new position would do this, this, and this. Tell me what you would do in this situation." I may learn something on the other side of the table that I hadn't thought of yet. You gotta know your stuff and be prepared for those questions.

MICHAEL: Let's talk about relevancy again. If you're job hunting right now, you need to, as my favorite three words are from Tom Hopkins, practice, drill, and rehearse. Go through a list of the most common interview questions and be prepared to answer them well. Tell me about a challenging situation at work and how you handled it. What did you learn from it? What would you do differently? You don't want to sound robotic, but you do want to have key points that you want to make, and then deliver your responses conversationally. But you've already practiced these over and over again. So, you're prepared.

Doug, tell everyone what to say and what not to say when they ask you to tell them about yourself.

DOUG: I've got one really good one in my mind that happened to me when I was working for a previous employer. I was a senior human resources analyst for the city, and we hired 911 dispatchers, a lot! We had an internal rule that someone from HR had to sit in on every interview panel. Dispatchers are a rare breed as it is. The really good ones are hard to find, and they're highly compensated due to the extremes of the position. It's not puppy dogs and balloons every day. They are hard to find and hard to keep because they burn out. They work a lot of hours, and they burn out fast. But I had one interview candidate, a female, that I really remember. We asked her, "Tell me something about yourself."

And she says, "Well, I'm really into tattoos." She picked her leg up, put it on a table, and pulled up her pant leg to show us this new tattoo that she had just had done on the entire length of her leg. It was nice, and it was her dog, but it was totally inappropriate for this interview setting.

That was the first question, and I was done. Sometimes, people don't think.

MICHAEL: **If you were a tattoo company, that'd be different.** ASK YOURSELF, IS WHAT YOU'RE SAYING IMPORTANT TO THE PERSON WHO IS INTERVIEWING YOU?

What would be an example of a great response to that question?

DOUG: So, again, relevancy. If I'm looking for somebody that's in public administration, I want to know they got their bachelor's degree here and it was in this. Also tell me how they took classes in marketing and business, for example. I want to know they did all of this and had an internship in a very similar situation to the job they are applying for with me. Sell yourself that way, and trust me, it makes all the difference.

If I'm trying to go for a job down the road, in the same county that I'm currently in, I can say that I'm very familiar with all the things within your organization. And because I did this, and I worked with the Boys and Girls Club, or I grew up going to the YMCA. Bottomline, I am a good fit for this job. If it's relevant to what you're looking for, then say it.

You also need to sound eager, because they're looking at 15 people that day, and you don't know what order you just came in. You could be the first one, the middle one, the last one. You can be the one that they just picked up because they had an open spot. Maybe they said, okay, pick one more.

MICHAEL: **Yeah. Show your eagerness. Another word for that is passion. COMPANIES WANT SOMEONE WHO REALLY WANTS AND DESIRES THE JOB BECAUSE IT'S MEANINGFUL TO THEM. Not just intellectually. Remember, we are emotional beings before we're intellectual beings. Communication is only 7% the words that we use. It's 38% tonality, and it's 55% body language. When Mom or Dad used to say, "Honey, it's not what you say, it's how you say it," they were right.**

I encourage everyone to record yourself, or even better yet, get that free version of Zoom. If you videotape yourself on Zoom, you can hit record, and you'll be able to see yourself answering questions as the interviewer will see you.

The only way to really know how you look to others is to tape yourself. I'm a professional speaker. I watch videos of myself. And sometimes, even as a seasoned professional, three quarters of the time, I look to the right side of the audience and not the left side. No one likes listening to their voice on

a voice recorder. They hate the way they sound. Don't shut it off.

But if you continue to play it over and over again, and practice it over and over again, you'll continue to get better. That's how we improve.

Also, remember that the power of tone and where you place that tone conveys different messages.

DOUG: That happens in email and text too. They're not supposed to have emotion, you know, but they do.

MICHAEL: When people put all caps, that means they're yelling. You need to be aware. And the only way to be aware is to ask for others' opinions and to take personality assessments like Myers-Briggs or Enneagram. THE BOTTOM LINE IS, WE DON'T KNOW WHERE OUR BLIND SPOTS ARE. So, you need other people.

If you slump over in an interview, the interviewer will subconsciously and sometimes consciously take note of that. Remember to show eagerness for the position. Whether you go in and set the tone for the 10 other interviewees coming in after you, or if you're the last one in, that could mean that you left them with the greatest emotion. You want this more than anyone else. People want to hire people who really are excited about making a contribution for the business.

PEOPLE WANT TO HIRE PEOPLE WHO REALLY ARE EXCITED ABOUT MAKING A CONTRIBUTION FOR THE BUSINESS.

DOUG: People give me a hard time because I wear a suit every day. But I'm prepared, because you never know when something is going to be more formal than you expect. My mom taught me to always dress for the job you want to get someday. In an interview, I'm the same way. NO MATTER WHAT LEVEL YOU'RE AT, DRESS FOR SUCCESS. You're selling yourself in more than just your body language and how you're sitting and how you're speaking to people. Make sure to make eye contact. You have to be able to talk to them and show them your passion.

MICHAEL: I often have to slow down because I can exhaust people. Because I go a hundred miles an hour, full war, all the time. That's just my natural tendency. But those of you who have quieter dispositions, that's fine. You can be intense just by saying things in a quiet voice.

DOUG: One of the things that I've found about myself is when I'm passionate about something, I'll get super fast. I lose people's focus. So, I generally have the word "slow" written on my piece of paper in size 28 font. Keep a joke in your pocket too. A mentor taught me that you have to have a joke on standby no matter what.

MICHAEL: Absolutely. We all have tendencies. If you're a quiet person, then what you need to do is make yourself a note when you practice. I know what my natural tendencies are, and I work on them.

DOUG: And your livelihood's on the line. If you're applying for a job, you're thinking, this is how I'm going to feed my family. So, when you're asked a question in an interview and immediately you just regurgitate the generic version of what you think they want you to say, take a tactical pause and think about what they said and how you're going to say it. You don't just have to spit it out that quickly. Don't look like you're dumbfounded and don't know the answer, but a tactical pause is really, really good. Especially when you find yourself in a situation where you're on your heels, take a tactical pause and think about it.

> THERE'S NOTHING WRONG WITH THE TACTICAL PAUSE.

MICHAEL: There's nothing wrong with the tactical pause. Zig Ziglar calls them "word whiskers," and then they take up time and space, but they have no meaning. If that answer doesn't pop right into the top of my head, I have these word whiskers that I just spread out and take no time to think of: "You know, Doug, I'm really happy that you asked me that question. I was really looking forward to that." So, as I'm saying that, I'm thinking about how I want to reply, going into the recesses of my brain and memory as to what my response is. So have those preplanned. You can pause, that's one great strategy. Another is word whiskers. Nothing but space, right? But that's giving you time to think of your answer.**

DOUG: And you can ask the interviewer to repeat the question if it's a long question, but don't do that too many times. That's annoying to the panel, sometimes, to have to repeat too often.

MICHAEL: These are two good tactics. First, you have to prepare. But sometimes, we all get stuck. And that's okay.**

Doug, if someone is looking for a job right now, and they've been rejected and rejected, what advice would you give them in terms of keeping their head up and going forward?

DOUG: I think that people are really going through tough times 100%. When someone's in an interview, they have a chance for an opportunity, and they're there to sell themselves to you. It is always good to leave them with something. Even if they didn't do great, you should always do a follow-up with a candidate. One way or another, you can give them some words of advice.

There's always a chance to coach somebody. You should never miss a good opportunity to give somebody a pointer if they're looking for it.

MICHAEL: **Flipping this around, what would you say to the job seeker? Should they ask what they could have done differently?**

DOUG: I had one of those just the other day for a very high-level job. They were surprised that they didn't get a second interview. And they said, "What could I do differently?" And, I'm sitting here thinking, well, you met all the minimum qualifications, so I can't say I was looking for a degree because you had more than the degree that I was looking for.

So sometimes you have to look hard for those kinds of things, because often the playing field is very even. It's a tough market.

MICHAEL: **Yeah. And in the end, the person who's going to hire you is going to hire you because you had more points on the scoreboard than anybody else. And all these little points add up is what we're trying to say here.**

You know, we all want to make a bigger difference and an impact on the world. And if we do that, we leave a better

world to our children and our children's children. I want to thank you for your contribution to the county.

Doug: Thank you for the opportunity.

ACTION STEPS

ALWAYS FILL OUT THE ENTIRE ONLINE APPLICATION. Do not fill space with "see resume." Copy and paste the relevant details, even though it takes time.

TELL A STORY WITH YOUR RESUME. Include specific, *relevant* examples of things you did in your job. Customize your resume and cover letter to each job description. Pay attention and don't make mistakes such as listing the incorrect job title.

SHOW YOUR PASSION IN YOUR INTERVIEW. Even if you're a naturally quiet person, practice your inflection to show your interest and excitement.

DRESS TO IMPRESS. You never know when the situation is going to be more formal than you expected.

IT'S OKAY TO TAKE A TACTICAL PAUSE during an interview to gather your thoughts before answering a question.

Idalia Perez

CEO & Founder,
beHuman HR Consulting

> ## CHAPTER FOCUS
>
> - *How to create a great LinkedIn profile*
> - *The importance of personality*
> - *Follow-up protocol for interviews*
> - *Keep up the hope!*

Idalia Perez is a dynamic, business-minded, global solutions leader with expertise in strategic planning and human resources. She teaches strategy, business process improvement, diversity, equity and inclusion, talent management, performance and productivity, coaching, change management, data analytics, and organizational effectiveness, all to drive a cohesive, well-blended, and organized environment. That's a lot! You're going learn a ton from her that's going to help you get a job. Idalia has studied a lot, is well-rounded, and has invested time. That's what people need to do today. Looking for a job is a full-time job in itself!

MICHAEL: You've been in the human resources game, hiring folks, for a long time. When you see someone applying for a job, what are the top three things that come off as, "Wow! This person is great!" What impresses you the most?

IDALIA: One for me is actually meeting the person. Personality means a lot to me, especially learning who I'm going to be working with, and who other managers or employees are going to be working with. I want to know, do they fit into our culture? How do they set the tone of the interview? Personality is a big deal.

> **TOP THREE THINGS EMPLOYERS LOOK FOR:**
> 1. PERSONALITY
> 2. SKILLS
> 3. DRIVE

Outside of this, making sure that they have the skills and the experience to do the job. Personality is number one. Skills is number two. And then three would be drive. Sometimes, you have people who have great personalities or skills, but they have no drive. You can definitely determine the drive and the determination of a person very soon upon meeting them.

MICHAEL: That's great. A lot of hiring managers may not think of that as being important, but we're people, and we're emotional beings. No one wants to hire someone they don't like. The way you feel about a person determines how carefully you listen to them. It's a science: how much you like them, or don't like them, influences how you hear, see, and internalize their message. Meaning, the more they like you, the more your message is going to be thought of in a positive way. And the more they dislike you, the more they're going to find flaws in everything.

Think of your significant other: when everything's hitting on all cylinders, every single feature of that person's face and body is beautiful. But all of a sudden, when things go south and you're fighting that Cindy Crawford mole that she has on her face that you thought was sexy last week... their physiology actually changes in direct relationship to how much you like or don't like them.

So, I know I went off on a tangent there, but I want to make the point that if someone likes you, and you have a good personality, and you're connecting and relating to them, that's going to go a long way to influence their reception of your message.

Let's go backwards. What are three things that you've seen in your career that make you say, "Wow. This is horrendous!"

IDALIA: Oh gosh. I've seen quite a few things. Here's a funny story about an interview I did with someone. They were living with their mother at the time who was elderly, and I could see her walk across the screen in the back, really slowly. And you can tell it made the person uncomfortable. They probably wanted to say, "Mom, I told you I was going to be on an interview," but they didn't. They kept going. So the mom walks back, but she walks to the drawer, and she opens up the drawer, and she pulls out a pair of underwear, like, "Do I want to wear these today?" It was terrible.

MICHAEL: That's absolutely hilarious. I once conducted an interview where the person only talked about the time they needed off. That's all they talked about. Like, I need this time off. Am I going to be working this time? Am I going to be working on the second? I was like, well, do you really want the job? Do you really want to work at all?

IDALIA: It's understandable to want to know about flexibility upfront. Am I going to be able to run and get my driver's license on my lunch break? Things like that are understandable. But at the same time, when you come in and you make so many demands upfront, it's kind of a turnoff. You haven't even gotten the job yet. We want to know if we can depend on you.

MICHAEL: So tell me about social media presence. As someone in HR, do you check LinkedIn? Do you check Facebook? Do you see what types of things people are posting or what kind of profiles they have?

IDALIA: I do like to go on LinkedIn, and I do like to see who I'm interviewing beforehand. I like to find out a little bit about them. I think just as you would research a job and know information about what year the company was established, what they do, what their partnerships are, I want to know that information about the person that I'm interviewing as well. I want to know what their experience is. I want to know if they have any references at the bottom of their LinkedIn or anyone has left nice comments for them. So yes, I do that.

MICHAEL: Excellent. And you brought a few things up that I want to dive deeper into. I love the fact that you said you check their LinkedIn profile to see if they have some references, because references are people who are third parties who are talking about you. Testimonials are always valuable. You want to make sure you have that. Let's say you haven't scheduled the interview yet. You, the recruiter or hiring manager, are looking at their LinkedIn profile to determine, "Do I want this person to come in for an interview?"

Do your research. We're going to circle back to that because we can't stress that enough. By doing the research, you separate yourself from others who didn't invest the time and, therefore, are sitting at home thinking, "Why don't I have a job?" If you do the research, it's a differentiator.

So let's go back to the LinkedIn profile.

IDALIA: I really like to see a *completed* LinkedIn profile. Sometimes, you'll just see profiles that were put together really quickly. There's an art to a LinkedIn profile. And it's important to me that any potential employee does go and invest the time or resources to find out how to build a professional LinkedIn profile.

MICHAEL: Is there any source that you can recommend that people can go to to get help building a killer LinkedIn profile?

IDALIA: LinkedIn is a good source. They have a lot of tutorials. Of course, you can go to YouTube. Everything's at the tip of our fingers now. What is even better is finding someone who specializes in LinkedIn profiles. There are individuals who are committed to this. They take the courses, they understand what headhunters and employers are looking for. And they can lead you through the process and say, "Hey, this is how you edit certain things. If you need to make updates, this is how you make changes." If it's within your means, I'd recommend you hire someone to do it.

MICHAEL: Yeah, it's an investment in yourself and an investment to get a job. If your LinkedIn isn't complete, then you're not going to get a call.

How about other advice? I'm guessing you shouldn't be wearing a bikini and holding a margarita in your profile picture. We know we've seen it—someone puts a picture of their cat up there. Listen, I'm good with cats, but if you want a job, I'm not hiring your cat. So, for the professional profile, take us from top to bottom. What are some of the things that you've seen that really resonate?

IDALIA: I definitely look at the profile picture, and let's just be completely honest, Michael, you're looking for someone that has a professional headshot. It doesn't have to be professionally taken, but it should *look* professional. You should look astute, serious about your work, and like you're going to get the job done. The picture *does matter*. Your image matters. The other thing that I think that is important is your intro, your tagline.

MICHAEL: Mine is that I'm an innovative and strategic leader, a business analytics champion, and it names off all of those unicorn items. I think that that is what grabs attention. You let individuals know with just a few words, right? Because you never want to be too wordy, but you let individuals know who you are, what you do, and what you're about in your tagline. So even if your tagline was something simple, like productivity, profitability, and proficiency, I'm already like, "Oh, I know what this person is about." I know that they're coming into my company, and they're going to make it more productive. I'm going to be more profitable as a result and, long-term, it's going to be proficient.

IDALIA: That tagline is really excellent! Another thing that I think is important is in that bio space that you open yourself up. If you're saying, "Hey, I'm looking for jobs right now," be honest, and say, "I'm currently seeking employment," or "I'm currently employed, but for the right employer, I'll move." Or, "I'm looking to relocate right now." You never know who might pop in your inbox and offer you an opportunity to relocate because you're being forthcoming and upfront with what your needs are. The other thing that I would do, and this is outside of the actual profile area, is go and make some connections in the field that I want to be in. Look at profiles that make you say, "Ooh, ah," and go and connect with those individuals.

MICHAEL: And when you're connecting with those individuals, don't just send them a request to connect, but actually enter something in the body and say, "Hey, Bill, I saw your profile. I thought it looked super interesting. We're in the same field," or maybe, "You're in a field that I'd like to come into, and I just want to connect and say hello." You'd be surprised. So many people write you back and say, "I'm so glad that you wanted to connect. Let me know if you ever have any questions." So, it's killing two birds with one stone. You're building out your LinkedIn networking community, but then, you're also looking at your connections at the same time to see where you can go. Now, what about your timeline on LinkedIn?

IDALIA: It should match up with your resume. When it doesn't, it sends a message of inconsistency. I think that it's incredibly important. Let me emphasize that you need to just be consistent across the board. You never want to put your whole resume word-for-word on LinkedIn, though. You want to give some good insights about who you are.

We want to let them know what we can do, what we did at this company. Some of the things that we accomplish, but we want them to talk to us to get all of the real, real details. We don't want to put every single thing, 55 bullet points of, "I delivered this, I manage this, I introduced this, I collaborated with this, I implemented this." We want to give an overall overview of what we did in that role. *Some* of the accomplishments that we made. That way, we keep them on their toes.

MICHAEL: **And it's been said before, marketing is everything. Most people think that job boards are where most jobs are attained. And the truth is, they're not. Over 60% of jobs are obtained through networking. When making introductions, you might also hear about positions that may not be posted yet. Networking is key. LinkedIn and Facebook have groups in the industry you want to get in. Start a chat with the people in these groups, asking questions. People genuinely want to help. Say, "I'm getting into this industry," or "I want to get into this industry. What can you tell me are the top three things I need to know?" and everyone will start responding.**

> CONNECTIONS ARE VALUABLE. REACH OUT ON LINKEDIN AND FACEBOOK, NOT ONLY WITH INDIVIDUALS, BUT WITH GROUPS.

Connections are valuable. **Reach out on LinkedIn and Facebook, not only with individuals, but with groups.**

What percentage of recruiters and hiring managers actually look at LinkedIn profiles, would you say?

IDALIA: I think quite a bit, actually. The workforce and the specific industry that you're going into might be more of a factor. So, if you're in a more corporate business environment, I think that it's closer to 65 or 70 %. People want to know who they're going to be speaking to. I think that if you're looking for a job in another sector, like work in a factory, maybe they're not looking at it as much. But that doesn't mean that you shouldn't have a LinkedIn profile or that you can't have a LinkedIn profile. I think you should always be prepared with one regardless of where you're at in your career or where you want to go in your career.

MICHAEL: You build your profile for where you want to go, not where you are. It's better to be over-prepared than under-prepared. You have a completed profile, and you checked all the boxes that we talked about.

Let's talk about other social media, whether it's Instagram or Facebook. Do you ever check those as a hiring manager, to get a little deeper look into the person?

IDALIA: I have heard of others who have, but I personally don't. From my perspective, I don't check Facebook. I don't check Instagram. I don't check any other social media, like Twitter or anything like that. I'm very respectful and understanding that individuals have a life outside of work. There's one way to be professional, and then sometimes, you just have to let your hair down and be who you are, and I don't want that to interfere with any decisions or assumptions I make. I always want to allow people to have their space, and I respect the space that they have.

MICHAEL: You have the right to free speech. I remember I heard a therapist say that regardless of how the bread is sliced, there's always two sides. You have a right to live your personal life, and you do social media the way you want to do it to express yourself. But with LinkedIn, understand that that's the majority of what business owners, hiring managers, and recruiters are looking at, and you want to keep that professional, because that's what it's used for.

So, are you pro or con cover letter? We've had both sides of this.

IDALIA: I don't care for cover letters, to be honest with you. I do think that they were needed a lot more at one time. But these days, I don't think that they're needed as much. The application process is much simpler these days. Instead of filling out a lengthy application, a lot of companies are going toward the point where they want you to enter your first name, your last name, your email address, how you heard about them, and upload your resume. That's it. So I think sometimes when we ask for all the extra, it turns away potentially good candidates. And of course, you have to sit and invest time looking for roles. But when you have a candidate who, all they've been doing is searching for jobs, at some point, you get tired of filling out applications. I'm not pro cover letter. I'm not totally against it, but I don't think that it gives you an edge over another candidate.

MICHAEL: What would you say regarding resumes? Have you been with organizations that use applicant tracking systems? If so, how much, and are you a proponent of customizing resumes?

IDALIA: Yeah, I am a proponent of that. Wording is everything. And because of these applicant tracking systems, you can be bypassed in an instant. You can be the perfect candidate, but not have the right wording. Can you imagine getting passed on by a six-figure job, because you don't have the right wording? So of course, study what they're looking for, and don't over-exaggerate your skills. Don't even exaggerate them a little, but be honest about who you are, and incorporate it with what they're looking for. Instead of saying, "Hey, I do technology," you should say, "Hey, I do a certain type of technology." Be more specific. It helps improve the resume. Those specifics help get it in front of the faces of the recruiters and the hiring managers and the people who need to see it. A lot of people don't know how to work the applicant tracking system. And when I say, "work it," that's what I mean, to be able to maneuver through it, to get the resume in front of someone's face.

MICHAEL: **This is important: 65% of larger companies use applicant tracking systems, which is software that scans resumes and looks for keywords that match the job description. And if it's not at whatever percentage they set it at, say, a 65%, 75%, or 85% match, it gets discarded. It could be a word that you put on such as a great "leader," but they may have "leadership." So you want to match those key words as best you can, again, without exaggerating. The better you do that, the better chance you have of getting through the applicant tracking system and ending up in the hands of someone who could actually call you in for an interview.**

IDALIA: Yeah, absolutely. If you're hiring or if you're recruiting, that statistic that you gave about 65%, that's correct. So yes, in my position, we want to see the resumes coming in. We want to see people applying. When resumes are discarded, we don't even see them. For instance, maybe we see a hundred people apply, but maybe five of those hundred people actually have a keyword in their resume that says you're looking for this job. But we only see the five, and we can't believe, only five out of a hundred? Slim pickings. So I have to pick my person from this five. Sometimes that's what the ATS system does. It produces slim pickings.

It's a blessing. And it's a curse. It's impossible to go through a hundred and some resumes; you'd be scanning resumes all day. That's why applicant tracking systems were created, to do the legwork for you just to get the cream of the crop. But everyone admits that a lot of great, qualified applicants are overlooked. They don't pass the applicant tracking system test, and they're overlooked because that person did not take the time to make their resume match the job posting with keywords and phrases. So do that. Even if you're qualified, understand that it's no guarantee that you're going to pass the applicant tracking system test. Make sure you match the words and the phrases in the job description.

MICHAEL: Do you have favorite interview questions that you like to ask and what kind of responses do you get? Tell us some questions that you might ask and what are some great and some horrific types of answers.

IDALIA: Yeah, sure. I'll start with a question that I wouldn't ask, which is, "If you were an animal, what type of animal would you be?" I've heard hiring managers, recruiters, and interviewers ask that. I guess you're making a judgment on that person based on the animal they choose. I feel uncomfortable with those questions, but to be honest with you, my whole style is to allow the interview to run like a conversation.

When you asked me at the beginning of our conversation what three things stand out to me about a candidate? Personality.

> YOU REALLY GET TO KNOW SOMEONE'S PERSONALITY BY TRULY HAVING AN EFFECTIVE CONVERSATION WITH THEM.

You really get to know someone's personality by having an effective conversation with them. An effective conversation does not mean that you're not asking questions or that you're not interviewing them while you're having that conversation. I like to make the person feel comfortable and to first get to know them as a person. I ask, "Tell me about yourself, and tell me about your background. Tell me why you're here today. Why are you looking for work?"

One question that I think is really important is if someone's leaving another organization, I always ask, "What's making you leave this organization?" I want to know what their answer is. We're always taught, don't speak negatively about your organizations. I don't believe in bringing that negative energy, but I do believe in being transparent. If it's a situation where the organization was extremely understaffed in their department, you might say, "I helped out as long as I could. I managed as well as I could, but I did that for about a year, and I did continue to ask my leader for help, but there was no room in the budget to get any help, or to hire a temp or another employee on. And that really took a toll on my work-life balance. It stressed me out, and I don't feel like I want to be a player in a place of stress at this point in my life."

I believe that transparency is key. The person that you're talking to might understand, or maybe they'll even tell you, "You know what? I want to be honest with you, the role that you're coming into, it's going to be a lot of work. You're going to be working days, nights, and weekends, but the salary is pretty decent. And I want to leave that up to you, whether you can handle this." Things like that are super important.

MICHAEL: You're right. Don't speak negatively, but speak truthfully. How do you speak truthfully if you left for a real, negative reason?

Let's go back to the questions I asked earlier. When you say personality, dive a little deeper. What does showing personality mean? Does that mean they smile? They make good eye contact? They speak clearly?

IDALIA: From a personality perspective, what I mean is, don't make me feel awkward in this interview. Invite me into your world. This is your interview, make it about the company and what you're going to do for the company. Make me see you here long-term. Make me want you to start right this moment.

Eye contact is key. I need to know that someone can look me in the eye. I know that nerves come into play, and sometimes it can be difficult, but really try to engage with the person that you're speaking with. Smiles are always good. Smiles are contagious. So when you're smiling, I guarantee you, someone else is going to smile too.

Those are a few easy things to make yourself more attractive. Focus on becoming an attractive candidate through your personality, because that is what you're selling. You're selling your personality, you're selling your skills. And, like you said, people want to know who they are working with. I don't think that it's great to dive into things too personal, but I think it's nice to make light of situations and talk about things when you have an opportunity to or when it comes up.

If they ask you, "Tell me about yourself," you can go back a little bit and give them a foundation from the very beginning. "When I went to school, I went to school for business administration, and I was a little confused at the beginning on what I wanted to do, but what focused me and grounded me in this area is this. And then from business administration, my first job was doing this, and you know what? It went terribly." And you can tell a short, terrible story, not a long story, about why it went terribly. "And it went so terribly because I did this, this, or this." And then go into how your career played out from that. "But from that experience, I learned that that was not the area that I was supposed to be in. I love the area that I'm in now, and I'm so grateful to have aligned that passion with what I know my purpose is. And that's why I'm here today." I think that everyone has a sense for what their purpose is and what they're here for. And I think that if you're looking for the right role, the right career, and if you're interviewing for the right thing, I think that it ignites something, and people can immediately relate to you. Just like you're purposeful and passionate about something, they're purposeful and passionate about something too. And then they know that you're going to stick with that role.

So, to sum it up, you have to be attractive, you have to win that role and win them. Let them know that can do that role. Nobody else. You were meant to do it in this season of your life. You were created for this purpose, for this moment. Maybe you don't want to be in the role for the rest of your life, but you better make them believe that for this season in your life, that's where you want to be.

MICHAEL: Excellent. And do you agree that as you're sharing your passion, you need to give quantifiable information as to results you have achieved?

IDALIA: 100%. You're selling yourself, but you're selling yourself honestly, because if you don't, you're going to end up in a role that you don't like, and that you're going to be trying to get out of in a little bit anyway. I do believe that you speak to your accomplishments. Talk in quantifiable measures. Talk about the accomplishments that you made. Talk about the accomplishments that you are looking to make. Then ask them what complex accomplishments they need you to make. They're realizing they need you to do this job. That maybe, finally, somebody understands.

MICHAEL: Right. And because you've done your research about the company by asking those good questions, it shows a level of interest greater than others who haven't asked. Good.

We heard that the pandemic is slowing down and that jobs are opening up. There's going to be lots of people applying. You still need to follow these steps to give yourself the best shot. What advice would you give folks today to really be successful? What would you recommend they do moving forward?

IDALIA: The first thing I would recommend you do is don't be discouraged. We've come from a tumultuous time. And the fact that you're reading this book right now means that you survived it. The fact that you're reading this book right now means that you already have the drive, the motivation, the energy to go after what you want. I commend you already because you want something better for yourself.

Maybe you've been out of work. Maybe you haven't been out of work. Maybe you just want another job. I don't know what your specific story is, but I would say number one, don't be discouraged. Jobs are opening back up. A lot of jobs are opening back up.

And one thing that I do want to say is that it takes about two months of consistently searching for a role to land a role. So this is two months of consistently searching. If you don't get something, I'm going to tell you something—I've been in the same boat. I've been looking for roles, and I've gotten the email that says, "Hey, sorry to let you know, we chose another candidate." Maybe you're at a place where you've gotten so many of those. Keep courage during these times.

You have to change with the times. You have to educate yourself. So your resume might change. It might look different. Look into opportunities to enhance yourself while you're looking for work. It's never bad to add a certification to your resume. There's so much free stuff out here. I don't know if you guys know, but Harvard University was offering free classes. It's easy to go in and say, "I took these classes at Harvard in this subject and this subject and this subject." You have to make yourself more appealing, more attractive, and adjust with the times.

My main piece of advice is don't be discouraged. Keep going. When you have an interview, follow it up with an email. If you can't email the manager directly, email the recruiter and say, "Please send this to the manager." Make sure that you're taking notes during that interview to understand what they need. And then, when you're going back through and writing that thank-you letter, list out those things they said they need and tell them that you'll be able to accomplish them. Sending a thank-you letter definitely sets you apart from other candidates.

If you don't get the role, it's okay. It wasn't for you. And just believe that what's for you, is going to be for you. Even if you get something that says, "Hey, we didn't select you for the role. We decided to go for someone else," then you should respond back and be truthful. "Wow, that's really disappointing. But I do wish you the best of luck with whichever candidate you did select. Have a great day, and stay safe." Because you never know what can happen. Maybe the candidate they select will drop off for no reason or they might have something going on. Then the hiring manager might come back to you, thinking, "When I dealt with Claire, she was so nice. And even though we didn't offer her the role, she got back to us. Something about that interaction, something about her transparency, struck a chord." Those are the key points that I want to leave with. Keep up with the times—they're moving, and you have to move along with them, whether it's technology, getting more education, or taking more classes. Send thank you notes. As long as you keep networking, as long as you stay hopeful, the right role will come along.

MICHAEL: Great information. For my readers, the time you spent here shows that you have a growth mindset, that you're learning and want to learn and want to get better. You're

willing to do more than most to get that job. Now you need to take action on what you've learned, because nothing happens without you taking action. And you mentioned a few times, Idalia, and I couldn't agree more, that it's about consistent effort with the right blueprint that is going to yield you the results that you want. So I just say, follow a Idalia's advice, do what she says, and you'll eventually hear those magical words, "Hey, you're hired!"

I want to thank you, Idalia, for having a big heart and a smart mind to offer all this great advice to job seekers out there.

IDALIA: No, thank you. And thank you for what you're doing. I truly had fun speaking with you today.

ACTION STEPS

LINKEDIN PROFILE – be sure it's complete and up-to-date. LinkedIn has good tutorials about how to build your profile, and there are many other good resources out there as well. If you have the means, hire a professional to complete it for you. It's an investment in yourself and your job search. Your LinkedIn Profile should have:

- A professional-looking photo.
- A great tagline.
- In the bio space, it's okay to say, "I'm looking for a job right now."
- Look for connections in the fields you're interested in.
- Your timeline should match the one on your resume.

LET YOUR PERSONALITY SHINE IN YOUR INTERVIEW. There are a lot of ways to do this:

- Tell a little bit about your background when asked the question, "Tell me about yourself." Be sure to explain what your passion and purpose are, and how they align with the job you're applying for.
- Make eye contact.
- Smile. A smile is contagious, and others will smile with you.
- Make sure to use a few keywords that tie into the job description, such as "I had this leadership role..."

ALWAYS SEND A THANK-YOU NOTE AFTER YOUR INTERVIEW. Even if you don't get the job, you can say, "Thank you for your time. I'm disappointed, but I wish you the best with the candidate you chose." You never know when/if that candidate will drop out, and your kind note might get you consideration.

DON'T GET DISCOURAGED. It usually takes two months or longer find the right job. Keep working at it, and, if you have the means, hire someone to help you.

Expanding:
Going Digital with LinkedIn, ATS's and Social Media

"Innovation distinguishes between a leader and a follower."
— Steve Jobs

Adam Meekhof

International Recruiter
for IQ Talent Partners

CHAPTER FOCUS

- *Applicant Tracking Systems: how to build an ATS-friendly resume and get more interviews*
- *How to organize your resume*
- *What if you're a student with no work experience?*
- *A word of encouragement*

I tracked down Adam Meekhof, because in order to succeed at your job market search, you need to learn all about applicant tracking systems. And Adam Meekhof is an expert! If you're not getting calls for interviews, and you're sending out a lot of resumes, this is the chapter you want to read!

Adam has been in the recruiting business for 15 years; he started in an agency and worked his way up the corporate ladder. Now he works for a Recruitment Process Outsourcing (RPO) firm called IQ Talent Partners. For the last three years, he has led, rebuilt, and started recruiting departments, implemented Applicant Tracking Systems (ATS) for two companies, and successfully does recruiting in eight different countries as well. Recruiting is his passion. He loves that every day he is able to wake up and help people, whether it's through finding new roles, building out a team for a manager, or training and developing new recruiters. Let's see what Adam has to say.

MICHAEL: Welcome, Adam.

ADAM: Thank you.

MICHAEL: My pleasure. There are three core challenges I've learned that job seekers face. One is, "I'm submitting my resume over and over and over again, and I'm not getting any callbacks." That is just deflating. It affects their self-esteem, and it's demoralizing. So I want to focus on how to get callbacks. One way to do that is through understanding the applicant tracking system, which we'll call the ATS. What can you tell our listeners about what an applicant tracking system is? How many different ones are out there? Who uses them? Give us your background and knowledge on that.

ADAM: Sure. There are tons of applicant tracking systems out there. I couldn't even give you the numbers. Everybody tries to create one because, at the core, an applicant tracking system is a system. So companies, recruiters, hiring managers, or whoever has to interact with a potential employee, use them help get to the candidates quicker. People have ATS because they want to be more efficient, more organized, to be able to get to the applicants to potentially, as you said, tell them the greatest words ever—you're hired. Right? And that's what the core is of an applicant tracking system.

MICHAEL: So tell us what an applicant tracking system is and what it does.

ADAM: Absolutely. Remember, people used to say you should go knock on doors and fill out paper applications. When you hand your application in directly, you have that face-to-face interaction. Well, that way of hiring has gone. Companies want to reach more people, find the most talent that they possibly can, and have a way to be more organized. If you've ever done any hiring back before applicant tracking systems, man, there were piles of paper everywhere, and it's not efficient to go through them. How do you go back through and remember that person that you were really impressed with that walked in last Tuesday? You can't do it. We're human. So THEY STARTED COMING UP WITH SOFTWARE THAT ALLOWS PEOPLE TO SUBMIT THEIR QUALIFICATIONS ELECTRONICALLY.

People can submit their resumes, and what we can do on the back end as the employer, potential recruiter, or hiring manager, is we can search for it. We can add keywords to our job description, or we can have people apply to a specific application electronically. And now we have all of our final files at the touch of a button, as opposed to the filing cabinets that used to stack up. So that's what ATSs are there for, to keep us organized and to find a way to get to the candidates quicker and more efficiently.

Some people think it's a great thing. Some people don't. I've been on both sides. I've been in the black hole of resumes. People apply. They never hear again. I've been there and wondered, "Why is no one reaching out to me?" That's part of what drives my passion of helping applicants understand ATSs.

MICHAEL: Okay. That's great information. Let's walk the reader down the path. Someone submits their resume to a job posting online. That would be step number one. What would the applicant tracking system look at to toss it away into that proverbial black hole where it's never seen by a hiring manager's or a recruiter's eyes? What can we do to get

through the applicant tracking system into the hands of a recruiter or a manager? Give us some ideas about that.

> A JOB DESCRIPTION IS SOMEONE'S WISH LIST.

ADAM: Yes, the submission is that first step for the candidate, but it starts before that. It starts with the job description. If you've written a job description before, you know that it's a wish list, and you start with this is what I have to have on my wish list. And here's what my must-have wishes are. And the hiring managers write those wishes by priority, and they are typically bulleted.

So that first bullet point you read is probably going to be the most important. The reason I'm telling you that is for the next step. Once you see the job posting online, and you start to read it, and you're starting to get interested, thinking, "Wow, I really like doing that. I've done this. I've done this well!" Or "I haven't done this, but I'm pretty close. I've got a good shot at most of them." And you submit. What happens next is if it's a recruiter, a hiring manager, when we start going through these applicants, we start trying to match up skills with what's on the wish list. And unfortunately, some companies get so many resumes, they have to do it quickly. That's why the job description and those bullet points are probably the most important, because if you can't hit that core, that is the untrainable stuff for this role. And then I can't move you forward. It's not that I don't *like* you as a person. It doesn't mean that you couldn't be good in this organization, but we have to have this core list.

So there's a couple of ways to get noticed. The first is, <u>**TAKE THE JOB DESCRIPTION THAT YOU'RE INTERESTED IN, AND MIRROR YOUR**</u>

RESUME TO IT. That that's the big thing. If you have five years of experience managing people and five years of management experience is their first bullet point, it should be your first bullet point too, because now that I know, I'm starting to line people up.

The other part is, a lot of times candidates (and I've done it to myself) take for granted a lot of things that we do on a day-to-day basis that we consider just basic things. Things like, "Oh yeah, I'm an accountant. I always balanced the spreadsheets there at the end of the day. I always balance everything out at the end of the month. It's my job. It's month-end close." Don't take that for granted. Are there some companies that are looking for that? They're looking for someone who is very efficient at closing out the books at month-end. YOUR RESUME IS YOUR LIVING ADVERTISEMENT OF YOUR SKILLS. So it should be living as you live in your job, right?

Typically, when someone gets a job, they take their resume, and they just throw it over their shoulder. Like, "I'm working. I'm happy. I don't care about my resume." As they get into their job and become experts, they forget to update their resume and what they're doing, and heaven forbid you get laid off or something happens to the company and it closes down. Now you have to go back and try to remember everything that you've done. So that's why I always say it should be a living master advertisement of you, of what you're doing. Create that document.

I don't care how many pages it is. You hear all these people say, well, I can't go past one page, or I can't go past two pages. Your template should be that master document that truly shows what you have done in your career. Celebrate it. I'm talking that if there's a statistic, celebrate everything that you've done and put it on that document. Now take that master document. As I'm looking at those jobs online, and I see that wish list, and I go and I look at my master document, how many of the bullet points have I done that matches that wish list?

And now I tailor a resume to that job description. I save that file as that company and the job. Then I apply with the document that matches that job description. And I can promise too, if you live that mindset, you'll have this master document of maybe six pages of what you've done. It'll pare down to one to two pages that match that job description. Now, when a resume is reviewed by a recruiter, we can see the recent, relevant, applicable stuff that you've done that matches the job. Most likely, I'm going to call you, reach out to you, and send you forward. Those are my biggest tips.

MICHAEL: **I love the fact that you said there's a hierarchy. Companies list these bullet points in order of what's most important to them in this job description, and you want to match your skills. The closer they match, the better they are going to be at getting through this applicant tracking system. I want you to touch on that. If you're off a little bit on the word, an applicant tracking system might not catch that. So if they say they want "strong leadership capabilities," and you put on "a great leader", would some applicant tracking systems not pick that up? Explain some of those nuances that you need to really match carefully or not match carefully.**

ADAM: That's a good point. A lot of times recruiters use what's called a Boolean search. I'm peeling back the curtain for you. *We* use a Boolean search. It's basically a way that you can string together words and phrases to find what you're looking for in resumes, LinkedIn profiles, or wherever it is that you're searching. And sometimes, if I search the word "leadership" and you wrote "leader", and I'm not experienced enough yet or haven't been doing the job long enough, or I'm just having a day where my brain's not quite clicking, they won't connect. They won't because one is "leader" and one is "leadership", as you said. So the great thing is with the searching capabilities that recruiters have, we have a way to say, "I want the word 'leader' and then anything that follows it."

A lot of recruiters are getting better about doing that, where we can tailor our searches, and it'll pick up nuances or semantics where one word might mean something else. We're getting very sophisticated in that. But yeah, we're all human. I always emphasize to everybody, even as a job searcher, a recruiter, a hiring manager, *we're human*. And sometimes we make mistakes. I've been on the wrong side of it when mistakes were made. I've been on the good side when mistakes were made. But we try our best, and we know we're not perfect, but we're continuing to come up with technologies that can help us be better and better all the time.

MICHAEL: **Great stuff. On a lot of my podcast episodes, I've talked to very talented hiring managers and recruiters, and everyone asks, "Did you do a resume?" I love the idea of a living, up-to-date, document list. If it's seven pages, let it be seven pages. Have a brag list of all your accomplishments, testimonials, references, and more, such as, "I increased sales by 120%." COMPANIES LOVE TO SEE THAT, WHEN YOU SHOW THEM SPECIFICS IN TERMS OF JOBS THAT YOU'VE DONE AND RESULTS THAT YOU'VE ACHIEVED IN NUMBERS OR DOLLAR NUMBERS. You can then** pare the six pages back to two pages that are specific to that company's job requirements. What's most important to them specifically and how your skills, qualifications, and all the results that you've achieved in that job transfer over to what would make you do a great job for them, with what they're looking for. Did I understand everything correctly that you just said?

ADAM: You absolutely did. **A RESUME USED TO BE A PIECE OF PAPER THAT WOULD JUST SHOW YOUR QUALIFICATIONS, BUT RIGHT NOW, IN THIS WORLD OF INFORMATION, IT HAS TO BECOME YOUR ADVERTISEMENT.** What's going to make me look at *you* more than this other person? Because, I'll be honest, I'm in the same boat. When I'm a recruiter, I'm a recruiter. I've been doing it for 15 years. I tend to think I'm okay at it. But I know, if you just put my resume down next to another recruiter who has been doing it the same number of years, and if I don't make it an advertisement, I'm going to be passed over.

The other piece that you mentioned that I would love to speak about: is there is a statistic, a data point, something that is *proven* that you can put into your resume, like "I increased sales 120%?" Wow. That changes everything, doesn't it? Because now, you're quantifying that you were successful. As yourself: did I help the turnover rate go down? Yep. Did my retention go up in sales? I increased sales by a certain amount of percentage marketing. I got an ROI on this last mailing campaign that was above the industry average. We know mailers usually reach 2%. If you get 2%, they say you're good. If you had one that was 4%, man! That better be one of the most top things that you talk about, because now you're showing, here's the standard. This is what I did. And now people will say, "Wow, I want to talk to that person because now I have a statistic behind it." We can say all the great words. You hear about it all the time. I can go in and source the heck out of my resume, but is it believable? Is it provable? Is it quantifiable? And is it recent and relevant? If it's not there, they might just pass me over. They may say, "Wow, this person can write well, but can they actually do the job that I want?"

MICHAEL: **Yeah, exactly. You've set up a perfect next question. As a recruiter, you've seen countless resumes and... well... some have sucked, and some are spectacular. As a recruiter who has seen thousands of resumes, what are the top three things that impress you, how much time do you spend looking at a resume, and what do you think the average recruiter looks for?**

ADAM: I've been told, I probably spend too much time on resumes. I'm way above average, and I'm spending typically at least a minute per resume, trying to really dive down into it. The industry average doesn't make us recruiters look very good because it's usually under 20 seconds.

MICHAEL: **At least five to 10?**

ADAM: This is where the brutal honesty is, because I've had to search for jobs, and it's taken me a while. A few times, I've had to get creative. I had to really examine my own resume and what I was doing wrong to where now I basically say I owe it to everyone that applies that I should give them at least a minute to look over it. Is there something I can grab hold of to go from there?

MICHAEL: Great, and certainly understandable. From your own personal experience, you want to give people a little more time that you feel they deserve. It's more than a job. It's their livelihood, taking care of the family. I totally respect that. So with that in mind, what are the top three things that you'd like to see on a resume?

ADAM:

1. **IS IT ORGANIZED?** I want to see visually that it is organized, so that it looks uniform. Headers in bold, certain sections for things. When I look at it, I want to see where they're currently working or where their last job was. Do I have to hunt for it or is it right there on top? And are the companies there, the dates that they worked there, and then their job title? And then specifically, what they did on a day-to-day basis. Some people try to write it in paragraph form, which maybe that works for them, but it won't work for me as a recruiter, because I have to look at so many resumes and try to talk to as many people as I can on a day-to-day basis. I need to be able to get to the information quickly, read it, and move forward. I know that sounds very harsh and that I'm not trying to look at these people as people. I am, but I also have a job that I'm being tasked with too. So I have to be able to be efficient. That's the first thing.

2. **IS THERE A DATA POINT** that I can reference that shows a tangible thing that they do, like sales? If it's someone that's programming, what languages do they know? How many years of experience do they have in that specific language? Are they writing code from scratch or are they modifying code?

People always worry that if there's a spelling error, I'll get upset, or this or that, but I always live by the motto that we're human people who are going to make mistakes. These people pour their lives into their resume, and you know what, they may be a single parent, and their kids are yelling in the background, and they have to apply. And an extra "a" got in there. If I fault them for that, I've taken the human element out of it. So for me, if there's a lot of errors, obviously I'm going to be a little bit more critical depending on the role. But if there's one or two spelling errors, it has never really ruffled my feathers, because, I always say, I hope someone would take the time to treat me this way.

MICHAEL: **So number one is make it easy for a recruiter or hiring manager to look at your resume and clearly see all the information they need to see at a glance. These are my qualifications, these are my skills, my accomplishments, my job history. You can see that they can go right to that category. And then from there, clearly you like bullet points versus paragraph form, is that correct?**

ADAM: I'm a bullet point person. It draws my attention. Now I will put a caveat in there—there are certain roles where I like to see resumes that look a little different, and that's going to be in your marketing creative space. If I'm a marketer or graphic designer, I want to see some of that creativity. I had someone that I helped recruit. She was a graphic designer, and she built a catalog for the company that I was recruiting for at the time. And when she came in for a face-to-face interview, she actually created her resume and turned it into a catalog for that hiring manager. She said, "Since I'm going to make a new catalog for you, here's my resume in catalog form." It was so creative, but the information was still all there. It showcased her creative design.

So there are roles where I love to see creativity, because it makes sense for the role. I just wanted to throw that in there.

MICHAEL: I love that. So beyond that, customize your resume. If you're an engineer, your resume will look different than if you're a graphic designer, because that's what's going to appeal to the hiring manager or the recruiter. I love that differentiator.

What would you put at the top of the resume? Would you put your name? Go down in chronological order of what the best order is for the information on a resume.

ADAM: Absolutely. So here's what I would do:
1. Your name.
2. Your LinkedIn profile, if you have one
3. Your email address
4. Then sometimes the city and state where you live because so many jobs are going remote.
5. Your website, if you have a public one

And then I want to see what you've done. If I'm young in my career, and I'm looking for a newer job, I'm going to put my education on top right after that. So I'm going to have my name, all that information that we just said, and then I'm going to put my education, because I really don't have the career that backs up what I want to do. And then, if I worked my way through college, or I had a specific co-op or internship, or even these major projects that we had to do, I put that in there, because there's a lot of things that students don't understand that are very important that they've actually done in school. If someone has an engineering degree and worked their whole way through college, that's very impressive. That is something that I could never do. I would not be able to do it with the rigor that comes behind that. So I want to see that.

Now I'm going to flip it. I'm going to go right into my experience. And then my education will be last. And then I always tell people, where do you cut off your experience? Because we have a lot of people that have been working for many years. I always say, when your career is no longer recent and relevant to what you're applying to, leave it off. So if I had a job 15 years ago as a machinist working in a manufacturing company while I was getting my degree, and now I've been in sales for the last 15 years, you don't need that. Not because being a machinist has no value, but because when applying for a sales position selling medical devices, it doesn't really apply. It's not recent and relevant to what I'm trying to do in my life now. You can put a caveat right in your resume that says, let's say from 2000-2005, I was a machinist. And then starting in 2007, I went into sales and then tell me *why* you changed careers. You can say, "Well, I saw that sales is where I'm at. I got a shot, and I went and did it. By the way, machinists, y'all are making bank right now. No one trains machinists anymore. There's my plug for skilled trades. But that's what I mean when it's no longer recent or relevant to what I'm trying to do, then I would start to remove that from my resume. And by doing that, you can typically keep it around one page long.

If you've been working for more than six or seven years in this world in a professional environment, throw a one-page resume out the window. You should have more to put down. But try to keep it around two unless there is something specific you're trying to say.

MICHAEL: I would add perhaps one more relevant thing. ULTIMATELY THE ONLY THING THEY CARE ABOUT IS ARE YOU THE BEST CANDIDATE FOR THIS POSITION? And I would say the acid test for this is what you're saying in your resume. Does it speak to the specific job that we want you to do in our company? And will you be able to do it well, based on this experience and the information you're providing? If it's relevant to that, if it's recent, and if it's something that will add value to our company and help us accomplish our objectives, that's ultimately what they're looking for.

ADAM: You nailed it. That's the hard part, because what we're really trying to do is ask you—while you're writing your resume—to remove the emotion toward yourself and your situation. And that's hard, right? If you've ever had to look for a job, there's a lot of emotion that comes behind that. It may be, "I need this job because I have to feed a child," or "I have to make this payment." And yet, I'm sitting right here and telling you, remove that emotion and go ahead and write a very concrete resume. It's easier said than done, but do it to the best of your ability.

MICHAEL: Yeah. I agree with you. We understand. We're not desensitizing how challenging and frustrating this is. We understand that this is hard. The whole purpose of my interviewing Adam is to you get a job. We want to help you fulfill the promise you made to yourself and your family. We're giving you the roadmap on how to do that.

As Steven Covey says in the *Seven Habits of Highly Effective People*, "Start with the end in mind." The end in mind is that you want to get a call for an interview. That's your first step. The first step you need to identify is what do I want to do?

What industry? What job? What's the ideal career? Where do my skills and qualifications align with those things? If you pivot in a new career, you have to think about how your skills and qualifications transfer over. But once you've done that and identify all the companies that you want to work with, now you have your target market. And then your goal is to get interviews. And second to that is to ACE the interview.

Also, you want a cultural and emotional fit. What are your passions? Are they aligned? All those things are good, but when you're producing this resume and you're delivering it to them, it has to be directly related to and relevant to, as Adam said, to what they want to accomplish. And you have to ask yourself that question at the beginning, during, and after your resume is written. Regardless of how important it is to you, it has to be important to them. They have a limited period of time, and they need to maximize that client with what will give you the highest and best result from the time they're spending on your resume. Does that all make sense, Adam?

ADAM: Yes. And then the next part is, if you don't get an interview, as discouraging as it is, don't give up. It can be so frustrating when you've applied to 50, 60, 70, sometimes over a hundred jobs and haven't gotten an interview. Reassess, look at your resume, look at the situation in front of you and say, all right, something's not going the way I want it to. How do I make it go in the direction that I want? One of them is start listening to podcasts like yours, Michael, or reading books like this. Maybe there's just one little nugget that comes out of this. It could just be the smallest thing we say, but you maybe never thought of it that way. And you just change one little thing, and the next thing happens. And then it just snowballs in the right direction. But whatever you take out of this, just <u>DON'T GIVE</u> <u>UP</u> because typically, when people give up, that's when they've almost broken through.

MICHAEL: That's great. This is sales, and as you said, your resume, it's an advertisement. You want to have the best advertisement possible and continue to tweak it to make it better. And the last thing is persistence and resilience. Two thirds of success is being knocked down, picking yourself up, brushing yourself off, and continuing to move forward, to learn, to get better and to continue to try. And also, just relentlessly call on more and more companies to say, "Hey, I'm here. I'm qualified. Interview me."

I couldn't say it better than you have, Adam... I appreciate the competence. Adam, thank you so much. This is gold, and I love your points. I want to challenge readers right now to take three things, not twenty, but three, and do them right now. THE GREAT END IN LIFE IS NOT KNOWLEDGE, BUT ACTION. You have to take action on to succeed, otherwise you will not get that job that you're looking to get. Adam, you were great, as I expected. Thank you delivering such value. And thank you for making a difference in so many people's lives.

ADAM: Oh, my pleasure. It's what I wake up for.

ACTION STEPS

KEEP IN MIND ATSs: When you write your resume, remember that it may be filtered through an Applicant Tracking System. Use keywords that highlight your goals and accomplishments, closely matching those on the job description.

ORGANIZE YOUR RESUME: A job description is someone's wish list. Make sure your experience and qualifications match those items on the "wish list." Bullet points are often best. The caveat is that if you are in a creative field, such as graphic design or marketing, you resume can reflect a more creative approach. But be sure your creativity doesn't interfere with the ATS searches.

REMOVE THE EMOTION FROM YOUR RESUME: It's all about the facts. Put in quantifiers, such as: did you increase revenue? Did you make more sales? Have you been successfully doing the job for a certain number of years?

IF YOU ARE A STUDENT SEEKING A FIRST JOB IN YOUR FIELD: Your resume will look different than someone with years of work experience. Highlight your education, work study, internship, or school projects that closely mirror what the company is looking for. Look for whatever qualifies you for that position.

NEVER GIVE UP: Job seeking is often a long, difficult, and lonely process. Identify your goals (which job you would like, which companies you want to work for) and hand-tailor your job search and resume to match the job descriptions. Often, when people are most ready to give up is when a breakthrough is about to occur.

Erin Urban

*Certified Career Strategist
and Development Coach*

CHAPTER FOCUS

- *Identifying your target market*
- *Avoiding the black hole of Applicant Tracking Systems*
- *Customizing the perfect resume*
- *The LinkedIn Lowdown*

I had a great conversation with Erin Urban about how to effectively identify what job roles are best for you, how to customize your perfect resume, and how to polish your LinkedIn to perfection so that you will stand out.

Erin Urban is a certified Executive Coach & Career Accelerator helping emerging and evolving leaders remove career roadblocks, unlock their potential, and elevate their careers. She firmly believes that your career success has less to do with your expertise and more to do with your presence and positioning.

As an industry-leading, certified professional development and leadership development coach, she is your results partner with action-based coaching to help you achieve the career advancement you want.

MICHAEL: Unexpected things happen. People don't build their careers expecting a pandemic to happen, and they certainly don't expect to lose their job because of it. One thing we can be sure about 100% is that crap happens in life. We're hit with obstacles that we had no idea were coming. And then we have to pivot and figure out how to turn those obstacles into opportunities. So where are the opportunities now? No one's going to say that it's easy to find a job during the pandemic.

Erin, you've been doing this for a while. In the years that you've been doing this, what do you see as the greatest change in the market and the greatest challenge that people are facing as they look for jobs right now?

ERIN: The biggest challenge I see is that people don't own their impact. It's very difficult for people to express their career contributions either vocally or in a written medium like in a resume, on LinkedIn, or in a networking conversation. People don't know how to express what they can bring to the table. What's your value? What's your ROI? What outcome can potential hiring managers get from hiring you?

Right now, there's a particularly competitive career market out there, and <u>WE NEED TO BE ABLE TO ARTICULATE OUR VALUE SIMPLY AND EFFECTIVELY.</u> It's great to be humble, it truly is, but we have to learn how to be the entrepreneurs of our careers.

> WE HAVE TO LEARN TO BE THE ENTREPRENEURS OF OUR CAREERS.

MICHAEL: I want to get some clarity for myself and for the audience. What percentage of your work is done with folks

that are already working? Or do you mostly work with folks who are unemployed and need a job?

ERIN: Probably about 50/50. I am what you might call a full lifecycle coach—I elevate careers. That starts with finding career clarity, developing an action plan, implementing that action plan, and then moving into more influence and income. It's a full lifecycle.

One of the things I find is, people don't know how to target their career action plan. That's really important right now in order to stand out. We can't be the Jack-of-all-trades or the Jill-of-all-trades. That just doesn't get traction. We need a specific target. So here's a tactical takeaway for anybody listening: understand where you want to go in your career.

The intersection of your strengths, expertise, and interest is your Zone of Genius. You want to leverage that. You want to seek relevant roles. Once you've found those relevant roles, you can reverse engineer from them to develop an action plan to get you where you want to go. You can analyze those job descriptions and then turn them into a question: "They're asking for x, y, and z; do I have an example of x, y, and z in my career history?" These questions can help you figure out where you fit and how to build your career action plan.

MICHAEL: **Let's talk about the target market. How does someone develop their target market?**

ERIN: So, for target markets, what you want to do is identify if your market is industry-based or role-based. Some roles are industry specific. Right now, you can go into pretty much any industry and you can be successful in sales. For the most part, that's a transferable skill. If you can sell *this* here, there is a high likelihood that you can sell *that* over there.

Once you define your role as industry-based or role-based - then you say, okay, based on this, what types of expertise do I have? If you're making a pivot, think; "what are my transferable skills? What kind of expertise can I leverage? And can I speak to those explicitly?" In other words, what are examples of times where I have leveraged that expertise and what was the outcome? That's where most people get off the bus. They can talk about what they've done, and the kinds of roles and responsibilities they've had, but they get off the bus when it comes to outcomes.

What we want to do is understand, where do I show up most powerfully? Here's a tip for you. I help my career clarity clients identify what actions and tasks in their jobs have historically given them energy, and which ones have drained them. Knowing that will help you identify your strengths, your Zone of Genius, and where you show up most powerfully.

Aim for the jobs that land 80% in your strength zone, the places that give you energy, and not 80% in areas that

> **AIM FOR JOBS THAT LAND 80% IN YOUR STRENGTH ZONE.**

drain you - because that will lead to unfulfillment and burnout. Be very cognizant and aware when you start your job search strategy so that you're aiming for the roles that will give you energy. **WHEN YOU'RE PASSIONATE AND POWERFUL IN A SITUATION, YOU WILL INTERVIEW SO MUCH BETTER.** You can be more authentic, and that shines through.

MICHAEL: So, what you're targeting as your first step is who you're going to be contacting. You want introductions to your networks. As you reverse engineer, you want to get in touch with these companies, and you're looking for industries, companies, and maybe specific jobs that are within the realm of what your passions are, what you're great at, the 80% of things that you would love to do, that would charge your battery, not drain your battery. Is that correct?

ERIN: Right. You want to identify whether your role is industry-driven or role-driven. You want to figure out where your common expertise is, whether the positions you're looking at intersect with your strength zone, and what big areas give you energy. To be fair, WE CAN BE REALLY GOOD AT SOMETHING THAT WE'RE NOT INTERESTED IN BECAUSE SKILL AND GIFTS ARE TWO DIFFERENT THINGS. You want to acknowledge your gifts, which often fly under the radar. They fly under the radar because they come naturally to you. Then, you'll think, based on this (your Zone of Genius), what can you do for a career? Analyze those potential avenues to define which one most strongly correlates with that key intersection.

MICHAEL: Great. So now we have a target. We have a list of companies. We say, okay, these are the criteria from which we're going to determine what companies to connect with in some way. Take me to the next step. Would you say that the next step would be the action step? What are all the things you need to do? Talk to us about that.

ERIN: The next step is defining and leveraging those job descriptions and those roles to help you reverse engineer your career contributions. You can talk about anything, but you want to talk about what is most relevant to the roles that you are seeking. This is extremely critical for multiple reasons.

Number one: applicant tracking systems (ATS) when you apply online for jobs. Inevitably you will, it's not just about the in-person networking. That's a component that's in three parts. One is your resume. The second is your LinkedIn. The third is your network, which is a little different now that we're more isolated. But, before we even get there, we have to be able to express our contributions in all of these areas. So, we leverage (reverse engineer) those roles to help you understand what the hiring managers are looking for.

MICHAEL: How do you know what the hiring manager is looking for? Ultimately it's about what they're thinking. What do they want, and how do I deliver it to them at the highest level? What will be meaningful to them?

ERIN: If you, the job seeker, are wondering what recruiters are looking for, really read the job description. That's what you have that is tangible and real. It's very difficult right now to talk one-on-one with an HR professional or with a hiring manager, so that is going to be your best bet.

What we want to do, most importantly, is to talk in terms of outcomes, talk in terms of deliverables, and talk in terms of impact. When you are thinking about the work that

> ALL HR MANAGERS, RECRUITERS, AND HIRING MANAGERS TELL ME THE SAME THING: I WANT TO SEE OUTCOMES.

you've done in projects or in daily routine work, think in terms of outcomes. Did you avoid a risk? Did you win more clients?

Did you make better revenue? Did you save money in overhead? Did you improve something? All of these things matter.

All HR managers, recruiters, and hiring managers tell me the same thing: I want to see outcomes. I want to see examples. When they see a document or LinkedIn profile that has this content, the outcome driven content, it makes you stand out from everybody else because few people do that. It's really very rare.

MICHAEL: **Yeah, I love that. When you can state specific numbers and quantify what success meant in your previous job, and you can transfer that over to what it will be in this position, that's everything. THE ABILITY TO CLEARLY AND EFFECTIVELY COMMUNICATE, THAT IS EVERYTHING.**

So let's talk about the resume. Are resumes as important or less important than they used to be pre-pandemic?

ERIN: I would love to say that resumes are going away, but currently, resumes still matter quite a bit. And, like I mentioned before, it's a three-pronged approach. YOUR FIRST STRATEGY SHOULD BE YOUR RESUME, THEN LINKEDIN, AND THEN NETWORKING. IF YOU DON'T LEVERAGE ALL THREE, IT'S GOING TO TAKE A LOT LONGER FOR YOU TO SEE RESULTS.

MICHAEL: **I will also share, though, that you can get a great job with just an outstanding resume that navigates applicant tracking systems. That's where a lot of people just go into the black hole. I'm being honest with you—they just disappear into the applicant tracking system.**

Can you explain a little bit about what an applicant tracking system is, what it does, and how to get through an applicant tracking system in order to get seen by someone who can make a decision to bring you in for an interview? What kind of resume can at least get through to a human being? Let's start there.

ERIN: That's where the rubber truly meets the road. You could have all the great contributions in the world in your resume, but if it doesn't get seen by a human being, it doesn't matter. And that's a huge waste of time. It takes around an hour and a half on average to apply for a job these days online. So we want to make sure that you are effectively and efficiently targeting and getting seen by real human beings.

What an applicant tracking system does is scan your resume against the job description and other criteria set by the job requisition manager. Even if you email your resume, they're going to scan it into their ATS system. Your resume needs to be around a 70 to 75% match to the job description, but no more than 89%. If you start getting a 90th percentile, you may be flagged as suspicious, because there are people that know just enough to put their name on that job description and turn it in.

You have to play the system a little bit, so don't be afraid to leverage those keywords, but keep it above board. Create an additional skills section if you feel like there's some additional content you need to include to get through the ATS.

Sometimes, what can keep you from getting through is plurals, because plurals matter. You might have "requisition" and the system is looking for "requisitions." It's kind of frustrating. If you see that there's a mismatch between your resume and the job description, <u>DON'T FEEL LIKE YOU HAVE TO REWRITE YOUR WHOLE RESUME FOR THE JOB DESCRIPTION. JUST MAKE SURE THOSE KEYWORDS SYNC.</u>

Now, I'm going to shock everybody by saying that at this stage, you want to have a three-page resume. If you're an experienced professional, a two-page resume makes it very difficult to meet the applicant tracking system job-match criteria. You don't have enough content. It's not possible. The system literally goes, "Do you have the right number of keywords, of key skills, or not?" It looks for education. It looks for other things too. They may have a certification they're looking for, but oftentimes, that's a check-the-box on the applicant tracking system itself. So a three-page resume is very important.

Now later, you may hear the recruiter say, "Well, the hiring manager really wants to see a two-page resume". That's fine. You want to talk to a real person who cares, but it's important to have that three-page document to give yourself some breathing room. Add the content you need to fully express your contributions. If they want to see a different format, fine. It is most important to get through to a human being first.

MICHAEL: **Let's touch on that for a second. If you're entry level, a new grad, or maybe mid-career, one page is probably fine. And then you hear two pages max. However, they're not necessarily speaking to how to get through the applicant tracking system. They're talking about their preference. What amount of time do you think a hiring manager or recruiter will take to look at a resume because of how many they receive? And number two, when they look at it, what** do they think is the ideal format? What should come first? Should you have certain things in boxes or grids, or should you bold headlines so the hiring manager can immediately see qualifications, experience, results, how to contact me, education, etc.? At the end of the day, we want to give real substance and good information to those listening who say, "I need a great resume." Two pages, or three pages? How do I format it?

ERIN: In order to get seen by a real person, let me give some formatting tips for applicant tracking systems. Avoid tables, no text boxes, no fancy graphics, and no heavy formatting. The resume work that I do with my clients is on a plain document with no fancy formatting to get them through the applicant tracking systems. Now, you *do* need to make the resume look nice for when it gets to a real human. But, when it comes to tables, text boxes, headers, and footers'; don't do it. A lot of them won't parse in and you lose that information.

When you *do* get to a real person, how much time do they spend on your resume? Recruiters only give you five to six seconds on average. They look at the first half of the first page of your resume. If you don't jump out as the ideal candidate immediately, you're gone. They only want to really look at around 20 resumes. That's all they're going to do. And they'll only call about 10 of those, maybe less—oftentimes, much less. Knowing that we're in the age of information and knowing recruiters only really give your resume five to six seconds, how can you stand out?

Let's talk about format. I'm finding that more hiring managers have less and less time. They're distracted. They've got a lot of things on their plate. One of the things I recommend right away is that you ditch a long summary. Please do not have a paragraph talking about how awesome you are.

What I recommend is that you have a short sales pitch—only three lines of text. Talk about the skills that you will leverage and what outcome you will give for that specific role and job description. You have to be relevant and you have to stand out right away. That is your sales pitch. It's a quick sales pitch about that job description and how you will show up and what skills you will leverage. Put it right at the top, right underneath your contact information.

MICHAEL: What I like about that is that it's very clear, concise, and compelling, and it's going to be meaningful to them and specific to the job outcome that you're going for. People don't want features. They don't want advantages. They want benefits. What's the benefit? Why should I speak to you?

You said no headlines for the applicant tracking system. Does that mean you don't bold things at all?

ERIN: Good question. You can use bold text, all caps, that's great. You can adjust the font size. That's fine.

Next, what you want to have is your core competencies. I prefer to call them your "professional expertise." This section is literally almost like a word cloud. You can separate those top core skills (which every job in the role you're targeting has in common) by dashes or by vertical slashes (or pipes). You want that front and center, right after your sales pitch.

After that, you want to include your career highlights. What are your select accomplishments? What are those things that really stand out based on the jobs you're applying for? The rest of your resume, the position descriptions, bullet points underneath each position, that all remains static. It's just that first half of the first page that changes with each application. It needs to flex depending on what job you're applying for.

MICHAEL: **There's nothing more important than what you put in your resume. Your resume cannot be general. It has to be specific. Don't take the shortcut and send a hundred of the same resumes out.**

> THERE'S NOTHING MORE IMPORTANT THAN WHAT YOU PUT IN YOUR RESUME.

ERIN: Amen. Getting past applicant tracking system and to a human being, is what matters. Here's the deal for those of you who just 'shotgun' resumes out there blind, not making any changes: you're wasting every second of your time.

For those of you who think, "Oh, I'm not a writer." Don't worry about it. Focus on the outcomes because your resume is meant to ignite a conversation, not close it. You want to hook them based on what they're looking for. Then you can talk with them in more detail in person. All that information is not going to fit in your resume, you can put more on LinkedIn.

May I liberate everybody reading this? I free you from the shackles of fear, because **NO ONE HAS A MICROSCOPE INTO YOUR WORK HISTORY.** Stop thinking that you have to be exact to the penny on any qualifications you share. Stop thinking, "Oh, I don't feel comfortable talking about this because I was just helping, I wasn't leading." As long as you can back it up in the workplace, in your new role, that's what matters. No one has a microscope into your prior work history unless you're going to work with someone you worked with before. Keep that in mind. Be smart about it, but also don't stress out about estimating the impact of your contributions. <u>**REMEMBER, IT'S YOUR RESUME, IT'S NOT A LEGAL DOCUMENT.**</u>

MICHAEL: Now, what are the pros and cons of a cover letter? And if you do a cover letter, what should it look like? How long should it be, and what should it include?

ERIN: Great question. Cover letters are read less than 8% of the time, and that figure was 12% a couple of years ago. A lot of job applications don't even have an opportunity for you to put one in. However, if they require one, you must have a cover letter to check that box. It basically says, "Oh, this person cares enough to have actually added one." You want to have about three short paragraphs as introduction to your resume. I would recommend creating a template, then customizing it as you go. Add a few statements about your expertise, then a closing statement. And that's it. Don't spend a ton of time on cover letters right now. They are dying on the vine very, very fast. Also, the first place anybody will go once you're flagged as a good candidate is to your LinkedIn profile. You have to have a good profile online.

MICHAEL: So if only 8% of recruiters read your cover letter, then spend only 8% of your time on that. If a resume has a 50% read rate, then spend 50% of your time on that. Spend your time working on the things that will have the highest likelihood of getting you a job.

Tell us about LinkedIn profiles. What makes a great LinkedIn profile? How many recruiters, hiring managers, and talent managers look at LinkedIn profiles?

ERIN: The stats are 95%. I argue that *every* recruiter is on LinkedIn. There's a feature called "LinkedIn Recruiter." Recruiters can search for viable candidates through that portal. Just know that they are out there, looking for candidates every day.

What's interesting is, if they find a candidate, the hunter-gatherer mentality kicks in. They're more likely to put that candidate forward over someone who just applied through traditional means. You want to be out there with your LinkedIn profile and have it optimized based on the roles you're targeting.

Your profile photo on LinkedIn is extremely important. Don't use one from 20 years ago or dress inappropriately for the roles you seek. You don't have to pay someone to take the picture either. Smartphones are fantastic. These days, they'll even blur the background, which looks very professional. Dress appropriately for the roles you're searching for. You don't have to have a suit and tie for every role, so use your common sense.

Also, don't do a straight on shot. It looks weird, like a mugshot. You want to have a slight side profile facing the camera. Smile or whatever is the best for your culture. In the Western world, a smile is extremely important because you want to look approachable. In the Western culture, the worst thing you can do is look overly-serious. And gentlemen, if you have a beard, please smile more and show teeth, because it's hard to see sometimes.

Now, number two—your headline is really important. Your headline is the billboard that advertises why someone would want to scroll any further. It tells them what you're great at. BE THE ENTREPRENEUR OF YOUR CAREER, and think in terms of outcomes. You can talk about your expertise and then include the expected outcome of working with you such as "operational improvements" or "top revenue growth".

For those of you who are currently employed and looking for new opportunities, be circumspect about this. You probably have your current position up there, and you can tweak it a little bit. Leave the current position title and drop off the company name. Put a dash in there and then put a little bit of expertise. Adjust it over time. That way, it doesn't send any red flags. Make sure to turn off notifications to your network if you're currently employed and are looking for a new job.

Next is your "About" section. So far they've seen your smiling face, they've reviewed your billboard (your headline statement) with your expertise and your outcomes. Now, what do you put in your About section that continues the theme of your professional introduction?

If you are actively in transition and looking for jobs, be aggressive. Go after it and tell them why you're awesome, what you do, what skills you leverage. YOU CAN'T TARGET SPECIFIC ROLES IN YOUR PROFILE, BUT YOU CAN TARGET THE ROLE TYPE. Pop in some top contributions or career highlights from your resume. Include those accomplishments that really stand out and demonstrate what makes you different.

Then flesh out your experience section. Drop off anything from before the year 2004. For those of you who are experienced professionals, please don't put your graduation date in your Education section.

For your certifications and credentials, you have to flesh them out. Really put the meat on that bone. If you are a professional who has a lot of credentials, pick the top acronyms to include after your name or in your headline if it's appropriate. It's not always a great idea to put 25 years of experience on your LinkedIn profile because you may be pricing yourself out of the market. So just keep that in mind. **WE WANT TO BE RELEVANT TO THE JOBS WE'RE LOOKING FOR.**

This next one is extremely critical for those of you who are actively in between jobs—*it's likely that you have put an end date on your prior role.* Currently, that means that you may not show up on popular recruiter searches. This is a problem, because what we've found is the most common search on LinkedIn Recruiter is current position title. What that does is - it drops off everybody who does not have a *current* position with that specific role title. They're not actively doing this to eliminate job seekers, but that's what's happening. What I recommend to anybody who's actively in transition right now is to create an "In Transition" position on your profile. The company can actually be called "In Transition." You don't have to be associated with a real company, per se. I wouldn't use "self-employed" or "contract" unless you actually are doing these things legitimately.

You want to include all the job titles that you're looking for. Oftentimes, it's not just one title, like "Data Analyst." It might be something else or a variation. As long as they're related positions, put all of them in there, separated by a dash or by a vertical pipe. Just make sure there's a space between the words and the symbol. Include all of the potential role names in there as your "In Transition" title.

Next, put descriptive information in your "In Transition" position. What are you great at? What are your core abilities? How will you add value in these roles? It's additional information outside of the About section, maybe a few more highlights about why you are an ideal candidate. This gives you a "current position" so when the recruiter does a "current position" search you will show up.

> **DON'T SHY AWAY FROM #OpenToWork**

Don't shy away from #OpenToWork either. It's not a bad thing.

MICHAEL: **You're giving away job secrets. It's perfect. In today's world, for those who are totally frustrated, what is the one thing they need to do to get a job?**

ERIN: Keep a positive, go-getter mindset. For those people who are frustrated, who aren't seeing results in their job search, it becomes personal. In American culture, our self-worth links to whether or not we have a job, though, in reality, they have nothing to do with each another.

<u>**REALIZE THAT YOU DO HAVE VALUE. YOU DO MATTER, AND A JOB WILL COME TO YOU.**</u> Pay attention to all the information that's being given to you here. Make your action plan. Don't set it aside. Mindset is critical to your success. If you have the wrong mindset, you won't follow through on the steps to success, and

you'll miss opportunities. So get your mindset straight. Clear your head and focus on the fact that you have a lot of value.

MICHAEL: That's a beautiful statement. I concur a hundred percent. You'll miss a hundred percent of the shots you don't take, according to the great Wayne Gretzky. Erin, it's been a pleasure and a privilege. I learned something, and I hope everyone else listening did too.

ERIN: Thank you, Michael. This has been a deep pleasure, and of course, there's tons of free resources on my website, coacheurban. com.

ACTION STEPS

DEFINE YOUR TARGET MARKET
1. Pinpoint your skills, gifts, and the things that energize you.
2. Match them to job roles that fit your gifts at least 80%. This will help lead you to a sustainable, energizing job.

CUSTOMIZE THE FIRST HALF OF THE FIRST PAGE OF YOUR RESUME TO STAND OUT TO A BUSY RECRUITER
DO:
1. Write a brief, three-line sales pitch and insert it beneath your contact information. This should include not just why you are an IDEAL candidate, but your OUTCOMES as well.
2. Include a list of your core competencies (or Professional Expertise) beneath your summary. This should target the high-level keywords in the job descriptions for the roles you're applying for.

3. Build a brief, bullet-point list of career contributions beneath your core competencies, showcasing how you are the best fit for the role you are applying for.
4. Use bold text, all caps, and adjust the font size to make things stand out on your resume.
5. Customize the first half of the first page of each submitted resume to the specific role you're applying to. Recruiters only read the first half of the first page before they make a decision.

DON'T:

1. Use tables, text boxes, graphics, fancy formatting—these won't parse into many applicant tracking systems, and your resume content will suffer.
2. Write a long-winded summary. Recruiters spend 6 seconds on a resume before they decide to move on. They don't have time to read a long summary.
3. Be afraid to submit a three-page resume, especially if you have a lot of experience! This is the only way to effectively include all the keywords the applicant tracking system is looking for.
4. Be afraid to game the system a little. Your resume is not a legal document. Target keywords that are authentic to you to make it past the applicant tracking system. Don't be afraid to list experience, even if it's something you've only done a few times. Makes sure you can back up your experience with examples.

THE LINKEDIN LOW-DOWN

1. A LinkedIn profile is a must. 95% of recruiters will check your LinkedIn page before calling you for an interview.

2. Upload a professional-looking profile picture. Most smartphones today can take photos good enough for LinkedIn.

3. Write an engaging, effective headline by targeting OUTCOMES that grab a recruiter's attention.

4. In your "About" section, continue the themes of your professional headline. Introduce yourself, tell readers what your value proposition is.

5. If you're currently employed and are looking for new opportunities, change your profile slowly over time so you don't raise any red flags at your current company. Make sure to turn off notifications to your network.

6. If you're in between jobs, create a placeholder position. The name of the company can be "In Transition." The job title should include all related job titles you're currently targeting. This will place you on more recruiter search results and is a valid way to put yourself out there.

7. Flesh out your experience section but drop off anything from before the year 2004. You want to show that you're relevant to the current job market.

8. Don't shy away from #OpenToWork. It's not a bad thing.

Resilience:
The Emotional Aspects of Job Hunting

"Don't get so busy making a living that you forget to make a life."
— Dolly Parton

Tony Deblauwe

Human Resources Leader

CHAPTER FOCUS

- *Exude Confidence and Energy*
- *Make them like you*
- *The art of effective follow-ups*

Tony is a Silicon Valley based Human Resources Leader. He has spent his career helping companies improve their culture and giving leaders and employees guidance on how to build great places to work. He has authored a book on how to address difficult bosses called *Tangling with Tyrants: Managing the Balance of Power at Work*, as well as created a mobile coaching app called iPocket Coach. I was excited to talk with Tony about hiring. Here's what he shared with us:

MICHAEL: **In your experience, what are the top three candidate dealbreakers? What should someone looking for a job absolutely not do on their resume, in their interview, or in general?**

TONY: The last year has been crazy. It's made job hunting, or even internal mobility, much more challenging than it already was. I'd say **THE NUMBER ONE CANDIDATE DEALBREAKER IS LACK OF PREPARATION.**

Make sure you can talk about yourself. Surprisingly, some people freeze up when they start to talk about themselves. Be prepared to talk about yourself and your highlights. Also, have you done any research on the company at all? A lot of these introductory calls are exploratory. They don't go into the weeds, but still, you need to do some homework.

The second thing is lack of enthusiasm and interest. You need to give me a little bit of energy so that I know you're excited. Having the right tone, attitude, and energy coming into the meeting, is key.

And the last piece is asking questions that allow me to get to know you better. I want to build a connection with you. Sometimes people come in here very scripted. They know what to say, and they've done this a million times. I don't always walk away knowing the person fully. So for some of the questions you ask, go off the beaten path a little. Ask, what does success look like? What are the obvious signs that somebody's not a fit for you team? These questions give me a sense that you don't just want to *get the job*, but you also want to *join the community*. You want to be part of something. When I don't get a sense of that, I feel like the interview is mechanical. It might be a fine interview, but I don't get the holistic picture.

MICHAEL: Yeah. We're emotional beings. Someone can be great intellectually and on paper, but if you don't have that connection, it doesn't matter.

So preparation. If someone comes in and they're totally unprepared, they're out. If you're not good when you're dating someone, it's just going to get a lot worse in marriage.

Even if you over-prepare, you can always ask great questions to the interviewer that shows that you did the preparation. And therefore, that will get you points. The interviewer will say, "He took a deeper dive," and that's going to differentiate you from the others they've interviewed.

I love the idea of being aware of your energy. And like you said, not robotic energetic, but natural and conversational energy. If you don't have passion in the beginning, they can't expect you to have passion once you're in the job.

So what can you do to impress a hiring manager? Would it be to be super prepared or energetic or would there be other things you'd throw in there?

TONY: All of those three detractors can become motivators. But again, confidence and energy are one of the most impressive things. When we talk about phones, we say "What's better, the Samsung, the iPhone, or something else?" And some people will say, "Well, Samsung is the better phone, but everybody uses the iPhone because it's pretty."

So in interviewing, it's not dissimilar. I could have somebody who is a Rockstar. I mean, their name precedes them, but if they are a lump on a log or they feel like they're too good for me to be interviewing them, that's a turn off. Especially coming through the lens of human resources.

I sit in on a lot of these leadership or executive level role decisions. This is going to be the same person that's going to be motivating a team, that's going to be driving goals, that's going to get people rowing in the same direction. Quite frankly, I don't care what your pedigree is. I care what you're going to bring to me right here and right now. I think a lot of your listeners should know a lot of company interviewers are bad interviewers. They don't come prepared, so you almost have to take over.

<u>HAVE CONFIDENCE IN YOURSELF.</u> Know your highlight reel. Make sure that you walk away feeling like they know that you're here to fulfill the job, but also do much more as part of adding to the culture. Those really become the most critical things above all else. I've seen engineers fail engineering tests and still get hired because they had this other stuff.

MICHAEL: **Do you recommend going over top interview questions and getting comfortable with your answer before you go into an interview? If you do that, maybe you'd be a little more competent and less nervous. Is that something you recommend?**

TONY: I think you hit the nail on the head. Your answers need to be comfortable, but not scripted. That's the difference. Somebody who does a great job but sounds scripted starts to create these concerns. Some of it's body language. It's this idea that there's a sincerity and authenticity to what you're saying. People want to have a conversation, and it really comes down to the basics. I'm going to be working with you 10 hours a day. So can I stand working with you or not?

MICHAEL: **So would you say likeability is part of that? I like this person. They come off as friendly and enthusiastic. Does that carry a certain amount of weight?**

TONY: Oh yeah. A hundred percent. IT'S ALL ABOUT SALES— SELLING YOURSELF, SELLING YOUR IDEA, SELLING WHAT YOU CAN DO. If you think about it in that sense, what do people want to be sold? What exactly are you selling? You're selling your skills. You're saying, "I can tactically do this job," but the factor that makes the decision between somebody who gets hired versus one who doesn't really is personality, that connection.

In psychology, you hear about mirroring your interviewer. The baseline of that is something called emotional contagion. If I yawn, then you might yawn. It's this idea that synergy is being developed. And some people can't quite put their finger on it. I don't know why I like Joe versus Linda, even though Joe's got these kinds of skills, and Linda has got these kinds of skills. Maybe one's more junior, but there's just something about him. It's that weird sort of unconscious feeling of a connection.

MICHAEL: Yeah. I'd call it connectedness. If you are genuine in your interview, then that's going to be transparent. They're not going to know why they feel good about you, they're just going to say that he was a great guy, or she was a great gal. They understood what your passions were. They connected and related to them. And that comes down to research. You looked them up on LinkedIn and you know they're dog lovers or something. And you brought that up conversationally.

But you're right. I think that's critical, because I always say HOW A PERSON FEELS ABOUT YOU, SHAPES HOW THEY SEE, HEAR, AND INTERNALIZE YOUR MESSAGE. So of two people with the same pedigree, the one they like more is going to get the favorable nod. What they're really saying is, "I like this person, and I want to be around them more."

What one question do you like to ask candidates that you feel tells you the most about them?

TONY: I don't actually always ask this question. I ask it if I'm on the fence about something that they said. And that question is, "Talk about your biggest personal challenge at work. How did you manage it? How did you overcome it?"

The reason I ask that question is because now we're not looking at the job description anymore. I want to know *you* better. I want to really tap into something that forces you into being more vulnerable and making that emotional connection.

Some people will give me a very personal answer, like, "I had a medical condition as a child. I had to overcome that, and that affected how I look at the world of work." But I always say, it has to be work-related. So the personal challenge could be something like, "I have a terrible manager, but I can't quit my job." It's those kinds of things that I want to understand, because it talks to grit. It talks to resilience, but it also talks to self-awareness, and that's so key in any job.

Certainly, with executives, self-awareness is very important. But even down to that junior level job, are you self-aware? If you can't even think of one challenge and how you overcame it, I can't understand the wheels in your mind. How do you approach problems? How do you resolve conflict? There are clues that come from the answer to that question that give me a sense of how they're going to behave on the job and if that approach is fine for our company culture. Is it fine for the team that you're going to be joining?

So, as I said, I don't always ask it, but it's usually when I'm feeling like I could go either way on a candidate. However, if it's a manager job or someone who is going to have people underneath them, I absolutely need to ask that because a non-self-aware manager usually becomes a toxic manager. So that has helped me gain insight into people and also understand fit.

MICHAEL: Have you ever asked the question, why do you want this job? What kind of response would be a great response?

TONY: Actually, I haven't. I've asked shades of it, like, "Why are you looking for this job? Why are you interested in this company?" If the conversation didn't naturally progress me to that point, where it's obvious why they're here, then there's no point in asking.

I want to get a sense that the person has been equally engaged in the conversation that we're having, paying attention to the flow and to the cues that we've taken along the way. It could be the kinds of questions I've asked, because that tells you so much. The truth of the matter is <u>EVERYTHING I'M TELLING YOU IN QUESTION FORM IS A PROBLEM WE NEED SOLVED.</u> I tend to look for somebody who comes in and says toward the end, "Based on what I've heard, I really feel like I can add a lot of value in these ways."

A lot of people move into that summary wrap and remind me of the top two or three things that they want me to walk away with without me having to ask. That's something that I look for now. You're judging us just as much as we're judging you for this job. So the more that I can tell you, the truth of what living in the trenches in this job is, and the better that you're able to respond to those questions, we're going to both walk away feeling like we know what to expect. It wasn't just this very high-level fluff stuff. I actually know what I'm up against.

So if I have to ask you why you're a good fit, I'm looking for something new. Something that closes the deal. It should resonate. Usually, the things people say that resonate aren't, "I've got 10 years of Java skills for programming." It's rarely those things. It's conversation. It's words that sound transformational. It's words that tell me that you're in control of how you're going to help us out.

I don't have specific bullets, but it's in those themes. How are you going to help us change? How are you going to take control of this situation? And why does that matter? And I've connected with you on why that matters. That that really is the wrap up. That makes a difference.

MICHAEL: And I love that because it also shows something else. It shows that they recognize what's important to you.

Have you ever asked the question, what are your greatest weaknesses? What kind of answer do you look for from that?

TONY: Well, first of all, I'll go on the record. I hate that question. I never ask that question, and I'll tell you why. A lot of times that's definitely one of those scripted things. It's a weird question. People get so crazy on weakness and what they're code for.

And I'm sure most of you have heard that you want to wrap a weakness in a strength. Like, I didn't spend as much time with my employees in our one-on-ones as I would have liked, but

I was working so hard. It's like, come on, I know what you're doing. But the other side of the coin too, I don't want to give the false idea that saying the truth is all good. If you say, "I'm a really terrible public speaker," but we're interviewing for you for a customer-facing job, what does that mean? So weakness is one of those weird things. I think asking for weaknesses is a weak question.

MICHAEL: I think some HR people still ask it.

TONY: They do. The way to go about answering that is have something that's not low-hanging fruit. Don't say something like, "There are times that I could have done more follow up, or I could have been more proactive in informing my stakeholders before I made this decision."

MICHAEL: You don't want to be stupid and say, "I hate people. I can't stand being around people," and you're interviewing for a team lead. You don't do that.

TONY: It reminds me a little bit of Seinfeld. There was an episode where George Costanza was trying to get a job with the Yankees. He was on this kicker to do everything the opposite of his natural instinct. So when he goes in, he's telling the interviewer off, saying stuff like, "Decisions you've made have ruined this great team!"

It's the same kind of idea. You don't want to be so blatantly honest, like with real honest-to-God weaknesses. You might risk going down a rabbit hole of

> YOU DON'T WANT TO BE SO BLATANTLY HONEST WITH REAL WEAKNESSES.

additional questions that you didn't anticipate. It changes the scope of the conversation, which might've been really good up until that point. So that's why you don't really answer that question as truthfully as you possibly can.

MICHAEL: **What makes a great resume and how important is a great resume? What do you look for in a resume and how significant are they today? Are they less significant than they once were, more significant, or about the same? What makes a resume stand out when you get a thousand of them online?**

TONY: Resumes are still useful. People still will look at a resume as they're sizing up somebody before they invite them to an interview. LinkedIn is great, but it shouldn't be your full resume. It should just tell where you worked, more of a chronological thing, so you can get a sense of what I've done. Maybe that sparks a phone call or an email reach out.

There's a different between highlights and chronology. Chronology is fine, but sometimes you need to prompt people a little bit more. That's why I always say, for a LinkedIn profile, you want to put highlights. Put two or three highlights at max. You don't want it to be overwhelming. If those highlights don't trigger them to say, "What else they do then?" Why would you want to waste your time?

People still expect resumes. When a resume's not used, typically it's because the person's very well networked, and it's a handshake and introductions and resume just because compliance or audit-wise, we need one on file. But the vast majority of people are still looking at resumes.

MICHAEL: There are applicant tracking systems that will scan and filter resumes out because there's so many online as far as resumes and how great they have to be. Are you a one-page, two-page resume kind of guy? What do you think is ideal from your perspective?

TONY: It depends on how many years of experience you have and the level of the role. If you have to stretch to three pages, that's okay. But if you're getting into six pages, something's wrong. If you're listing your thesis and your patents, include a link to a personal page where people can look at them if they want. The resume should focus on what you did and when you were doing it. And some interesting anecdotes of what you did while you were there. And then here's some skills or education. That's really it.

MICHAEL: Another big question I hear, is how to follow up and how often to follow up. When do you become a pain in the butt?

TONY: It'll vary from person to person and can depend on the type of day they're having. If they're having a bad day, it's going to seem like you're bugging the heck out of them as opposed to a day that they really want to hear from you.

MICHAEL: In general, what do you like to see? What do you think the right amount of follow-up is?

TONY: Generally speaking, email's fine. People aren't really answering their phones these days. So it's going to be mostly email or, depending on how the hiring is done, it might be in something like a chat tool, like Slack or Teams. I definitely am in the camp that a thank you note, if you can get all your interviewers' emails, is really important.

MICHAEL: You said email, not sending a card to the office, right?

> A FOLLOW-UP THANK YOU NOTE IS REALLY IMPORTANT.

TONY: It depends on the role and on the industry. Sometimes a handwritten note is best. Because you definitely will stand out. I've told people a million times to do a thank you note, but they still don't do it. So I'd just go the digital route. It's easier. If you don't have their emails, you can ask the recruiter to give their emails to you or to forward the email on your behalf.

So thank you is number one. That's the first follow-up.

MICHAEL: What do you suggest someone puts in this follow up? Is it one or two lines? What are some of the things you would include in that?

TONY: Keep it to just a couple of simple lines. Reinforce your interest in the role, remind them of the great conversation that you had, and make them feel like you definitely want to work with them. Let them know that if they have any other questions that they can reach out.

MICHAEL: So here we have two types of follow-ups—the thank you note you do right away. Then, when should you reach out again if you haven't heard anything?

TONY: That's assuming I wasn't told what the process was. Somebody might say, it's going to take us a week to get back to you. Okay, great. But if I wasn't told anything or didn't ask, I would wait three days. Then, if you still haven't heard, send another note after a week.

Some people will immediately apologize. Some people will get annoyed. In my world of tech, there's this expectation that talent is so hard to find, especially technical talent, people will tell you that we need to go from interview to decision to extending an offer within three days. And some people do that. A lot of startups do that because they know they need to take this seriously. When we find the right talent, we're not going to wait around. I wish more companies would think that way, but that's not normal.

Let me throw this other piece in, which is something I think all job seekers need to understand. **HIRING MANAGERS KNOW WHAT THE BEHAVIOR OF INTEREST VERSUS DISINTEREST LOOKS LIKE.** Everybody's gone through it. If they know the people that they like, the process moves really fast, or they're quick to follow up. Know those telltale signs. Maybe you went through your second interview, and they were on top of things, and then nothing. And again, I'm not even at the ghosting stage yet. They're just slow to respond.

MICHAEL: **Is it okay for a candidate to ask when they can expect to hear back at the end of an interview?**

TONY: Yeah. I don't think there's anything wrong with that. It's back to this dance of this is a mutual interview. Even if you're absolutely desperate to get a job, you should never, never let

> EVEN IF YOU'RE DESPERATE TO GET A JOB, YOU SHOULD NEVER, NEVER LET THEM SEE YOU SWEAT.

them see you sweat. You have to come with that confidence. I am what you want. I do have the right skills. Yes. I've been ghosted and told "no" 50 times in the last month, however, this one I'm going to get. I can add to the community. I can add to the culture.

I think one of the things that I dispel with people is that six months for a job search is not unusual. I mean, it may feel like it's the end of the world because it's so long, but it's actually not. It's not surprising. Some people think, "Oh my gosh, in 30 days, I haven't had any offers. I've been on tons of interviews. Something's wrong with my resume. Something's wrong." Actually, probably not. The things that are the most obvious problems are your resume was full of typos, or you didn't feel prepared. Or you were all over the place in your highlight reel.

A lot of the time, people do a decent job of interviewing, but it just takes time. People say it's a numbers game. **IT'S NOT A NUMBERS GAME. IT'S A WILLINGNESS TO SAY, THIS IS WHAT I WANT.** And these are the companies and the profiles I've matched to what I want and what I can do, and I'm going to express that to them. There's a stat that 85% of jobs are hidden. I don't know if it's that high, but I've heard that one before. It's "trying to get the job before the job is posted" logic. So this is what I want. Here's how I show up. And here's how I show up after the interview. All of those things are very key, but understand that between the company's process, which could be good, bad, or just normal timing, don't get so hung up that you did something wrong.

That's the way it is. So when people ask me how long the process will take, I take it as a sign of respect. I try to do it myself to the interviewees. I try to let them walk away saying, "Hey, we've wrapped up. You should expect the following because that's how I roll." It's a good process. But when they ask, even better, because I know that they're serious and they want to know because they may be interviewing other places as well. So I think it's another sign of a well-prepared interview.

MICHAEL: You should always look for ways to improve and do better on your next interview, because we should always be raising the bar. You can tell, this is the peak performance guy coming out. Now you should always raise the bar and say, "Okay, I did well on that, but how can I do even better?" How can we be better prepared? How can I answer questions better? How can I look better in terms of my dress?

TONY: Right, that goes back to the self-awareness thing again. As long as you're in that space, you should be fine. The other self-positive, motivating thing I tell people is, "It's the company's loss." Everybody has a unique offering to give. If you don't have a job, and you're paying the bills and supporting a family, you get into that emotional state. But take yourself out of that and say, "Okay, I'm going to look at this objectively as a project plan. And the project plan has these components. I have to do research of where I want to be and what I have to offer." If you can put yourself in that mindset and take the emotional part out of it, it actually becomes a lot easier.

If you're in sales, you have so many customers to call. You need X percentage to make your commission. You can walk through this and really objectify your job search. And for people who are just nervous, or they haven't interviewed much, you need to learn to treat this more objectively. And that will inform being clear and concise around your messaging, whether it's before the interview, after the interview, or during the interview. I'm not saying it's easy. We're all emotional beings.

> **IT'S OK TO THINK OF JOB SEARCHING AS A PROJECT.**

It's okay to think of job searching as a project. When you go to the movies, and you're sitting there eating popcorn and there's two people fist fighting on screen, you don't get the sense that you're in danger. You're watching and taking it in. You might have some reaction, but you're more or less neutral to what's going on. The more objective you can be about this as a project, it's got a beginning, a middle, and an end, the better off you will be in control of your process in the search.

MICHAEL: I would add to that then, you want to practice and make sure you're comfortable with everything. So when you go in, you will be comfortable.

If you're prepared and you do your best, and you're thinking, "I'm doing this for the right reasons," and you're yourself, all those things play into what will make you feel more comfortable and less nervous.

Tony, if there was one piece of advice you could give to job seekers, what would it be?

TONY: Understand that this does take time. You can always improve, like you said, and it's important to be self-aware, but sometimes these things take longer than you expect. When you realize that that's normal, up to six months for a search, it's comforting to know that even the most prepared people can take a while to find a job.

I would say, sometimes you need a community of people to encourage you and to motivate you and to remind you that you do have something good to offer. It's just a matter of time. Stay diligent. Be resilient. And don't be afraid to talk to people, even if it's just digital talking. Reach out to people on LinkedIn. All of those things are additive to get you to your goal. Just be patient, and it will happen.

MICHAEL: **Tony, thanks a million for being on the show.**

TONY: Thanks, Michael. Thank you for having me.

ACTION STEPS

TAKE THE RIGHT TONE AND ENERGY in an interview the moment you walk in—exude confidence and energy. Ultimately, we're emotional beings. Connect with them. If they like you, they're more likely to hire you if you have all the qualifications.

HAVE CONFIDENCE IN YOURSELF. Know your highlight reel (best moments). Make sure you leave them with a full understanding of what you can offer. Don't be afraid to include a summary wrap of the top three reasons why you are the perfect fit for the job.

ALWAYS SEND A THANK YOU NOTE after an interview—an email will usually suffice. Remind them that you're excited about the job and let them know that they can reach out to you if they have any questions.

DON'T BE AFRAID TO ASK how long the hiring process will take at the end of an interview. This shows that you care for and respect their time and their company.

TAKE THE EMOTIONALITY OUT OF JOB SEARCHING. Sit back and create a project plan.

HAVE PATIENCE! Job searches often take up to 6 months or more.

Damon Burton

Business Owner,
Search-engine marketing guru

CHAPTER FOCUS

- *The "secret sauce" as to why a business owner would hire you or not!*
- *The importance of soft skills*
- *Creative ways to get the attention of the head of the company or hiring manager*
- *How to be human and yet land the job of your dreams*

Over a decade ago, Damon Burton beat a billion-dollar company by outranking their website on Google. He knew right away that he was on to something special and has gone on to build an international search engine marketing company that's worked with NBA teams, Inc. 5000, and *Shark Tank*-featured businesses. I had the good fortune of speaking to Damon recently, and you'll be impressed with his knowledge, as I certainly was. He is super successful and has hired many people over his career. He's a small business owner, and along the way, he's hired a lot of people and *not* hired a lot of people. He's going to tell you exactly what you need to do and not do in order to get the attention of hiring managers, gain their interest, and get to hear those beautiful words, "You're hired!" Damon and I have had a lot of laughs, so we're going to have some fun with this discussion. Without further ado, let's see what words of wisdom Damon Burton has for us.

MICHAEL: Hello, Damon!

DAMON: We did it. Man, we're on a whirlwind romance here. I've known you for officially 26 hours or something like that. Now we're best friends already.

MICHAEL: We really are. And it's great that we're both connected in terms of our values, which is really the cornerstone of how we live our lives. We both want to make an impact. We want to make a difference. We want to leave the world better than we found it. So tell us a little bit about how, during the course of your business existence, you've hired many people and not hired many people. What were the one, two, or three things that really impressed the heck out of you when you interviewed someone, that made you say, "Wow, this is great. I've got to have this person on my team."

DAMON: All the opposite things than the listeners probably think. It's not the flashy resume; it's not the huge accomplishments. For me, it's the soft skills. So to give a little context to the type of efficiency that I put into the hiring process, I'm going to explain the business-owner side for a minute for the benefit of the job-seeker side.

For the business owner, turnover sucks. They don't want to waste money. They don't want to waste time and resources investing in somebody who eventually leaves. They want to make the right hire. I myself have been fortunate enough to never have an employee quit in the fourteen years I've had the agency.

Well, I've had *one* quit, but I'm not going to count it, and maybe we can talk about why later. I've only fired a few, and even then, it's super rare.

Let me give some context to what I hire on. My agency works on internet marketing and web design. When I'm looking for these designers, these developers, these copywriters, I can find a million of those types of people, but I can't find a million that have morals or can follow and read instructions and directions. What I do to pre-qualify and pre-screen those without wasting my time is, once I vet the talent that they can do— web design, copywriting, or whatever the thing is— then I hire based on morals. I ask myself, "Will they fit

> I LOOK AT SKILLS FIRST, AND AFTER THAT, I HIRE BASED ON MORALS. CAN I TRUST THEM? WILL THEY FIT INTO THIS COMPANY?

in with the company?" **MY NUMBER ONE THING IS TRANSPARENCY.** If there's the slightest inkling of some BS story, to me, that plants the seed that they can take any other story and stretch it out, that one inch into a mile kind of thing. So I hire largely based on transparency and morals. I'll look at the skills, but once that box is checked off, that's not what I'm hiring for.

MICHAEL: That's interesting. I find there are tons of people that are qualified skill-wise to do the job. So in this competitive marketplace with 10 million people looking for work, the differentiator for you, the person making the hiring decision, is going to be based on trust. You want to be sure they're a person of their word, and have good values that match your corporate values. How would someone be able to effectively demonstrate those things, and by virtue of that, differentiate themselves in your business?

DAMON: There's going to be a couple of different opportunities, and I think it depends on the hiring process and the business. I can only give insight as to the hiring process that I go through. Since my business is largely digital and remote, I have never met the majority of my team in person.

I'll walk you through my process as a business owner, and then you can glean from it whatever opportunities present itself from the job-seeker side. A lot of the job listings that I post obviously go online, and you have to pay attention to the details of these job listings. I'm going to give you a very literal example. Who knows what other businesses are doing this and putting subliminal things into their own job listings, just like I'm about to explain that I do.

When I put out a job listing, I put an easter egg right in the middle. I stack my job listing in a specific format. On the top it's, "How do I relate to the job candidate?" Because I want somebody that I can work with too, that can fit well in the team. So I have to say, "Hey, here's why our business is cool. You're cool too. We should be a good fit." But then what I do is I skip to the bottom, because the next thing a lot of these people are going to look for is compensation and what's in it for them. That's fair. So then, in the middle, here's where my first safety net is. For my first screening mechanism, I put in something bizarre. Like I say, "Don't message me on this job board." Instead, my preferred method of communication is Skype when I'm talking to candidates. So I say, "You must Skype me." So that's check number one—Do they message me on Skype, or do they hit my inbox on the job board? Then the next thing is, if and when you message me on Skype, you have to copy and paste, "I love Tyrannosaurus Rex cheeseburgers." It's something that nobody in their lifetime would ever send me in any other circumstance, because I want to know if you follow directions. Those are the tiny things that have a massive impact. And here's why, because when I first started going through those processes of saying, "How do I prescreen some of these candidates?" I would get distracted by the shiny resume. I would go check the inbox because they're there, and I want somebody.

These businesses want to fill the role just as much as you want to take it. I would get distracted by the resumes, and it never worked out. Those tiny things, those tiny qualifiers, are there for a reason. If a potential problem presents itself early on, it'll probably stay, so you need to have the thoroughness and willingness to go through and say, "Hey, can I play by the rules?" And if you can't, that's fine. Equally, you've got to find a job opportunity that works for *you*. These are the types of things that employers are putting out. There are these little, subliminal things, because they mean bigger things.

MICHAEL: I love that. There's certainly overlap when you speak to business owners and recruiters and hiring managers that I call the common denominators of success. I use this example a lot: it's like when you're dating someone, and they don't hold the door for you, or have good manners, and they always show up late. Do not expect that to get better when the ring is put on the finger. So exactly what you're doing is kind of an acid test before you consummate the relationship, right?

DAMON: Yeah.

MICHAEL: **People should always put their best foot forward and follow instructions during the interview process. If they don't do it then, don't expect them to do it later. And if they don't put the extra mile worth of work in at the beginning, don't expect them to do what you want once they're in the job.**

DAMON: Especially when it's something so simple as copying and pasting a little silly text. If you can't do that when it really matters, what can't you do later?

MICHAEL: **Yeah. I couldn't agree more. Now you mentioned something earlier, Damon, about how you only had one person ever quit. I'm not going to ask you about that one person who left the company.**

DAMON: Oh no, we can talk about him.

MICHAEL: **I know you can't wait, but we're going to hold off on that. What I want to know next: turnover costs companies lots of money. But this is not about the company, it's about the employee looking for work. However, that being said, I want you to talk about and share with the audience the importance of it being a right match for both parties. You, the job seeker, need to ask good questions, and a good match will mean that you're waking up every day and not going to work a day in your life. That you're working and getting paid for your passion. That you're going to have longevity because no one likes to hire someone who has been skipping jobs. If you saw somebody who went from job to job to job, what would that mean to you? And also, how important is it for** the job seeker and you as the employer to make sure that you are a good fit for each other?

DAMON: Well, it's super huge. It's just like your relationship analogy. How many listeners are in, or have been in, that toxic relationship that they just stick out for one more day, one more day. And then next thing you know, it's five years later, and you're more miserable than ever. The longer you stick it out, the deeper the hole is going to get. I've been fortunate to be in a position where I can have a little more freedom that allows me to further analyze the circumstances that I'm in and that the people around me are in. We all know that toxicity is bad. **WE ALL KNOW THAT YOU SHOULD WORK AT A PLACE THAT YOU ENJOY WORKING.** If people hate their job, you see the dying inside that you know is there, but they don't want to admit it.

Now don't get me wrong, because the current circumstances are a little bit abnormal. You've got to put food on the table, right? So there's going to be some circumstances where you've got to put food on the table. But if you have a little bit of freedom to stick it out a bit longer to find the right job or to hunt for the right job, or to choose between job A and job B, do it. You don't want this to come down to entirely a financial decision as long as you have those base needs met. As you said, this is something like a relationship. If you don't wake up every morning wanting to go into that job, then you're not going to perform as well. And then it's eventually just going to spread in all the other facets of your life. So the short answer is, I guess, that I totally agree. The long answer is I could probably ramble and take this down lot of different paths. So I don't know if that answers it.

MICHAEL: Yeah. It does. So you believe firmly that it's as important for them to be a good fit for you as you for them. What are some of the ways that you as an employer know that you like a perspective employee? Are there certain questions that come to mind that they could ask that make you say, "Wow, that's really insightful. I'm glad they asked that question"?

DAMON: This may sound egotistical, but what becomes attractive is when they ask about what the long-term goals and interests of the company are. Because then, that tells me that they have a long-term interest in the goals and success of the company as well. What is off putting (yet understandable), is when they come straight in and they say, "What's in it for me?" Because then you're not going to be a team contributor. That's not to fault protecting what's in it for you, but you also have to understand on the other side, the company is hiring for what's in it for *them*. You have to find a happy medium where you can come in and say, "Okay, are my needs met?" You can ask those things. You just have to ask in a respectable way, because the company wants to know what you will provide for their team.

I hope that I can give my team long-term opportunities. I hope that they never choose to leave. But if they do, because there's a need that I couldn't meet or they have new aspirations in life, then I want to support them in those choices. So now that you opened up the relationship door, (I'm going to continue to abuse that analogy throughout the rest of the discussion), it's much like a relationship. When somebody comes in, you want to know how you can equally foster each other's growth to the benefit of the overall relationship. In this case, the overall job and company goals.

MICHAEL: Yeah. Now that's perfect. And you can use that relationship analogy anytime you want. I work on a dollar royalty every time that story is used.

DAMON: Ha ha. Yeah.

One of the things that comes to mind on a slightly different topic is the transparency thing. I understand that life happens, and sometimes there is miscommunication, but anytime I have a job applicant that shows up late or sends me a message the next day saying, "Sorry, I was at the doctor," I'm going to guess they probably weren't, because it's pretty staggering how many people are job applicants that happen to go to the doctor the day that they have an interview. So just based on statistics alone, I'm going to lean toward that they are probably full of crap.

The applicants that come to me and say, "Crap, I was late because I had to go buy diapers. Crap, I was late because I got..." whatever. As long as it's not a car wreck, a doctor, all the typical go-tos. And if it is true, then it is true, that's fine. When you come at it from a realistic perspective and just say it like it is, I am going to infinitely trust you more. Then, the fact that you then went through something together as a job seeker and a hiring person, is a little bit of a bonding moment where you established a little seed of trust by just being transparent.

MICHAEL: Yeah. For a person to share, I love that. And by the way, you said that they're full of crap and they went out and got diapers. I like how you pulled that together and didn't even realize that diapers and crap go together. It was just flawless. This is probably too much information, none of the listeners want to hear. But I said, "Well, that's pretty clever.

He didn't even realize that that was put together like that."
But my point is that—

DAMON: I like that. I guess half the readers are going, "He's a
dad."

MICHAEL: Yeah. Definitely. That's a dad joke. So no doubt,
Damon, when you have those challenges and own up to
them, you show your character more. You don't want to do
these things on purpose, but how you handle them really
speaks to the kind of person you are. Because when they're
working for you, they're going to have issues come up. We all
do. How they handle that before, during, and after the job
interview, I think, really builds strength that says, "Well, this
person is honest, has integrity, dealt with it, apologized, and
did all the right things."

DAMON: Just owned it. Yeah.

MICHAEL: So what are the one, two, or three other big no-nos
or some things that you've heard that you just say, "Wow, I
can't believe this person said this, or didn't say this, or didn't
say something they should have." What are some that are
just a turn off, that make you decide you are not going to hire
them? You mentioned some. Do any others come to mind?

DAMON: I'm going to keep going down the transparency
path. I'm a little bit biased, because I have those prescreening
mechanisms, so I have really good relationships with my team.
And so those safety nets tend to protect me from a lot of these
things that usually come down later. Let me give you an example
that just happened today. One of my team members messaged

me with a frowny face and that was pretty unusual, because she's usually upbeat and the context of our conversations are never really drama filled. I won't get into too many details, but she sent me a screenshot of some personal issues that her best friend is having.

And she says, "I don't know how to handle this." I loved the fact that she was willing to discuss this with me and say, "Hey, I might not be productive today, but here's why." I

> TRANSPARENCY GIVES YOU (THE JOB SEEKER) AND THE HIRING MANAGER MORE FREEDOM TO BE HUMAN AND BUILDS A TRUSTING RELATIONSHIP FROM THE START.

will let her check out any day that she comes to me and says that, because what I don't want to happen is all of a sudden, she's gone for the day. Let's say she didn't say anything. And then she's gone for the day, and I'm either checking hours, or I'm checking productivity, or I'm checking whatever, and I could see that gap. Then it becomes weird that I have to even bring it up, because I don't like to micromanage. If I can notice a gap, I have to address it. I don't want to come to her. She's going to feel even more weird, then what's she going to say? "No, no, no. Really my friend, this other person, not me." And then just the whole thing becomes weird. And so the fact that she's just transparent about that helps, and that happens all the time.

I have my team hit me up. Just yesterday, another one of my team members messaged me super late, and I wrote him back, and I said, "Why are you working?" And he says, "Well, we have production deadlines for Monday that you need to review by Friday, so we can push them out on Monday." And he was sick, and I knew he was sick, so that's why I asked. And I said, "I care more about you than I care about that production deadline. Go to bed." So the fact that these guys have the willingness to come and present that transparency in the relationship, it opens up. It makes it better for *you*. You the job seeker trying to sound perfect, does more damage to the relationship, the job opportunity, the job and your freedoms, than just being transparent and saying, "Look, here's the reality of things. I'm not perfect."

MICHAEL: **Right. I love that. So I want to dive deeper because you do something that's unique. You do a lot of vetting, good questions, whatever you want to refer to it as, before you get too far into the process. I'm thinking of one of Marcus Buckingham's books, "GET THE RIGHT PERSON ON THE BUS." You get the right person on the bus. So once you get the right person there, everything is... I don't want to say it's on autopilot, but you have the right teammates. We know with the professional sport teams, it's all about getting the right people, the right team, together. So you do a lot beforehand. Let's talk about that because that's important.**

If someone wants to be on your team, what are all the things that you do to test them or vet them, or whatever you want to call it? Such as making them follow certain steps. What does a job seeker need to do with their LinkedIn, resume, and all that stuff?

DAMON: Well, I'll touch on a couple of things, and maybe to preface this is, I hate micromanaging. I DON'T WANT TO MICROMANAGE. The way that you said it, get the right person on the bus. That is totally me. And even the job seekers or other people at hiring roles that say, "I am a micromanager," or, "My boss is a micromanager," even if they *are* a micromanager, they still hate it. So either you don't want to do it and you hate it, or you do want to do it and you still hate it. So nobody wants to micromanage. They're looking for somebody, like you said, that can get on the bus. So for me, the first check is obviously, "Can they do the thing?" But once you qualify that, then it's largely transparency and personality. So transparency, I think we've hit on pretty well in the most recent touchpoints. But then personality is a big part of it too, because nobody wants to work with a difficult person. Some business owners may not care. To them, it's a dollar-in, dollar-out kind of thing.

But most of us want a healthy environment to work in, and personality comes with that. A lot of times, I'll look for anything that stands out. You don't have to be the most amazing, hilarious person at all. But when you're looking at 10,000 resumes, that one tiny, little thing is going to stand out.

What's interesting is, about an hour before we jumped into this conversation, there was a gentleman who sent me a message on LinkedIn. He had shot me a message a couple days ago and said, "I'm looking for new opportunities," and this and that. He wasn't hitting me up for a job, but I asked him, "Where are you at in life? What are you doing?"

And so he said, "Here's my resume, if you can point me in the right direction." And so I went through it, and I recorded a moment of video for him where I said, "Hey, I hope now that we're internet best friends, that I have the freedom to crap all over your resume." I gave him honest feedback. And what he wrote back, I have the words right in front of me. It says, "I hate my resume, so I very much appreciate you taking the time to walk through it. I don't know why, but when I sit down to work on my resume, I just get cross-eyed. One of these days, I'd love to connect with you on the phone or take you to lunch." Everyone has something going on right now. So you taking your time to help a stranger is a welcome blessing.

What I want to point out from that little moment is how important it is to get an outside perspective on your resume. He self-admittedly said he hates looking at his resume. Even if you *like* looking at your resume, you're going to become blind and numb to it. And I'm not going to go into the details of his resume, but the short answer to his problem was to simplify. This guy had so many amazing skills. I didn't even look at any of them because I just saw a big wall of text. He needed to simplify. You need to have your calls to action. He had his job history first, and then the summary of his skills. I don't care what his job history is until I know what his skills are.

> YOUR SKILL SET AND RESULTS (SUCH AS INCREASE IN REVENUE) SHOULD BE AT THE TOP OF YOUR RESUME.

So I told him, "Put the skill set up top and be really brief and be candid in what the results were. Don't give the fluffy 'I'm an excellent leader striving to...' and all the mumbo jumbo words that we all hear in resumes. Cut out all of that. Even if it's accurate, half of the people that look at resumes are going to ignore it because it's the same crap they see on all the other ones. Don't use fancy words. Simplify things. You have to realize that the people reading these resumes aren't going to read it until after they skimmed it. So give them the keys to skim it, to be attracted, then maybe they'll read it after that.

MICHAEL: You mentioned something. You and I are super personable people. We're rapport people. We like communicating with people like ourselves. We joke and we have fun, but we also understand the seriousness of the situation. When someone's applying for a job, they can never dismiss the fact that there's going to be multiple people qualified for the job. When you're sitting in front of a person or a screen, your ability to relate and connect and develop rapport with that person sitting across from you is going to influence how they hear, see, and internalize you and your message.

What are some of the things that folks can do, besides being transparent, that develop that rapport and trust with you to show that they are a team player? Every hiring person has their own style. Some are more relationship-driven. Others may be less relationship-driven. But the bottom line is, if someone can't stand you, no one's going to buy just from facts. They want to like the person sitting across from them, trust them, and believe they can be part of their team. They want to know that their team players can like them and trust them as well. What are some of the things you look for when you're having that conversation that makes you say, "Yeah, I liked this person."

DAMON: That they cut the crap. I think that there's a lot to be said about not trying too hard. That goes down a couple of different paths. When you come in, and you're super rigid... understandably, you might be nervous and you're not going to be faulted for that, but it's how you handle those emotions that's going to reveal a lot too, depending on the job you go into. If you can't handle your emotions, then the person doing the job hiring may misinterpret that to an extreme. That you can't handle the pressure of whatever job you're applying for. So there's a lot to be said about just being conversational. We've touched on this in a couple of different ways. You can be the most skilled, but skills can be learned. You can go to school for skill set A or skill set B. You can go to apprenticeships. You can go do internships, or whatever.

It's a lot harder to teach soft skills, relationship skills, and conversational skills. I would much rather have somebody apply for a job that is just okay at it, but I know will grow because they're open-minded, they have the soft skills, they're willing to listen, and they're willing to adapt, to become a sponge, and to learn. I would way rather take a person who's going to take me another extra six months to train, but then they're going to be perfect after that, than to hire the perfect guy on a resume that I know is going to be a train wreck and can sabotage the whole company unintentionally because of his toxicity. THERE'S A LOT TO BE SAID ABOUT SOFT SKILLS OR JUST YOUR WILLINGNESS TO COME INTO SOMETHING THAT SOMEBODY HAS BUILT AND SEE WHAT YOU CAN CONTRIBUTE TO IT, AND WHAT YOU CAN BRING TO THE DISCUSSION.

MICHAEL: Great stuff. Really, really good. What's your favorite question to ask that just gives you tons of valuable information to either qualify or disqualify that candidate?

DAMON: I do have one. I ask them a two-part question. I ask them A, "What are you good at?" and B, "What do you like to do?" Those can be dramatically different answers.

MICHAEL: **What are some of the positive and negative things that you've heard?**

DAMON: I'm paying attention to the latter half of the question: what do you like to do? They may be good at something in the first half of the question, but if they don't enjoy it and also mention it in the latter half of the answer, then they're not going to last. Eventually, they're going to burn out on the job. They're going to lose interest. They're going to take the job for the paycheck, but at some point, they're going to leave because something becomes more important than the paycheck. A good example is, one of my team members works on our social media asset creation. When I go and do interviews and podcasts and webinars, she'll chunk those out into shareable social media bites. And she's been doing awesome for a while now. And then I had to revisit with her, and I said, "Hey, we're really growing in this space. So let's start over with this relationship, and let me ask you, "What part of this do you like doing? And where do you want to go with it? Where can we grow together?"

And one of the interesting things that she said was, "I hate doing the captions. I feel like I spend so much time doing the captions." So to give an example, she might take a picture of me from an interview and then put a little caption underneath it about what I said. She has to capture that moment in time and add context in that little caption. And she did an amazing job, so I would have never known had I not asked. But she just didn't feel comfortable. Two things were wrong. One, she didn't feel like she was the right person for that job. And two, it was taking her a lot of time. So even though she was doing well at it, she felt she was spending more time than that task was justified to take. And so that gave me the opportunity to free her up from that so she could focus on the things that she liked doing, and then bring somebody else in that *did* like doing that and that could do it better and more efficiently.

MICHAEL: **And they like it?**

DAMON: Yeah. It really is two questions, but I say it in one sentence. I say, "What are you good at, and what do you like doing?" And then I clarify. I very literally tell them, "Those can be different answers," because I don't want them to lie. Here's a red flag: "I'm really good at spreadsheets, and I like spreadsheets." Not going to fly because now what's happening in my mind is you're telling me what you think I want to hear. I want different answers, or at least some deviation in the answers.

MICHAEL: **Okay. Great. So what kills that is if they give you a prescribed answer, based on just what you want to hear. That's a turn off and a no-no, and you're going to disqualify them.**

Next question. So at the end of the day, this is a tough climate for anyone to get a job. If you were going to give people who are looking for work one bit of advice today from what you know, and you know there's every type of job, small companies, big companies, what bit of advice would you give them?

DAMON: <u>TRY TO FIND AN ECONOMICAL WAY TO STAND OUT.</u> I'll give you a couple examples on the economical and the non-economical side. On the non-economical side, there's the guys that will go get a billboard on the freeway that says, "Here's my resume," and they're looking for a coding job. And then the verbiage on the billboard is in code. So it attracts the ideal type of job position, and everyone else is going to say, "I don't know what that means." Great, because it doesn't matter to them. And so that really stands out.

But you can find economical ways to do it too. One of my jobs that I had about 16 years ago was in web design. During the interview, the job recruiter made a joke about the employer and pet rocks. He said something like, "This guy is an entrepreneur. He's always being innovative and creating new things. He could probably sell a pet rock because, 'Boom, that's a little gold nugget right there.'" So what I did when I went home was I built an e-commerce website that sold pet rocks and then I put my resume on it. I sent the link to the recruiter, and I said, "Here's what I think this guy needs. It shows my personality, proves my qualifications, proves that I was listening, and makes me stand out." It took me maybe an hour to do that. Didn't cost me anything financially. And I guarantee you, I got the job. So I have no idea what anybody else did, but I guarantee nothing was close to that. So look for the little ways to showcase your skillset and, as equally important, to showcase your personality.

MICHAEL: First of all, brilliant. And since we're on that track right now, I'm going to share as well. You got me going now. A lot of times we want to get through to the decision maker. How do we stand out? Here's something I'm going to suggest to everyone reading this. If you're looking for a position, I suggest you send what I'm about to tell you to the hiring manager, the recruiter, and the president/CEO of the company. Here's what I did. I wanted to get a product that I created into Barnes & Noble. Well, Barnes & Noble has

buyers, and they're all backed up and it takes time to get in, and the numbers are working against you.

So I said, "How can I break through the clutter? How can I stand out, like what you did, and get right to the decision maker?" There is a book called *Selling to VITO*. VITO is an acronym for very important top officer. "How do I get right to the top? I want to get where the top person says, "Hey, listen, you need to talk to this guy or this gal." I went online, bought silver platters with handles and they were beautiful. They looked like they cost $60, and they cost $14. Okay? I put my product and a letter on top of the silver platter, meaning it's going to be delivered on a silver platter to this person. And then when they got it, the secretary must have given it to the decision maker, the hiring manager, because they said, "What do you want me to do with it? It's not just a letter. It's a letter on a silver platter. Let me see what it is." So the curiosity gets to them, and the secretary or hiring manager can't throw it away. So it gets to the destination, that's first and foremost. The second thing they said is, "What is it? There's an envelope on it. And it says to Mrs. Jones or Mr. Smith or whatever." And out of curiosity, they open up the letter and there you have just separated yourself from 99.9% of all others who were trying to get in and have the resume read. Just by investing the $14 and $6 shipping you spent 20 bucks to get your resume read by the top people in an organization. And by the way, I got a call with the CEO of a $5 billion company.

I called him up after five o'clock—by the way, this is another lesson for those of you listening. I called after five o'clock, and his secretary didn't have his voicemail on. He picked up, and he said, "This is Jim Jenkins," or whatever his name was, I forget. And I said, "I don't know if you remember me, but I sent you a silver platter with my product on it." How many people did that? So immediately he said, "I remember getting it, and I gave it to our director of store sales." And I said, "Do I have your permission to speak to that person, and tell him that you referred me?" He said, "Yes." So he remembered who I was because I did something different and that's what people need to do in this very crowded job market.

DAMON: I'm going to speed date three other examples of that exact thing. One is I got a friend that wanted—

MICHAEL: **Wait a second, wait a second. We're not going to play, "Can you top this?" Because I can go on buddy.**

DAMON: No, we're not... No, no.

MICHAEL: **I'd like to... Listen—**

DAMON: I'm going to win this. Now, these are—

MICHAEL: **So those are the benefits. This is all value.**

DAMON: Yeah. They're ideas for job seekers. Exactly. They emphasize the point of standing out. I have a good friend who wanted to get his product in front of this big podcast host, so he sent him a mannequin leg with the product inside the leg. And the leg was full of BBs so it's going to rattle. No matter which way you move this plastic mannequin leg, it's just going to be making obnoxious noises. And it's a freaking mannequin leg to your silver platter! So they are saying, "What are you going to do with the mannequin leg?" Well, he got in. Not only did he get his product to this person, but he sent me the video. I can't remember the guy; it's some big media guy. And the guy even commented on it in his podcast and gave free exposure to the guy being like, "What do we have now? A freaking mannequin leg." So that is one. Second one—

MICHAEL: Wait. I want to comment on that. Most people say you want to get your *foot* in the door. He got his mannequin *leg* in the door. Okay. Go ahead. Your next one.

DAMON: So the next one is, I have a business-owner friend. He sells software, and his theme is something like Caesar with swords and stuff like that for his product. And this will make sense when we're talking about it from a job hunter perspective. But his cost per lead to get a new client was averaging about $200 per lead. What he did was he found—I don't know if it was on Amazon or Etsy or eBay or whatever—but he found these real metal swords that were about 18 inches that he could have engraved. Got them down to $20 or $25. And he gets in the door on dang near every single person he sends that to. Brought his cost per lead from X amount of hundreds of dollars down to $25. Same concept—he's getting in the door to whatever target audience he wants. Now, the last one, I say the last one because it'll be more of a recognizable person.

MICHAEL: I always like to end with a comment about that. So basically that's cutting edge technology.

DAMON: Oh my gosh. Things are getting worse by the moment.

MICHAEL: I'm trying to get back to the story. I think that's a really short comment. Well, go on.

DAMON: That's it. We're done. We're done.

MICHAEL: Go ahead. Okay. Yeah. So at your risk, shall we go to the last one?

DAMON: The last one is getting in front of Grant Cardone. So my other friend was trying to get some face-time or some talk time with Grant Cardone. And he knew that Grant Cardone smoked cigars. We've seen him smoke on videos. My friend found out which type of cigar he was smoking, and it ends up being this certain fancy cigar. He went and got a box of these cigars and fashioned them in this little locking safe. He then took a picture of it and taped the picture on top of the safe and sent it to him and said, "Hey, Grant, I know you like cigars. Inside are your favorite kind. Here's a picture for proof. If you want the combination to the lock, give me a call." Guess who got a phone call?

MICHAEL: I love it. But you know what though? When you look at that, of all the attempts that you mentioned earlier, that was the *safest*. This is so good.

DAMON: That was so good, it was bad. Or so bad, it was good. One way or another.

MICHAEL: Or both. Let me say that—

DAMON: I thought you were going to say, "That one was smoking," or something like that.

MICHAEL: By the way, we might be joking, but as you're reading this right now, do these things. They absolutely work. I've spoken to the top people in the world, and I've had success in getting through to them. I'm friends with one of the Sharks from *Shark Tank* by doing this exact technique. Now, one of the original Sharks, Kevin Harrington and I, we spoke on the platform together. This is after I did this special technique that we're talking about now. They cost nothing. So here's the story: I went to this convention. Kevin Harrington was doing a *Shark Tank* pitch fest for the National Speakers Association. I'm a professional speaker. I actually had a display booth at a trade show there. I was displaying a product line, the one I actually wanted to get into Barnes & Noble. And I was displaying it there, and someone came into my booth and it was Kevin Harrington's assistant.

And I told her about the product, and she said, "I'll bring him by tomorrow." And tomorrow came and went. I stayed an extra half hour in the booth. Everyone left. He didn't show up. I was leaving to go to my hotel room (the convention was in a hotel) and who was walking toward me, but Kevin Harrington. Now, let me tell you what I did the night before and emphasize how important research is. The night before, because I knew I was going to meet him the next day, (or rather, I didn't know that I wasn't going to meet him), I watched everything I could online about Kevin Harrington. I knew how significant this meeting would be. Now, years later, he's done testimonials with me. We golf together. I spoke to him this morning. We're doing a big deal together. I mean, this was big time, right? A Shark from *Shark Tank*! He spent $5 billion in sales and is the creator of the infomercial. So I did all this research on him, and here's what I found when I watched him being interviewed by people: he carries a little quote in his wallet that he has had since he was a young entrepreneur in his early twenties. And it's meant a lot to him. It's by Paul J. Meyers from the Success Motivation Institute. When he was being interviewed, he was asked, "What had the biggest impact on you?" He actually pulled it out of his wallet on air as he's being interviewed, saying, "This is my guiding light, my focus, my whole life." So there I am, laying in my hotel room watching all these videos. Next to my hotel bed was a little pad of paper and a pen. I wrote down exactly the words that he lives by, that created his success. And I put that folded up piece of paper in my wallet, so when I met him, I could say, "Kevin, you won't believe this. I knew I was going to meet you. I have to share with you this mantra that I've lived by my whole life. May I share with you, it'll only take a second?" and I pulled it out.

So that didn't happen that day at the booth, and then I see him in the hallway. He's in the lobby, walking to get into his car to go to the airport. And I said, "Kevin!" It was just like I had planned it in my head. I said, "Nice to meet you." And he just kept walking. I said, "I got to share with you something because I had a feeling that I was going to meet you today. I was hoping you'd be in the booth, but this is fine." I said, "I've lived my whole life as an entrepreneur. I've made millions and lost millions according to this one mantra. And it's, "Whatever you vividly imagine, ardently desire, sincerely believe and enthusiastically act upon must inevitably come to pass," by Paul J. Meyers from Success Motivation Institute.

> "WHATEVER YOU VIVIDLY IMAGINE, ARDENTLY DESIRE, SINCERELY BELIEVE AND ENTHUSIASTICALLY ACT UPON MUST INEVITABLY COME TO PASS."
> - PAUL J. MEYERS SUCCESS MOTIVATION INSTITUTE

He said, "You won't believe it." And he didn't know that I did what he did. And he pulls out his wallet, and his wallet was filled with stuff. And things were falling all over the place. And he pulls out, twenty-five years later, the sheet of paper that he still carries with him to this day, all tattered. And he said, "This is my motto." At that point, he gave me his home phone number. I met him in St. Petersburg, Florida. And that was the start of our relationship, which has only gotten bigger and better, all because of that. Did it cost me anything? Zero. It was a little time, a little creativity, and a little action. And that's the magic.

DAMON: Yeah. Just a little on tank goes a long ways.

MICHAEL: Yeah. So—

DAMON: I don't have any catchy follow-up like you do.

MICHAEL: That's a Sharkey story—

DAMON: Hold on. Now I got one. That story was money, because it was in the wallet.

MICHAEL: I like that.

DAMON: So that's how I'm going to say it.

MICHAEL: Okay. Because now I'll tell you what I'm thinking of you. You tell the stories, and I'll do the punchline at the end.

DAMON: Yeah.

MICHAEL: Okay. Let's finish with this. What crazy story— good or bad—or give me one of each. I love the fact that you're a storyteller, Damon. What's the craziest story you have about a person you hired who did something either funny, entertaining, creative, or a combination thereof? For example, I had a salesman with a very high energy sales job who was in the coffee business, applying for a job. I said, "I'll be with you in a minute. I'm on the phone." And I looked over, and he was sound asleep in the chair. What do you have?

DAMON: It has to be to about hiring?

MICHAEL: **Hiring or is it someone you didn't hire?**

DAMON: How about I tell my one employee that left me story?

MICHAEL: **That's it! Okay. I'm glad you mentioned that. Go ahead.**

DAMON: So at the time, this guy, he was my number two, right? We would talk daily, and one day, he called me on the office line, and I could tell right away that something was wrong, because we'd been working together for a long time. And he didn't even say more than, "Hey, Damon." It was nothing. But I knew him so well that just in that short comment, I knew something was off. And so I just called him out and said, "You all right? You sound like you have something to say." And then he starts stuttering a little bit more. And he says, "Well, yeah, I do. I got this call, and I went and talked to this one guy..." and he's dancing around it. And long story short, he goes, "I have an opportunity to take a job with another company."

And I said, "Okay, well, let's talk about it." And this will go to support what we were talking about earlier, that I hope to provide the opportunities for my team and grow with them long-term together. And if I can't, then I want to support them in those other decisions. And so what had happened is, he wasn't looking for a job, but his ex-wife had somebody who asked her if she knew somebody who did marketing. And so she told him, "My ex-husband does marketing. And maybe he can give you some pointers." And that just evolved into an opportunity. And it was substantially more pay with unique opportunities. And so he was vested in my company a little bit, and I said, "Look, go for it. I have no reason to tell you no. There's business Damon and there's friend Damon. Of course, as business Damon, I'm going to have to figure out how I fill those gaps. But I have no reason to tell you no. You may have some opportunities, and this could be long-term that will pay off pretty substantially, and they may be able to bring you a little bit bigger wins faster."

So that's the only person that I've ever had leave. I think that goes to reinforce a lot of what we talked about, about how **RELATIONSHIPS MATTER ON BOTH SIDES** of the thing. He felt bad leaving, and then of course, as the employer, I didn't want him leaving either. So once you get that basic need of putting food on the table met, then there's a lot to be said to sticking it out or continuing the search to find the one that you can, using the relationship metaphor, the one that you can marry. Then everybody in both parties ends up living happily ever after.

> FIND THE JOB THAT YOU CAN "MARRY," AND THEN EVERYBODY ENDS UP LIVING HAPPILY EVER AFTER.

MICHAEL: That's awesome. And you want that growth. You want to show that growth projection, that both you and the company can grow. It's not always going to be a perfect fit forever because circumstances change. And we can't always predict that.

I knew this discussion would be a lot of fun. I had no idea it would be this much fun. And the value that you've brought, the ideas, and also the perspective that you brought, Damon, about how important the soft skills and the relationships goals are. I love that. I love the questions that you ask when someone is looking at the job posting to vet that person out, or make them feel included, like, "This is someone I want to talk to." I like that if they don't follow the instructions properly—I don't know, I probably wouldn't get the job. I forget whether it was Tyrannosaurus Rex or—

DAMON: T-Rex. Yeah.

MICHAEL: Yeah. Well, you got that.

DAMON: T-Rex. You're in.

MICHAEL: That's a winner. All right. And that, I think is brilliant. So look a little closer when you're applying for a job, at what could be the meaning behind these questions. Just don't answer them as black and white. Look at the meaning behind them, because this reflects to them how you would be in the job based on the quality and depth of your answer. Are you communicating in a good way? And I really liked the fact that you say, we're human beings first. Transparency, honesty, integrity; you'll earn so many more points with that than by trying to be perfect. You can be imperfectly perfect and that would get you much more ground than the other.

DAMON: Yeah. I think that applies to pretty much everything in life. Even for me on the business side of things. When I'm looking for business, theoretically, those clients are my employers that are going to be paying me and my company. And it's the same thing; we grow because of that transparency. We don't spend any money on advertising. We don't do the crazy things, but we do the silver platters. We do the unique mannequin legs. We show the personality. I have 30 employees, and we have a pretty successful agency, and it's all based on the same concept: putting relationships and personality and transparency first. So I think you can apply these rules to everything.

MICHAEL: That's great. I can't top that. That's perfect. And brother, thank you so much for delivering so much value. For making it fun for the listeners. We're going to help people get back to work. Help their families. To us, it's not just the job that people lost, it's the ability to take care of their family, their identity, putting food on the table, and so much more. And your help with this means the world to me. Together, we can certainly make this place better for everybody. So thank you.

DAMON: Yeah. Thanks. Good luck everybody.

ACTION STEPS

THINK OF CREATIVE WAYS TO GET YOUR FOOT IN THE DOOR. Is there an interesting way to display your resume? How can you reach the CEO or hiring manager directly? Be respectful, and nobody is off limits.

SOFT SKILLS ARE IMPORTANT. Make sure you put your best self forward. Be conversational and do your research ahead of time, so you can carry on a conversation with the hiring manager.

COMPANY CULTURE MATTERS. Sometimes you have to get your basic needs met, but if you have enough food on the table for now, take some time to find the right job fit. You want to land a job that you're passionate about and can stay in for a long time.

BE HUMAN: TRANSPARENCY can often get you further in the door. Do your best, but be honest. If you are late, explain what the crisis was. Don't try to cover it up, because that breaks trust.

Ken Eslick

President of Summit Careers

CHAPTER FOCUS

- *Make every hiring manager fall in love with you*
- *Spinning bad breakups with previous companies in a good light*
- *Gaining confidence points with your interviewer*
- *The "why" of finding a new job*

I had a great conversation with Ken Eslick about how to ace an interview by gaining confidence points with your recruiter and understanding the "why" of your job search. Ken is the President of The Leaders Lab, a talent acquisition firm specializing in placing leaders with Fortune 500 companies. Prior to starting Summit, Ken was the VP of Sales and Operations for Cintas. While with Cintas, Ken led teams as large as 1,000 and was the dealmaker on more than 50 acquisitions totaling over $300,000,000 in revenue. Earlier in Ken's career, he served in the U.S. Army, and started and sold his first company to Cintas.

MICHAEL: **Ken, tell us a little bit about your background. What drove you to recruiting? What is your biggest word of advice to someone who is looking to be placed in a senior level position?**

KEN: When I decided to leave corporate America, I thought about where my skills and talents could best be used and what my passion was. I've always enjoyed working with people, leading people, and developing people. I was really good at bringing people into our organization, even when that wasn't my primary job. It was just one of the many hats that I wore. So I decided to do that on my own when I left corporate America.

To get more specific, when I was 18 and 19, I was going to college but not really *going* to college. One day, I had an epiphany. I was in class, and I thought, "I'm going to be a loser if I continue on this path," which was an amazing thought for me to have at that time, because all I could think about were girls and how to get enough money to buy a 12-pack of beer on Friday night. That was the level of my thinking. But one day, it just hit me that I had to get out of there and do something different.

So I joined the Army. I never finished college. When I got out of the Army, there weren't a bunch of opportunities waiting for a college dropout, even with four years of military service. I didn't know how to go about getting a job, and I didn't know how to get the right job, and I didn't know how to get in front of people or how to be noticed. So I started my own company as a result of not being able to market myself to others.

Now it ended up working out okay for me, and I wouldn't trade that experience, but I have a real passion for people because of it. There are so many great people out there with awesome experience. And military people are really in my wheelhouse, because there is so much leadership there, but they often don't know how to translate it into their civilian career. I think everybody's got gifts. Everybody has something to offer, and the ability to bring that out and to connect them with corporations, it goes beyond just serving them. It's surveying them.

MICHAEL: What are things that a job seeker should do that would help them the most?

KEN: I would say the number one thing is preparation. And I know that sounds basic, but I'm just shocked by the number of people who don't prepare that much. For some people, job searching is like car shopping. You think, "I don't know if I like this one, so I'm going to go to the next one." But when you're interviewing, you can't be so laissez-faire about it.

You want to be more like the Bachelor. You want everybody to want you. If you're going to eight interviews, you want to be able to have all eight opportunities as options. You can't have that attitude of, "I'm just checking it out, so I'm not going to invest too much time in it." That's going to come across to all eight employers. **YOU DON'T GET A SECOND CHANCE AT A FIRST IMPRESSION.**

Once your chance is gone, it's gone. If you're taking the time to drive all the way to the interview and to sit there for an hour, then you can take 30 minutes figuring out if the company is publicly traded, what their stock has traded for recently, and if they are growing or contracting. We're in such a great day and age right now, and any of that I just mentioned can be found in a five minute Google search. Figure out what their culture is, which informs how you should dress. Map out your route to the interview the night before. Print resumes. Not everyone's going to think of doing that for you before you get there. Preparation is key.

Also, make sure not to ask questions too early in an interview process about how *you're* going to benefit. You want to ask questions about how you can serve them.

The first question you ask should not be, "How many vacation days do I get?" First of all, if you're using a recruiter, you never need to ask that question, because the recruiter can ask all that stuff. Second, that's more of a question for HR. Third, if they don't have HR, like a small company, you ask that after they've already bought the Ken Eslick package. That should be the last thing you ask. If someone starts with a question like that, they tend to have 10 questions like that. When does my bonus get paid? How often are my commission checks? How much do you guys match on my 401k? I'm not saying these aren't important. These are very important pieces of information. It's just not the line of questioning that you want to enter into as a candidate in an early-stage interview.

A better question would be, "Hey, I know that your company is growing at 12% year-over-year internally. That's amazing. How is this individual location doing? And what do you see as your three biggest challenges over the next year?" Boy, that's somebody that you feel will add value the minute he starts at the company.

MICHAEL: Right. He did his research, so he's going to do his research when he works for you.

KEN: Exactly. It is an indicator of what they're going to do moving forward. If the interviewer asks you a question, you can relate it back to the research that you've done, and kind of do a little bit of a humble brag along the way.

MICHAEL: Absolutely. Along that line, what question do you ask that you think reveals the most about a candidate?

KEN: I can find out 90% of what I need to know about somebody by how they talk about their current or previous employers. Their ability to navigate that, especially if it was a bad breakup, is really eye opening. You can figure out if it was a bad breakup without them being unprofessional in how they go about it. Navigating that choppy water tells me a lot about how they're going to handle conflicts in the workplace and how they're going to talk about us if things don't work out. That's one of my number one areas to ask about.

MICHAEL: Let's take a deeper dive. Tell me your stories. Give me some examples of those that you've spoken to. Tell me about the ones that totally flubbed it, and about the ones that answered the question perfectly.

KEN: I get some that are rock stars in how they handle this. And I get some that are awful. So, a typical question might be something like, "Tell me why you left Target and went over to Amazon." And they say, "Oh, gosh, well, you know, I didn't see things the way they saw it at Target. Ethically, we weren't aligned, etc." They're already starting to get into pretty dangerous water right out of the gate. And then they just keep going. As a recruiter, do I throw them out at that point? Is this guy going to be a cultural fit with where I want to place them, or are they just young and maybe need some career coaching along the way?

The ones that really blow my mind are the ones who, even after I tell them that going down this path is a red flag, they just keep going and going. And again, what it shows is not only that they're not being professional with their old employer, but they're not showing that they're able to compartmentalize things and know when to speak out and not speak out.

Sometimes, I'll ask a question that implies that I'm trying to trap them, but I'm really not. I'm just trying to find out their hot button. A question I might ask would be, "Hey, it sounds like you've got a great thing going with company X. If you were to make a move, what would be three things that you would change about your current situation in a new situation?" So basically, what are your must-haves?"

Now, the ones that handle this really, really well are the ones that don't answer directly out of the gate. They start with saying all the things they like about their previous company. They'll say, "Amazon has been great for me in terms of career growth. They brought me on in a fast-changing environment, etc." They say all the good things first, and then they'll say, "But that being said, we were on call seven days a week, and I have a new baby now. That's not Amazon's fault, but it presents a challenge for me because I'm a young parent."

There's a right way and a wrong way to get your point across. Be honest. What are you really looking for? It's not really on them. It's me. I've just had a baby. I've changed my circumstances, and now it doesn't fit Amazon as well, even though they're great.

MICHAEL: Absolutely. IT'S ABOUT COMMUNICATING AND FRAMING YOUR RESPONSE IN A WAY THAT IS PROFESSIONAL.

KEN: There's also a way to be even more direct. Let's say there was someone who was on a VP level where the real reason they left might've been a conflict with the vision of the company. You can still say that in a really good way. Like, "These guys have been awesome to me. I've grown so much, I've learned so much, but now we are at this crossroads. The company is more focused on a profitability model now, and I'm a growth guy. I want to build a sales organization." That's great. They didn't bash their old company at all. They just clearly stated where they were in their career. It's almost like being in a marriage that was good, and you still have shared custody of the kids, and everybody's happy, but you go separate ways. There can be amicable breakups.

MICHAEL: **Yeah. It's about relationship. Even if you hate the company, and you may hate your ex, there must still be some good things, because you married that person in the first place. They're not all bad. I think the same thing applies when you get a job with a company: they provided you an opportunity. There are things you learned. State the positive things about the company. What do you like about the company? What value do they deliver to their customers? And that will set the tone.**

KEN: Exactly. <u>YOU ONLY HAVE SO MUCH TIME IN FRONT OF THE DECISION MAKER. DO YOU WANT TO SPEND IT BASHING YOUR PREVIOUS EMPLOYER?</u> Is that going to help you get the job in any way? Even if it doesn't knock you out, none of that information is increasing your status as a candidate.

MICHAEL: **Right. Everything is about preparation. We talk about this on every single one of my podcast episodes. But people aren't doing it. Preparation puts you in a whole other category. Get on a zoom call with yourself and videotape** yourself answering the most common questions. Tell me about your greatest challenge and how you overcame it. What are your greatest strengths? What are your greatest weaknesses? If you got this position, where do you think you would shine, and why would you contribute?

We have a whole list of them. Have you prepared the best responses? Not that you're going to read like a robot, because people want you to be conversational and real during the interview, but are you prepared with those one, two, or three key points? When you're asked that question, you need to be able to articulate those answers clearly.

We are in the age where there's no excuse not to research. Go online, go

> PEOPLE ARE PEOPLE FIRST. CONNECT WITH THEM.

on LinkedIn, and not only know about the company, know about the person who is interviewing you. What are their passions? What charities do they believe in? People are people first. Connect with them. Relate to who they are and to what they want. They're interested in the value you can deliver, why you're the best candidate. You have a limited period of time, so you want to use it well.

KEN: When you're answering questions, answer with as much detail as possible. I don't mean that you spend a long time answering. I mean be as specific as possible. Tell me how you did with sales: "Oh, I always beat quota, and in the last five years on average, I made 121% of quota. I also made the president's club the last three years in a row. I'm up for promotion to sales manager." Okay, that I can sink my teeth into.

All of those awards, all of those letters of recommendation, achievements, call outs, emails, etc., you should have a little stack of those. Don't send them electronically but have it with you as a "brag book." When someone starts going down that line of questioning and you just flop it in front of them, it's almost like, "Here's all the evidence of me being awesome." Just drop it on the table. It looks like a lot of evidence. Now, as a recruiter, I don't think I need to dig into your history as a sales guy anymore, because now I'm looking at it in a hundred pages of documentation.

MICHAEL: Yes. You're offering proof sources that raise your credibility. You're not just saying it now, but everyone else is saying it. You're not just blowing smoke, which a lot of people will do. Everyone's going to talk a good game, but who do they actually believe?

KEN: I know you've listened to Tony Robbins in the past. He talks about the six human needs: uncertainty, significance, love, connection, growth, and contribution. We all have them. We all value them at different levels and at different times in our lives. But we all lead with two primary needs. I can tell you right now that a hiring manager highly values certainty. When you're making a new hire, you don't want to screw it up. You want to hit a home run. You want somebody who can come in and contribute. The more certainty you can provide that you're the right choice, the easier the choice becomes.

Once you get hired, that's how you get promoted too. If you and I have the exact same results in the same job, we've been there the same length of time, and we're both up for promotion, the person who's going to get it is the person who gives the boss the most certainty that they're ready for the next role.

So then the question becomes, how do you give them certainty? It's usually through the evidence of what's in the job, either above you or the one that you're going for. If you just pull the job description and go, "Oh, they're looking for someone who's done medical equipment sales in small offices. I've done that before, maybe not with medical devices, but I've done it with whatever. I'm going to talk about that now." But you would never have known to talk about that if you didn't do the preparation in the first place.

MICHAEL: I read a book 30 years ago by Charles B. Roth called *Secrets of Closing Sales*. And he said, "There's only one reason people don't buy, and it's uncertainty. There's only one way to raise the threshold of certainty, and that's through reassurance. There's only one way to reassure, and that is proof of evidence."

Everything you do or don't do will either add confidence points or reduce them. If you're talking negatively, that's not going to add any confidence points in that hiring manager's mind that you're the right candidate.

KEN: Right. You have this limited amount of time. So even with your own answers, even when you're adding points, you have to think, am I taking too long? If I'm a basketball team, I can't take four minutes to get down the court, even if I score a basket. We need to be more active than that, so that's where you want to be direct. Clarify the question, get to the point. Boom. You want to score a lot of points, so ask me a question, boom, and serve it back.

MICHAEL: And to do that, you have to be prepared. If you're not prepared, you're going to ramble. You're not going to know the right answer. And IT'S THE TIME YOU SPEND PREPARING THAT'S GOING TO PUT YOU IN A POSITION TO BE CLEAR, CONCISE, AND COMPELLING IN A SHORTER PERIOD OF TIME.

What are you doing that's gaining competence points?

KEN: As a candidate, you should want all of the jobs. You want every employer to make you an offer. You want this to be your choice. It might not be the company I'm going to be with forever, but I want to have an offer. I want to have something to think about at the end of this. If you just get in that habit, then it's not even something you have to think about that much.

MICHAEL: So here's the big question. Why don't people do what they need to do to prepare and ace an interview? There was a book by Fred Harvey called *Selling is Simple but Not Easy*. We can tell people where to go, but actual preparation is going to take time. It's going to take time to work out a game plan. One of my favorite quotes is a Sun Tzu quote that Bill Belichick of the New England Patriots often uses: "Every battle is won before it's fought."

The bottom line is that it's hard to prepare, because it takes effort, and people don't want to make an effort. Ken, tell me your spin. What can we do to help people get on the bandwagon and do what they need to do?

KEN: I think it comes back to what we were just talking about with human needs, certainty and uncertainty, and all of that combined with identity. If I'm looking for a job, and I'm going to do all this preparation, it's because I see myself in a certain position. I see myself as being a top candidate. If you get your identity down first, your brain will follow.

But your brain is designed to keep you comfortable, to play it safe and to play it slow. So your brain will say, "Why do you want to leave your current job for this other job? It's not so bad the way it is now." Our brains don't want to play that game with us. **OUR SOUL WANTS MORE, AND OUR BRAIN WANTS TO PLAY IT SAFE.**

I think people aren't intentionally half-assing it. It's more that they don't realize that there's something better waiting for them right now. And so they check themselves out. It's like if you and I play a competitive game of some kind, and I don't really try that hard, and at the end, I say, "Well, I never really wanted it. I never really competed to begin with." That's a way of protecting yourself.

I guess I would look at it this way. I used to weigh 50 pounds more than I do now. One day, I had an epiphany, and I said, "I need to get my butt in shape, and not only get in shape, I need to thrive." What I tied it to was the fact that my kids were getting older. They were going to have families of their own, and every single thing that I did was not only going to be replicated by my friends and my immediate family, but now by my grandkids and their kids. If I was to become a slacker in this area, what that means to me is reduced longevity and quality of life for my entire family tree from me on down. And it's true.

When my wife and I changed our health and fitness, our kids changed their health and fitness too.

And now our grandkids have different attitudes. This is an example of getting leverage on yourself to change your why. How do I do this with career? The example that you're setting right now—are you living to your fullest potential? And if you're not, it's not just you that you're disappointing. It's all the people that look up to you and count on you. I believe that when you can get that kind of leverage on yourself, you can make massive change, because **WE WILL OFTEN DO MORE FOR OTHER PEOPLE THAN WE WILL DO FOR OURSELVES**. I think that's just human nature.

MICHAEL: The bottom line is, if you don't do this preparation, you won't feel like showing up all the time. The reason you're doing it is more than just getting a job. Why do you want that job? When you continue to ask why, you continue to peel back the onion and dig a little deeper. I think that's going to drive you to do the things you don't feel like doing, and that's going to help you become more successful in landing a job. While you're doing that, you're building your character, and you're making an impact on the people who are watching you and who are learning from you and who are emulating who you are.

KEN: Our mutual friend Rod Thomas often says that **HOW YOU DO ANYTHING IS HOW YOU DO EVERYTHING**. That is such a simple statement, but if you get in the habit of showing up for every interview, at your best, with preparation, with all the things that we're saying, then that's just who you are. That's how you will show up to everything. Whether you're up for a job, not up for a job, or up for promotion, you're just a professional person always. You do your homework, and then suddenly, it becomes part of your character. It's part of who you are. It's not something you're going to think about eventually.

Or you can be the tire kicker. The one who sometimes does their research when it really matters, when there's an immediate payoff.

MICHAEL: You need to understand things about yourself that are holding you back from becoming the better version of yourself, that are holding you back from doing the things you need to be doing, to get the results that you really want to get.

At the end of the day, the bottom line is your action, your discipline. THE THINGS YOU DO TO GET A JOB ARE INEVITABLY GOING TO BE THE THINGS THAT SEPARATE YOU FROM THE PACK. The more work you put into it with the right blueprint, the better the results you're going to get.

Ken, what is your one piece of advice for someone who's looking for a job but is getting frustrated?

KEN: I always like to flip the unemployment picture a little bit. If there's 8% unemployment in the US, then 92% are employed. That sounds a lot more like a glass half full, instead of saying 8%

> I ALWAYS LIKE TO FLIP THE UNEMPLOYMENT PICTURE A LITTLE BIT. IF THERE'S 8% UNEMPLOYMENT IN THE US, THEN 92% ARE EMPLOYED.

unemployment, which sounds high. So if 92% of people are employed, can I be one of those 92% in a job that is at least going to serve me right now? Because now I can start to internalize that yeah, that seems realistic. Can I do the preparation that is going to be putting me in front of the right people? If you're reading this, you can.

I think this is a really good time if you're employed to start looking around for other opportunities. You might be thinking it's not a great time to look around because of COVID, but I don't know if there's ever been a better time to look, because entire industries are being born. Others are pivoting. Things are moving around. So if you can be flexible and watch the landscape and do the preparation as we've talked about, I feel like there's a lot of opportunities sitting in front of us. There's a lot more for the people that prepare and show up. There's still going to be the people on the couch, wondering what happened and blaming COVID, but the reality is there's a ton of opportunity right now.

I work with Fortune 500 companies that deal with smaller businesses, and so I get snapshots of the economy through their hiring practices. And it *was* dead. I'm not going to try to sugarcoat it. It was really, really dead from March until September or October of 2020. And then there was this gradual pickup, and it's very busy again right now.

I know you and I both have sales in our background, but a lot of people don't have that, so it might feel unnatural to show excitement or enthusiasm. To "close" as we say in sales, all you need to say is, "I really enjoyed meeting you, and I'm very excited about this opportunity, and are there any reasons you wouldn't be moving me onto the next step?" If you want to, just ask them three very simple things like that. That's enough. That's all you've got to do. You don't have to make it anything more elaborate than, "I like you. I like the company. I'd like to know if I'm moving forward or not."

MICHAEL: Yeah. I love that. We really want to help transform lives. We know it's more than just a job, because we spend more time at work than anything else. It's meaningful to folks that are not working right now. Just remember that 92% are working, and you could be part of that 92%.

Thank you so much for being on the show and for making such a big contribution.

KEN: Thank you, sir. It was a pleasure. For anyone that needs any help with anything, please feel free to reach out on LinkedIn, or you can find me at the Leaders Lab as well.

ACTION STEPS

PREPARE FOR AN INTERVIEW BY DOING A QUICK, 5-MINUTE INTERNET SEARCH. Make sure to do the following:

1. Read through their website to get a feel for company culture—this can inform how you should dress.
2. Browse recent news headlines to understand what the company has been doing—have they recently acquired a new company? How are their sales? Knowledge of recent events can set you apart from the pack.
3. Search for your interviewer on LinkedIn. Understand what they're passionate about. At the end of the day, your interviewer is a human being, and human beings care about connecting on a relational level.

NAVIGATING QUESTIONS ABOUT A BAD BREAKUP WITH A PREVIOUS COMPANY

1. Always begin with the positive things the company did for you. Even if there were negative elements, acknowledge that the company did give you an opportunity and that you did learn things by working there.

2. When speaking about why you left your previous company, focus on how your goals no longer aligned. Emphasize that it isn't the previous company's fault, but that you are in a different place in life now and need something a little different.

ASK THE RIGHT QUESTIONS

1. Don't open with questions about what the company can do for you (how many vacation days do I get?). Always focus on how you can serve the company.

UNDERSTAND YOUR "WHY"

1. Understanding why you are searching for a job can help you do the preparation you need to do for every interview. It can keep you from having a laissez-faire attitude.

2. Keep asking yourself "why" until you have peeled back the layers of the onion and have found a motivation that fuels you.

3. Put in the work required to reach your goal—it doesn't take long to prepare for an interview. Do you research and practice common interview questions. Show enthusiasm and be positive.

Stephen Lutter

Recruiter for Mass Mutual, New York

CHAPTER FOCUS

- *Older individuals in the job hunt*
- *Research as a tool for job-seekers*
- *The importance of self-care*

Stephen Lutter and I had a great discussion about how to make the right career move, focusing on older individuals who have been in the work force for years. We also discussed how to stay motivated during a long job hunt, among other things. Stephan previously served as an active duty Army officer prior to transitioning to the Army Reserves. He is an MBA candidate and an active member in his western New York community. He serves on numerous nonprofit boards and volunteers for Say Yes to Buffalo and Breaking Barriers Buffalo. He and his wife, Madeline, live in Elma, New York and have an English bulldog and two cats.

MICHAEL: Stephen, you're a young guy (at my age, everyone is a young person), so tell me a little bit about your sensitivity and awareness to what's going on out there in the job market and what are you seeing as a recruiter in terms of where people's heads are at and what you're dealing with.

STEPHEN: I participate in a lot of career support groups, and what I'm finding is that <u>IT'S A VERY DIFFICULT TIME FOR EXPERIENCED</u>

FOLKS. Folks who are mid- to senior-level in their careers are combating age-ism. They're combating having archaic resumes, or they were in a job that they thought was safe. And if COVID taught us anything, it's that no job is

> IF COVID TAUGHT US ANYTHING, IT'S THAT NO JOBS ARE SAFE.

safe. For example, in our western New York market, one of the biggest companies we have is Delaware North, and they do a lot of gaming; they run casinos, entertainment, things like that, and that went away very quickly. They had to furlough a lot of people. But prior to COVID-19, that was as safe as it could get. It was a bolstering company. But now, COVID has punched a lot of people in the mouth, and I think what it's done to the psyche of the job seeker, is it has made them focus on what they want to do and be a little choosier in where they end up next. But they're fighting picky recruiters and picky companies who want to bring in the right people, so it's a challenge. If you're a college student graduating right now, you probably have a lot of opportunities available to you. You're going to have a lot of years ahead of you and a lot of people in your ear offering their value proposition as to why you should come to their company.

I think you need to make a choice that is guided by your own values. Where do *you* see yourself. You don't have to listen to your parents, to others, even sometimes to your spouses; make sure *you're* making the choice as a job seeker. Find the job that's right for *you*.

My heart goes out to the folks who are mid- to senior-level and struggling. It's tough to get noticed. I speak to some Baby Boomers and Gen-X folks who might not have their LinkedIn profile up-to-date. Job seeking looks different now than it did in the 1980s and 1990s. I offer whatever support I can with mock interviews,

> JOB SEEKING LOOKS DIFFERENT NOW THAN IT DID IN THE 1980s AND 1990s.

resume prep, and LinkedIn optimization to help folks in that category.

MICHAEL: That's really nice. Stephen, there are a few key things that I'm sure resonated with different folks based on their situation. Tell us first about aging out and how perception is reality. And tell me if this is something you agree with: when you're in your forties or fifties or sixties and someone's interviewing you and they're in their twenties, thirties, or forties. And they're thinking when they see someone older come in, that this person, they're on the tail end of their career, they've slowed down a little bit. Do they really have that growth mindset? Are they really interested in learning new stuff at that age or stage in their life? Can you teach an old dog new tricks? Do you think they're dealing with those preconceived notions on the recruiter and manager's mind?

STEPHEN: Yes. I think whether or not we want to admit it, the psyche of the 20 to 30-year-old recruiter has a little bit of imposter syndrome, almost defensiveness, about where they're at. And it's awkward. It's awkward for me to interview folks in their forties and their fifties who could be my parents, my aunts, my uncles. But I think HR folks and recruiters have to take a hard look at their own biases, their own stereotypes, and work to combat that with formal training. LinkedIn also offers a lot of great courses on how to combat that in the hiring process, like what questions you should and shouldn't ask.

I know our recruiter in western New York tells me not to Google a candidate before they walk in your door. He says to just base your impression on the resume and the objective standards of how they meet the ideal candidate profile. If you're going to move forward with them, you would do a background check and social media check, obviously, but *before* you meet with them in person or via Zoom, don't Google them, because subconsciously it could play a part and add some bias.

MICHAEL: **That's really interesting. So with the influx of all the resumes, all the candidates looking for work right now, which we know is crazy, like eight to 10 million people, how do you then have the time if you don't filter out folks? You'd be spending all day doing interviews.**

STEPHEN: Yeah. So if I'm looking for salespeople, it's up to the candidate. **THE CANDIDATE HAS TO HAVE AN INTRINSIC DESIRE, A BURNING FIRE IN THEIR BELLIES TO SUCCEED**, otherwise, they're going to hit obstacles and get a note from a client and crawl into their shells. I used to recruit for the military. I can recruit thousands of people, but ultimately the candidate has to choose, because it's a hard life, you know, going the military route. It's a hard life going into a commission pay structure as well. But I'm telling you, there are people in my office who are in their late thirties, early forties who are financially free, and don't have to work. They golf frequently. They take vacations when they want. It's an exciting opportunity. So there are people out there who are ready and willing to go for it.

MICHAEL: **Sure. You bring up some great points. I've heard this before, that it has to be a match more so with working in a sales field, where you eat what you kill with straight**

commission. There's going to be resistance. There's going to be downtime. There's no steady paycheck. You're looking for a match, and they should be looking for a match. It should be a win-win, whether it be a straight commission job or any other job where your skills, qualifications, desires, and passions all align with the company's culture, your qualifications for the job, and the role that you'd be fulfilling.

So, since we're talking about that, let's go back to the aging out, the mid- or senior-level. What can they do to improve their odds of getting in and getting interviewed?

STEPHEN: Yeah, Michael, I would say, unless the job is a public job, or unless that job 30 years ago is applicable to the job you're applying for now, don't be afraid to take it off your resume. You only really have to go back about 15 to 20 years. Just highlight the older stuff, and moving forward, remove any sort of potential for leaving yourself vulnerable for bias. There are also old resume formats, typed in Times New Roman and bulleted. Please avoid copying and pasting your job description from that and onto your new resume. **MANAGERS WANT TO SEE HOW YOU MADE AN IMPACT ON THE BUSINESS THAT YOU WERE SERVING IN**, not just a copy and paste.

Everybody is responsible for daily operations, we get that, but highlight the big time accomplishments you had in the role. And know that it's not bragging, it's advocating for yourself. Lastly, I would say, the skills section: things like proficient in Microsoft Office, proficient in Microsoft PowerPoint—you can go ahead and remove that. It's almost a given nowadays to be proficient in that. Lastly, look for people in your network who have really stellar LinkedIn profiles and ask for recommendations. Include your volunteer experience. Take free LinkedIn classes on personal branding and marketing and how to sell yourself.

And, so you know, I agreed to be on Michael's podcast because I looked at Michael's profile and saw that he was legitimate. I thought, 'he's doing a lot of great things, and I'll absolutely be a guest.' So it's important to have those things listed on your LinkedIn.

MICHAEL: **Yeah. Yeah. And thank you for that. By the way, I was going to say, you looked at all my stuff and in spite of that, he got on the show, and you know, maybe likes me as well.**

STEPHEN: I hope I look as good as you when I'm 60, and I hope to be in Boca Raton and golfing as much as possible. I'd love to get a tan. I don't get a tan like you when I'm in Buffalo, New York.

MICHAEL: **Well, yeah, that would explain it. But you know, as you get older, you change your habits, rituals, and routines. Now, every Sunday at 4:30, my wife and I go to the beach. We're ten minutes from the beach. We go to the beach, and I listen to podcasts or something on Audible, or I read a book. We should all dive into things and continue learning. If you're not reading LinkedIn articles or reading about ways that you can advance your career or doing anything that will help you land and ace more interviews and be clear on a career path, you need to start, or you're not going to put yourself in a position to win. It's as simple as that.**

STEPHEN: Yeah. And I would also say, if you're a job seeker, personally invite 20 people *per day* within the network of companies that you're interested in to join your LinkedIn network. Secondly, make sure you're taking care of yourself. Job hunting can be physically, emotionally, and mentally draining, and you can quickly fall into a pit of despair. So dial up the self-care, pull yourself out of that hole of self-pity, and get networking. Get out there. Attend free and paid networking events. Request referrals from insiders in addition to informational interviews. You'd be surprised how many people are more than willing to let you interview them for information, and they don't have to be in HR. As a matter of fact, I would suggest *not* going the HR route, because they might be a little more standoffish, but request informational interviews from insiders in the company that you're interested in. You never know.

MICHAEL: I hear more and more about the power of networking, and that most jobs are achieved through networking and not necessarily through job posts. Talk to your doctors, your lawyers, your accountants, your kids, your coach; talk to ex-employees; talk to everybody. I love the idea of 20 new invites. And if it's hard to do 20, there's a great book by James Clear called *Atomic Habits* that may help. He says to start small: do three a day. And then if you do three a day, the next day, do four, and build up gradually. Build momentum. So remember if you speak to 10 people, you're going to have 10 times the opportunity, potentially, as opposed to if you only spoke to one person. The numbers are in your favor here. And know the right things to ask for. I'm a personal fan of asking them, "Would you be kind enough to do an email introduction?" And that email introduction puts you in touch with that person you want to speak to in the company; you have their email address. Now you have a warm introduction, something flattering, and you're on your way to setting up the next appointment, which is what your goal is for an interview, either in person or over the internet. So, yeah, all that networking is huge. Those are the things that are going to separate you in this competitive job market.

So many people, Stephen, are thinking about career changes. What are some critical things someone needs to be thinking about studying and doing to really get clear on that career path and to do it successfully?

STEPHEN: I would say take personality tests such as the Kolbe Assessment Strength Finder, Myers-Briggs, etc., and read those profile assessments. Know who you are, and what your motivations and your intrinsic values are, and be choosy about it. **DON'T TAKE THE FIRST JOB THAT'S OFFERED TO YOU IF IT DOESN'T ALIGN WITH YOUR VALUES.** That's okay. You know, a lot of people are still riding out unemployment, and they're making a good penny with that. So be choosy, and refuse to lower your standards. Despite the long job-seeking process, make a deliberate choice to put a foot on the ground and say, *I offer value.*

It's important to get on the internet. I mean, people are making so much money just getting referrals from Instagram or Ted Talk. It's a new world out there. And don't forget Clubhouse.

So here's what I would recommend:
1. Choose what you want to do, and be open to different industries.
2. Make sure that you're not only looking into the interview process but are getting informational interviews, gauging

the work culture, and asking, "Is this a healthy place where I'll feel psychologically safe to bring my ideas forward? Is this a culture where I'll be encouraged to collaborate and invest in my future?"

3. Realize that it's okay to hop around, but you know, ideally stay in a job a year. As job seekers, we kind of have the upper hand. *You offer value.*

4. Take those personality assessments, and also, just ask your colleagues and prior supervisors, "What do you see in me that I'm not seeing?" Lean into those assessments, and take those seriously, and be choosy about your next opportunity, because no one wants to work at a place where they feel like they're a robot punching the clock nine-to-five.

MICHAEL: I think that's such sage advice. My son, who is 29, did go from one company to the next to the next until he found what was his home, the right foster, the right culture, the right growth trajectory, so I love the idea of what you said, Stephen. I just want to reinforce that WE DON'T SEE THE WORLD THE WAY IT IS. WE SEE THE WORLD THE WAY WE ARE. **So what you see may not be what others see, and by getting this subjective roadmap as to who you are and what you are, and to know what you'd be ideally matched to, asking other people, getting other perspectives and opinions... it's all valuable.**

But also, a lot of times, you've just got to try it. I get that. I'll use an analogy: it's like going shopping, and you see a beautiful shirt on a rack in a clothing store. You say, "Oh my gosh, this shirt is amazing." And you take the shirt off the rack, and you try it on... and it looks like crap. It looked

great on the rack, but it looks terrible on you. And then, conversely, you see a shirt on a rack, and it's like, eh, I don't know. And your husband says, "Just try it on." And then you get it, and you try it on. And all of a sudden that shirt looks super-hot.

It's the same with jobs. It may not seem ideal, but you want to align these things as best you can and have others help you with assessments. You want people who know you to say, "these are your talents, your skills, your qualifications, your passions." Then you have to figure out how to align those with the company's culture, their product services, the job description, and who you'll be reporting to. Read their LinkedIn profile. You're interviewing them just as they're interviewing you to make sure it's a fit for both. Does that sound accurate to you, Stephen?

STEPHEN: It does. And I just want to share, when I left active duty in 2017, I applied for the police academy, and I applied for project management roles. I tried to go the credential route. I wasn't listening to myself or listening to others. Then I started taking these assessments, and found out, no, you're not detail oriented. You're people focused. You're good at networking. And you're very extroverted. So you should not be in a detail-oriented project management position. You should be outwardly seeking connections. So now I laugh at what the jobs were that I applied to in 2017, like operations supervisor, project manager type roles, and it's laughable, you know, but I learned the hard way, and I'm finally in a role where my values align with my work style, with what I do on a daily basis. Now work doesn't seem like work. I'm happier, and you will be too if you follow your intrinsic nature.

MICHAEL: So, Stephen, from what you've seen, if there were three greatest weaknesses that you see when people come to you for an interview, what are they? What do they need to do better next time?

STEPHEN: Here's what I suggest:

1. **DON'T ELIMINATE YOURSELF FROM A JOB BEFORE THE RECRUITER DOES.** If you don't

> YOU'LL MISS 100% OF THE SHOTS YOU DON'T TAKE.

   at least interview, then you don't stand a chance. So I encourage you to apply for jobs that you're interested in, and don't eliminate yourself from a job because of self-doubt.
2. **DON'T SELL YOURSELF SHORT:** In the interview process, be proud of the accomplishments you've had in your previous roles, and recognize that the company was better off with you and the team was better off with you in it.
3. **ZOOM:** With Zoom interviews, make sure you're presenting yourself as you would in an in-person interview. Have the proper background, reduce noise, dress professionally, at least from the waist up. Don't do the Zoom from the car. You get the point.

MICHAEL: So, at the end of the day, how do you differentiate yourself?

STEPHEN: Do research about the company. It is a huge differentiator when a candidate has gone through the website, knows the executive leadership team, understands where the company is headed, and understands where the company is looking to go. That's a huge differentiator. It so rarely happens. Maybe one of every 10 candidates I speak to does the research.

MICHAEL: **When an interviewer see that you did research, it's not that you know about the new acquisition they made. That's a feature. It's not that you know that the company has a new product launch in medical devices that's going to solve x or y problem. That's nice. That's a feature. What it *shows them* is that this person does research. This person does homework. This person is exceptional, because they're doing what nine other people applying for the job didn't do. And that's the type of person we want working for us.**

STEPHEN: You nailed it on the head. And if you can already predict the points of a business acquisition, a new product launch, or say, "I noticed this product isn't really taking off in this geographic region. Here's what I would do to help that boom," you're already offering value through the interview process.

MICHAEL: **And lastly, what about common courtesies at the end of the interview?**

STEPHEN: The worst thing I can have is when I ask, "Do you have any questions?" and there are no questions. How are there no questions? Even if we have an hour together, we're talking about something you're about to spend 40 hours-a-week doing, how do you have no questions?

Another common courtesy is <u>**DON'T UNDERESTIMATE THE IMPACT OF A SIMPLE THANK YOU**</u>, even if it's just an email or a LinkedIn message. One time, I could see people were really down from job losses, and I brought in bagels to a company with a thank you. That really differentiated me.

MICHAEL: Yeah. That's great. And I want to touch on three things.

1. If you meet an employer's or recruiter's or hiring manager's

> **THE GREAT ONES ARE COMFORTABLE BEING UNCOMFORTABLE.**

expectations, it's meaningless. It is meaningless because meeting expectations leaves people neutral. You don't want to be a candidate. You want to beat others. You want to create a raving fan, a zealot and ambassador, someone who can't wait to talk to their coworkers about the guy who brought in bagels, because that's a differentiator. Doing that is not reaching expectations. It's *exceeding* them.

2. And then the second thing, is doing something thoughtful, caring, understanding. Those little things, like if you knew your interviewer was late for an interview because their child was sick at school, the first thing you need to do on that call is say, before we get started, how is your child doing? Is he or she feeling better?

It's those little, thoughtful, kind, considerate gestures that are differentiators. And when you add all these little things up, like the research, the good questions, the thoughtfulness, the thank you card, they subconsciously recognize that you did all those thing, and it has greater impact, right? THE SUCCESSFUL PERSON WILL DO WHAT THE UNSUCCESSFUL PERSON WON'T DO. When I coach peak performance coaching, I tell people to do one extra thing today.

Do you have a question that you ask, Stephen, that kind of helps answer a lot of questions in terms of the person's heart, the person's intelligence, the person's clarity, whatever it might be?

STEPHEN: Yeah, I believe in behavioral based questions, but my favorite of them is, "Where do you see yourself in two to five years? And how are you going to get there?" It's purposely open-ended. It tells me your goals, your drive, your initiative, your ability to plan ahead and, and ultimately, where you want to be. A candidate who can say, "I'm going to get there by ideally moving forward with this role and getting five years of great experience under my belt, working with a diverse pool of clients, and then eventually going out on my own to be a career agent for the firm," tells me a lot.

MICHAEL: **What would you say about the situation as it exists today, with eight to 10 million people unemployed; what words of advice do you have to give?**

STEPHEN: Most importantly, take care of yourself. My version of self-care is going to the gym. I put my ear buds in, and it's just me and my zone for an hour. And if I don't get that in, I'm less pleasant to be around during the day. So first and foremost, take care of yourself. What do you love to do most when you wake up on a Saturday morning, and you have nothing planned? Whatever you go do on that Saturday morning, do that every day. Do it when you wake up, at least for a half hour to an hour, and that'll put you in the right mindset. Practice meditation, or maybe, for you, that's prayer. For me, it's the *Calm* app. I do Morning Savers, which is 10 minutes of silence, followed by affirmations of where I'm headed in the day, visualizing what I'm going to accomplish, and then exercising for at least 10 to 15 minutes. If you're not a huge exerciser, read some sort of article, and write down what you're going to do that day.

MICHAEL: **Morning savers. I love that. And you know, I'm always improving with that. We call them morning rituals, and you don't have to follow what Stephen does. You don't have to follow what I do either, but you can create something for yourself. I'll share mine. The first thing that my wife and I do in the morning is we pray. We're believers in the Lord, so we start our day with prayer. We end our day in prayer. The next thing we do is make our bed.**

STEPHEN: Absolutely. That way, even if your day was a failure, you to come back to a made bed.

MICHAEL: **Go online and just read about what are good morning rituals and do one or two things that get you started in the right way and add to those. And the rest of the day has a better chance of being successful.**

Stephen, you've dropped so many gems for job seekers and for people who are down on themselves. And you've given a lot of people hope. All they have to do is listen, take notes, and take action. And they'll start to see positive results. That's how it works.

STEPHEN: Thanks for having me, Michael.

ACTION STEPS

IN ORDER TO NETWORK WITH THE COMPANIES THAT YOU ARE INTERESTED IN WORKING FOR, SEEK OUT THOSE COMPANIES ON LINKEDIN. THEN:

- Add 20 people per day to your LinkedIn connections.
- Request information interviews from insiders.

AVOID THE THREE WEAKNESSES OF A BAD INTERVIEW:

- Self-Elimination
- Lack of research
- Failure to do common courtesies at the end

REMEMBER:

- You bring value. Don't underestimate yourself.
- First and foremost, take care of yourself. Create morning rituals and positive self-talk that start your day off successfully.

FOR JOB-SEEKERS WHO HAVE BEEN IN THE WORKFORCE A WHILE:

- Update your resume and join LinkedIn.
- Eliminate older, generalized job descriptions, and update with what you specifically brought to the company
- Don't be afraid to look in different industries.
- Through assessment tests or by asking others, find out your strengths, and what you love to do, and do it.

Acknowledgments

As I reflect on the magnitude of this undertaking, I am reminded of the interviews that take place at the end of every NFL game. Typically, one or two players who had outstanding performances that led their team to victory are selected for a post-game interview. I remember waiting with great anticipation to hear what these amped-up stars of the game were going to say. Yet, unremarkably, the interviewer always started the interview the same way, by praising the player for his stellar performance, and the player always responded the same way, by giving credit to his team, saying he could not have done it without them. Well, I feel the same way about this book project. Although, it's the author who typically gets the praise, I have to tell you that I truly could not have created this book without an amazing team behind me. The time, love, support, guidance, encouragement, dedication, and hard work that they all poured into me is the reason this book was born. I am grateful to you all. Thank you from the bottom of my heart.

To my Lord and Savior, to you I give the highest praise.

To my amazing wife Emi, my awesome son Kyle, my terrific stepsons, Dex and Julian, your unwavering love and support mean the world to me. I'm truly blessed and love you all.

To my mom and dad who influenced me in ways they will never know. Leaving people better than you found them, with a smile on their face and laughter in their heart, was truly a precious gift.

To the highly talented hiring managers, recruiters and career coaches I interviewed for this book—Josh Love, Twila Alexander, Adam Meekhof, Alberta Johnson, Damon Burton, Ken Eslick, Erin Urban, Andrea Hoffer, Linzee and Steve Ciprani, Dan Sell, Tony Deblauwe, John Baldino, Becky Krueger, Stephen Lutter, Doug Baber, Idalia Perez, and John Maihos—the tips, strategies, and insights you provided in this book were off the charts, but what struck me even more was how much you genuinely cared about helping job seekers land the job of their dreams. Your contributions will change lives.

To my good friend Kevin Harrington, your ongoing support of me and the work that I do means a lot. Thank you!

To Mike Alden, whose friendship is valued beyond words. You are love in action by always being there with great advice and great encouragement. You are a key reason this book is being published.

To Kevin Brody, David Nekava, Michael Norton, Peter Velardi, Jon Lavin, Kris Bonocore, Matt Eggen, Andrew Lassise, Tom Doherty, Tod Weston, Patrick O'Hara, Justin Kasper, Jake McClusky, Mitch Russo—your friendships and council continuously push me to elevate my game and make me a better person. I'm grateful to have all of you in my life!

To my best friend of over 50 years, Richie Diamond, you have taught me the value of loyalty, integrity, persistence, and resilience. I treasure those lessons, and above all I treasure our unwavering friendship. I love you, buddy.

To my super talented writer and editor, Pamela Gossiaux, thank you for pouring your heart, mind, and soul into this book. And thank you to your talented team of proofers and formatters for their great work.

To Mary Puskas, Jim Thomas, and all the mentors at Lake Grove Job Seekers for your continued time, insight, and support that helped take this book to the next level. I'm very grateful for all your invaluable help.

To Bruce Serbin, the best PR guy in the business—I'm grateful for all your hard work in getting the word out so we can help more people get back to work.

To Mary Cheddie, who selflessly connected me with some of the top hiring managers and recruiters from across the country who became great contributors in this book—a HUGE thank you.

To David Guggenheim, my podcast producer who was there from the very beginning, creating a strong foundation that *GET HIRED* was launched from. Thank you for always being there and for your great work.

So to my amazing family, friends, and colleagues, I thank you from the bottom of my heart. You are my battery chargers and bright lights that make me a better person and in so many ways. It's because of all of you that this life-changing book is now a reality.

Learning Resources

- *GET HIRED With the Job Gladiator Battle Plan eBook (FREE)*
- *The Job Gladiator MASSIVE ATTACK Plan eBook*
- *Group Career Coaching*
- *One on One Career Coaching*

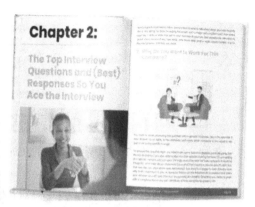

GET HIRED

With the Job Gladiator Battle Plan eBook

LEARN HOW TO:

- Land More Interviews (Faster)
- Ace the Interview (and get more offers)
- Successfully Make a Career Change

FREE ($39.00 VALUE)

To order go to: www.JobGladiator.com

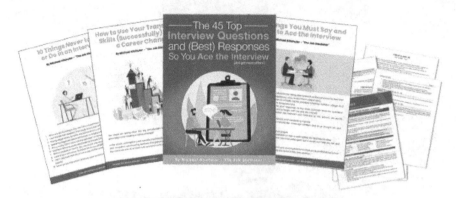

GET HIRED IN RECORD TIME!

Insider Secrets on How to Ace the Interview and Get More Offers!

THE MASSIVE ATTACK PLAN INCLUDES:

✓ The Ace The Interview Book... The Top 45 Interview Questions and BEST Responses...*Total Value: $129.00*

✓ 10 Things Never to Say or Do in an Interview... *Total Value: $25.00*

✓ 10 Things You Must Say and Do to Ace the Interview... *Total Value: $25.00*

PLUS... 2 FREE BONUSES:

✓ Top 10 Resume Templates...*Total Value: $120.00*

✓ How to Use Your Transferrable Skills (Successfully) During a Career Change...*Total Value: $75.00*

TOTAL VALUE: $374.00

NOW ONLY $9.95

To order go to: www.JobGladiator.com and sign up for the FREE Job Gladiator Battle Plan, you'll then be directed to the order page for the Job Gladiator MASSIVE ATTACK PLAN eBook.

Expert Group Coaching

Finally, get the Expert Group Coaching you need to stay motivated and fully prepared to get more interviews, and, more offers! On each coaching call you'll be joining a very select group of other job seekers ready to up their game! It's time to land the job of your dreams... *fast!*

REG. PRICE: $69.95/MONTH
Exclusive offer: only $19.95/MONTH

✓ Join Weekly 'LIVE' 30-Minute Zoom Calls w/ The Job Gladiator or Other Career Coaching Experts

✓ Hear Relevant Q's & A's That Deliver Real Results

✓ Get Access to The Career Coaching Video Vault

✓ Access to Exclusive Discounts with Our Partners

✓ Get Ongoing Support, Encouragement & Motivation

To learn more go to: www.JobGladiator.com and sign up for the FREE Job Gladiator Battle Plan, you'll then be directed to the order page for the Job Gladiator MASSIVE ATTACK PLAN eBook ($9.95) and the last step is you'll be given the option for to sign up for the Expert Group Coaching. That's the Trifecta for landing your dream job!!!

One-on-One Career Coaching
with a *Job Gladiator* Certified Coach

Get personalized one-on-one coaching that will take a deep dive into what's holding you back from getting more interviews and offers. This one-on-one coaching will accelerate your success in landing the job of your dreams.

Reg price $500, Now $250. (for a limited time)*

*Each coaching call is 45 minutes in duration and is delivered via Zoom.

To schedule your coaching call with a certified Job Gladiator coach, please email your resume to: support@jobgladiator.com A Job Gladiator coach will get back to you with available dates and times within 24-48 hours.